Judgeships in Iran: Step Down, You are a Woman
A Legal Analysis of International Human Rights

JUDGESHIPS IN IRAN: STEP DOWN, YOU ARE A WOMAN

A LEGAL ANALYSIS OF INTERNATIONAL HUMAN RIGHTS

A History of Women's Rights in Iran and Women Judges in the United States

DR. DELARAM FARZANEH

JUDGESHIPS IN IRAN: STEP DOWN, YOU ARE A WOMAN
A LEGAL ANALYSIS OF INTERNATIONAL HUMAN RIGHTS
A History of Women's Rights in Iran and Women Judges in the United States

Dr. Delaram Farzaneh

Published by:

Vandeplas Publishing, LLC – May 2017

801 International Parkway, 5th Floor
Lake Mary, FL. 32746
USA

www.vandeplaspublishing.com

ISBN 978-1-60042-288-1

To my mother, the first woman of strength in my life

To my father who supported my dreams

To my mentor,
whose encouragement allowed me to flourish as a scholar

NOTES ON TRANSLITERATION BY AUTHOR

The transliteration used in this book is according to the standards adopted by the *International Journal of Middle East Studies* (IJMES).

TABLE OF CONTENTS

Chapter 1

History of Women's Status and Rights in Iran: Ancient to Modern Times

Introduction

The rights of women in Iran have gone through an undeniable evolution throughout its long history as one of the world's oldest civilizations. Since the beginning of the 20th century alone, Iran has gone through three different government changes, each with direct impact on the legal status of women. The earliest part of the 20th century, which includes the landmark Constitutional Revolution, certainly counts as the birth of the women's movement in Iran. For the first time, women courageously participated to challenge humiliating patriarchal social norms and laws that counted them as second-class citizens. De jure discriminatory laws considered women as mindless and incapable of bearing political rights and responsibilities. The end of the Qājār Dynasty[1] and the establishment of the house of Pahlavī[2] in 1925 counts as the beginning of embracing the most progressive, yet controversial, policies concerning the lives of Iranian women. Then, after well over fifty years of continuous transformation and progress in women's rights, the previously attained progressive rights were thwarted when the Islamic Republic of Iran was established in 1979. The new government pushed women two steps back to their status of half a century earlier. Once again women are systematically discriminated against, yet this time it is in the 21st century.

Today, the de jure discriminatory Law on the Qualifications for Appointment of Judges exemplifies the pervasive systematic and systemic discrimination against women in Iran. This makes it essential to examine, first, the historical pathway of women's challenges in removing social taboos and legal hurdles to advance their rights. Demonstrating an historical background on the legal rights

1 The Qājār Dynasty ruled Iran from 1795-1925.

2 The Pahlavī Monarchy was the found by Riżā Pahlavī in 1925 that was later succeeded by his son Muḥammad Riżā Pahlavī in 1941, whom was overthrown by the Islamic Revolution in 1979 by the leadership of Āyatullāh Khumiynī.

of women in Iran is informative and will assist in understanding the significance of the setbacks on women's rights after the 1979 revolution.

This chapter will examine and analyze the historical aspect of the legal rights of women in Iran since ancient times until today. To place the relevant critical events in perspective, this chapter will begin first to assess women's status during early key historical times, including the Arab invasion and subsequent rise of Islam in Iran. Considering the significance of landmark events and birth of the women's movement in the early 20th century, the legal status of women during the final years of Qājār will be analyzed next. This will be followed by unprecedented social and legal developments for women during the Pahlavī era. The last discussion will examine the beginning era of women's rights under the Islamic Republic of Iran after the 1979 Islamic revolution.

Status of Women during Ancient Times Prior to Arab Invasion

There are no reliable sources regarding the socioeconomic, cultural, legal, and religious status of pre-history Ārīyans[3] (periods without written documentation). However, it has been speculated by the historians that Ārīyans were part of Indo-European tribes.[4] Also, it has been speculated that during pre-history times the social status of people were based on tribal traditions. This meant every household was under mothers' guidance and fathers were considered the guardians of the family.[5]

The ʿīlāmīyān were the first group of people to establish a civilization and legal system centered in the far west and southwest of what is now modern-day Iran, almost 4,000 years prior to the birth of Christ.[6] It is notable that the ʿīlāmīyān's legal system, after their defeat by the Ḥamurābī king, was influenced heavily by the *Qānunnāmiyi Ḥamurābī* (Code of Hammurabi).[7] This code is one of the oldest deciphered texts in the world.[8] According to the ancient Code of Hammurabi, for example, a man could divorce his wife only if she was unable to bear a child and in that case she was entitled to receive her entire dowry from

3 The reason behind the migration of Ārīyans to the Iranian Plateau is not clear to historians yet. However, it has been speculated that their migration was due to increased inhabitants and lack of lands. Ḥasan Pīrnīyā, Tārīkhi Irān: Qabl az Islām [Iranian History before Islam] 29 (8th ed., Niqāh Publication 2012). (Translated by author, hereinafter TA).

4 Ḥasan Pīrnīyā, Tārīkhi Irān: Qabl az Islām [Iranian History before Islam] 27-28 (Niqāh Publication, 8th ed., 2012). (TA)

5 Siyid Ḥasan Amīn, Tārīkhi Ḥuquqi Irān [The History of Law in Iran] 42 (3d ed., Dāʾratulmaʿārifi Irān Shināsī Publication 2012). (TA)

6 *Id.* at 44. *See also* Pīrnīyā, *supra* note 4, at 35-36.

7 The Qānunnāmiyi Ḥamurābī, hereinafter Code of Hammurabi, is a Babylonian law code of ancient Mesopotamia, which goes back to about 1750 BCE. The Code consists of 282 laws including various legal issues such as slavery, marriage, inheritance, family, judgeships, ownership, and legal responsibilities and punishments. Amīn, *supra* note 5, at 50, 51. *See also* Pīrnīyā, *supra* note 4, at 44-46.

8 Pīrnīyā, *supra* note 4, at 46.

her husband. Acceptance of having multiple wives for men was possible only if his first wife was suffering from sickness.[9]

According to the *ʿīlāmī* laws, women and men were treated equally. In some cases there are even records of women being treated as legally superior to men. For instance, in one of the discovered ʿīlāmī tablets, a father in his will equally divided his entire assets between his children but mentioned the name of his daughters first and before his sons' names. In a different tablet, a man gave his entire estate to his wife and he asserted that after the death of his wife, these assets would go to his sons only if they treated their mother with kindness and respect.[10]

In the absence of historical evidence regarding the legal system of the early Ārīyans, most of what we know today about them is based on ancient national stories written by masters like Firdusī[11] in his masterpiece Shāhnāmi (a long epic Persian poem), which is considered the most important evidence of the early lives of the Iranian identity.[12] During the pre-Ārīyan time, it has been speculated that for a long time women were in charge and the society was based on a matriarchal system. In marital traditions, though, it was not common for a woman to ask a man to marry her; however, her opinion was respected after being asked by a man to marry him. There have even been stories in the Shāhnāmi that girls got married without acquiring permission from their fathers.[13]

The Median tribes, who were early Ārīyans, established the Median Dynasty. However, due to lack of archaeological and textual sources from this time, historians do not have much knowledge about their religion, culture, language, chirography, creed, or art.[14] However, it is known that they were tribal communities and their family units were based on patriarchal authority. Also, the tradition of multiple wives among Iranians goes back to the Medians. Fathers as sole decision makers had all exclusive rights over every single person in their families, such as making marriage choices for everyone.[15]

---

9 Amīn, *supra* note 5, at 51.

10 *Id.* at 53.

11 Abul Qāsim Firdusī Tusī was one of the most celebrated and influential Persian poets and the author of the epic of Shāhnāmi.

12 Amīn, *supra* note 5, at 60.

13 *Id.* at 68-70.

14 Pīrnīyā, *supra* note 4, at 70. *See also id.* at 79.

15 Amīn, *supra* note 5, at 80.

To analyze the status of ancient Persians, the most important hurdle for historians has been a lack of factual and written archeological discoveries from the ancient times. Scholars who have done extensive research regarding the status of women in those times have clearly noted that most of their information about women belonged to the behavior of individual females who belonged to the Persian royal household. However, they have been unable to uncover factual information regarding non-royal women or impoverished women.[16]

To learn about the status of women in pre-Islamic Persia, historians depend on the often hostile, limited and secondary sources of the Greek and Roman writers, which tend to focus on particular aspects of the lives of royal Persian women or use specific descriptions for historiographical purposes.[17] A fascination for Persian women already existed in ancient times, especially in the fourth century when writers of philosophical and historical literature mentioned Persian royal women. However, the information that has been preserved in all historical writings is a selection of stories. These stories were chosen because they were particularly exciting, fitted into a specific narrative context, and confirmed the opinion, which contemporary Greeks already held about Persian life.[18]

The Hakhāmanishī Empire was the first Persian Empire, and the largest empire in the ancient world, founded by Cyrus the Great.[19] During this time the Hakhāmanishī kings introduced their reign as an endowment from the Ahurā

16 Hassan Toqranegar, Ḥuqūqi Sīyāsī va Ijtimāʿyi Zanān Qabl va Baʿd az Pīruzīyi Inqilābi Islāmīyi Irān [Political and Social Rights of Women, before and after the Islamic Revolution of Iran] 53-54 (The Center for Islamic Revolution Documents, 2010). (TA)

17 *Women i. In Pre-Islamic Persia,* Encyclopaedia Iranica, *accessed at* http://www.iranicaonline.org/articles/women-i.

18 When deeds, actions, customs, and behavior of foreign cultures need to be evaluated they are often compared with and judged against one's own cultural standards. The Greeks were far from able to create an unprejudiced record of Persian life; their comments on Persian royal women reflected what the Greeks thought the behavior of royal women was like. What was permissible or socially accepted behavior for women in Persian society was judged by the Greeks, not within the framework of Persian culture, but by the accepted Greek standards of behavior. It is also vital to realize that once the story has been selected it becomes subjected to the principles of the wider narrative. In this regards, women lose their individual historical identity and become figures equipped for the sake of the story's development with characteristics that are not uniquely applicable to Persian women. They became gender specific characteristics of women in general. There has been a tendency among ancient historians to accept the Greek viewpoint on Persian royal women uncritically. Maria Brosius, Women in Ancient Persia (559-331 BCE) 2 (Oxford University Press 1996).

19 Hakhāmanishī Empire (550–330 BCE).

Mazdā (the founder of the Zoroaster religion);[20] which made the foundation of their sovereignty and rulings divine.[21]

The Hakhāmanishī Kings had the highest authority in legislative, executive and judicial matters. According to historians' limited information, during this time judicial matters and verdicts were solely controlled and judged by the King, especially regarding sensitive matters like national security of the kingdom.[22] They also were in charge of the appointment or removal of the judges. Judges were among the highest judicial authorities in the society in resolving public and private legal issues. Nonetheless, they lacked independent judicial authority because kings had the ultimate authority to modify their judgments, or pardon the convicted, especially in national and criminal matters. The unlimited power of the king as the sole representative of the executive authority made the judiciary part of the executive power.[23]

Our knowledge about the status of women during the Hakhāmanishī period depends mainly on the sporadic and limited information left from Herodotus and later Greek historical writers about individual females who belonged to the royal household. This has led to generalizations about royal women that lack any substantial foundation. The stories that found their way into written archives were those, which were sensationalized and politically motivated by the antagonistic relationship between Greece and Persia. Instead of speaking of "Persian women" in general, historians found it more useful to examine the actions of a few individual women as queens, because very little is known even about the majority of royal women. It is important to note that the information on their legal, economic, and cultural status and activities is similarly limited.[24] The most invaluable evidence for the discussion of women in the Hakhāmanishīyān period is based on the later discoveries of the Persepolis Fortification Tablets that were found during the excavations conducted by archaeologists in the

20 Zoroaster is one of the world's oldest religions founded in the ancient Persia. The Avistā (Avesta) is the primary collection of sacred texts of the Zoroastrianism.

21 Amīn, *supra* note 5, at 81.

22 *Id.* at 120; *See* Amīn, *supra* note 5, at 82, 90.

23 *See* Amīn, *supra* note 5, at 82.

24 Maria Brosius, Women in Ancient Persia (559-331 BCE) 1, 105-106 (Oxford University Press 1996).

1930s. They shed light, for example, on the titles for royal women and their economic status.[25]

During the Hakhāmanishīyān period, two groups of women had an active role in the political life of the Persian court: royal women and noble women, which included royal daughters married to nobles and daughters of noble descent. The most important motivation for their political involvement was the welfare of their family, such as saving the life of a family member or maintaining the position and the continuity of power of their family. Women could only act within well-defined boundaries that made them unable to take the law into their own hands. They needed to consult the king and to obtain his consent; if they ignored his authority and acted for themselves they also became subject to the king's punishment.[26]

Royal women were able to express their opinion on certain King's decisions. They could inform the king about possible disturbances arising in the palace; however, they had no power of judgment regarding judicial matters. Certainly, women did not have a direct role in other matters like politics, military, or in deciding the succession to the throne. Once the verdict was given, however, the women could seek to alter the method of punishment.[27]

Based on the hierarchical order among the female royal families, according to the Greek sources, the most important woman at the Persian court was the "mother of the king" who had direct access to the king. The mother of the king could express her main concerns to protect her family from harm and death. She could play a role of mediator in order to save the life of a member of the royal family at the Persian court and could appeal to the king to change royal verdicts.[28]

The second most important royal female was the "wife of the king." Information about the position of the wife of the king, other than being the mother of the heir, is difficult to construe from the sources. Responsibilities of the king's wife were similar to the tasks of the king's mother. Both often had great wealth and could manage estates, villages, and towns across the empire.[29]

---

25 Encyclopaedia Iranica, *supra* note 17. *See also id.* at 9-10.

26 Brosius, *supra* note 24, at 119-120.

27 *Id.* at 120-121.

28 *Id.* at 122.

29 *Id.* at 180, 187-188.

During the Hakhāmanishī Empire, the absolute power of fathers in families started to decrease, and every individual in the family started to gain some autonomy. Girls after wedlock came under the guardianship of their husbands and later under the guardianship of their sons. It was during the Zoroastrian time that women gained ownership rights and could inherit, and could participate in their family, social and political affairs. During this time, marriage was considered a religious and according to the Zoroastrian faith, and thus women and men were considered equal in all their marital affairs and responsibilities. Despite some gains for women, it was also during the Hakhāmanishī time that seclusion for women during their mensuration became mandatory, and upper class women were strictly banned from appearing in the public arena during menses.[30]

There is no written or archeological evidence that suggest royal Hakhāmanishī women lived in the seclusion of a harem; it is quite to the contrary, royal women were among the few people at the court who had direct access to the king and joined him, for example, at breakfast and dinner.[31]

The Persepolis Fortification Tablets also shed light on the titles for non-royal women and female workers.[32] In addition they also allow us to learn about the economic situation of Persian royal women who enjoyed considerable independence. The independent position enjoyed by royal women is evident from their use of personal seals and their ability to give orders to their officials in form of the letters. They had administrative facilities available to them similar to ones available to the king.[33]

The Fortification texts allow a unique insight into women's further involvement in the employment of work groups and the status of female workers. For example, it has been disclosed that there were work groups headed by a female chief.[34] Even though women did not hold any office within the royal administration, it has been shown that women worked alongside men and children.[35] There were two groups of workers identified that were characterized by predomi-

30 Amīn, *supra* note 5, at 97, 98, 99.

31 Encyclopaedia Iranica, *supra* note 17.

32 *Id.*

33 Brosius, *supra* note 24, at 180.

34 *Id.* at 181.

35 Encyclopaedia Iranica, *supra* note 17.

nantly female workers; there are no comparable texts identifying a workforce consisting mostly of men.[36]

According to the texts, it is clear that distinctions were sometimes made within professions based on different levels of expertise and skills. The texts also reveal that men and women were represented in identical professions and that they received equal payment as skilled workers. But overall, history seems to say that women received one third less payment than men. However, before interpreting the lower payments for some women as an indicator for unequal payment based on gender, it is important to discover whether the male and female workers engaged in the same kind of work.[37]

According to the Greeks, the Persian royal family appeared to engage in both polygamy and incestuous marriages;[38] but it is hard to determine their credibility.[39] It has been speculated that a king's decision to enter into marriage with more than one wife reflected particular circumstances and not custom. For example, some marriages were politically motivated, as in cases where the king needed to secure his legitimate right to the throne, or to bring peace to his kingdom.[40]

Another ancient dynasty is the Ashkānīyān Dynasty, also known as the Pārtīyān Dynasty. There is no reliable evidence on the status of judges, judiciary and penal traditions during this time.[41] However, there are few documents that enable historians to learn about women during that time. This does not permit a detailed discussion of the possible political influence, economic independence, and legal situation of women during the Pārtīyān. The few documents available reveal nothing more than a few names and titles of royal women and their status. Historians are unable to discuss about the legal and economic status of non-royal women. However, they can only assume that, based on the Hakhāmanishī and other practices, Pārtīyān royal women owned land and estates.[42]

---

36 Brosius, *supra* note 24, at 186.

37 *Id.*

38 *Id.* at 35.

39 Encyclopaedia Iranica, *supra* note 17.

40 *Id. See also* Brosius, *supra* note 24, at 36.

41 The Pārtīyān Empire (247 BCE-224 AD) was a major political and cultural power in Ancient Persia. Amīn, *supra* note 5, at 106.

42 Encyclopaedia Iranica, *supra* note 17.

During the Ashkānīyān, the family unit was the most important pillar of the society and families ran according to patriarchal traditions. During this time, women had fewer rights and did not participate in any social and political affairs. Women and children were under the guardianship of men and considered inferior. They were forced to cover themselves and were banned from appearing in public areas. Single women belonged to their paternal families and after marriage they belonged to their husband's families.[43] Not only did political marriage alliances occur during this time, but royal women were also used as pawns in the creation of political alliances.[44]

The last powerful and leading empire before the invasion of Arabs and the rise of Islam in ancient Persia was the Sāsānīyān Empire.[45] It is undisputed that after rein of the first Sāsānī king, Ardishīr Bābakān, the entire legal system was deeply transformed. For the first time, rules and traditions of Zoroastrian religion became the most important pillars of the Sāsānī's legal system; creating religious and customary jurisdictions. Religious figures became the most important persons and the highest class of the society, competing with the king. The average and common people made up the lowest class of the society.[46] The judicial power in general and judging, especially in penal, private, family, and religious matters, were kept within the religious tribunals judged by the Zoroastrian clergy. Administrative, military, national security, and sometimes highly anticipated criminal matters became the authority of state tribunals, judged by judges who were supervised by the kings as the ultimate lawmakers.[47] The discussion of women during this time has been influenced by two key assumptions. First, ordinary women were not depicted in Sāsānī art. Second, the title "Queen of Queens," used as a reference to a king's daughter or sister, signaled the woman's status as a wife of the king, and thus gave proof of incestuous marriage alliances within the Sāsānī royal family.[48] Based on numerous seals, finger rings,

43 Amīn, *supra* note 5, at 108.

44 Encyclopaedia Iranica, *supra* note 17.

45 The Sāsānīyān Empire (224-651 AD) ruled more than 400 years and it was the last powerful empire before the rise of Islam. It was during this time that Zoroastrian became the official religion of the country. Prior to this, Persia did not have an official religion and people had freedom to choose their religion. Pīrnīyā, *supra* note 4, at 248. *See also* Amīn, *supra* note 5, at 108.

46 *See* Amīn, *supra* note 5, at 114, 117.

47 *Id.* at 120, 121, 123, 128-129, 167.

48 Encyclopaedia Iranica, *supra* note 17.

and silver vessels, it has been understood by the historians that there were high-ranking women during the Sāsānī time. Royal Sāsānī women also possessed their own seals authorizing them to conduct transactions and official affairs. The Sāsānī kings were polygamous to meet the king's need to produce numerous male offspring, choosing the best heir to the throne from among them.[49]

Civil laws were based on the Zoroastrian rules and traditions and organizing affairs such as marital relationships, financial and personal matters in a family, marriage, divorce, and birth were in the complete control of the Zoroastrian clerical figures.[50]

By the end of the Sāsānīyān period, even with having limited historical sources, it appears that all the information that we have today is about the status of royal and noble women in ancient Persia. There is no reliable evidence about the legal status of non-royal women during those times. Having limited resources and speculative secondary stories even about royal and noble women does not allow us today to confidently pass a judgment about the status of women during ancient Persia.[51]

49 *Id.*

50 AMĪN, *supra* note 5, at 128-129.

51 *See* TOQRANEGAR, *supra* note 16, at 55-56.

Status of Women Post-Arab Conquest

The Arab invasion and conquest of Persia in the mid-seventh century destroyed the Sāsānī legal system, which was based on social classes and therefore privileges that discriminated; instead introduced a system that was based on equality and elimination of class-based discrimination. The expansion of Islam beyond the borders of Arabia brought vast social and political changes into all aspects of Persian people's lives including women.[52] This was the beginning of the gradual replacement of the Zoroastrian rules and traditions with Islamic principles and laws. It has been well documented that during the Umavīyān and Marvānīyān Dynasties, the legal systems were extremely discriminatory and anti-Iranian, which laid the foundation for the establishment of the ʿbāsīyān Dynasty due to the extreme discontent of the Iranian people. For the first time, the foundation of an Islamic legal system was established during the ʿbāsīyān.[53] It is noteworthy that many dynasties were established and collapsed after the Arab invasion, certainly with significant influence on the role and status of women in the society. Nonetheless, examination of women's legal status during the many centuries and dynasties after the invasion of Arabs requires keen analysis and summarization based on reliable sources that is beyond the scope of this paper. This section will include only a general overview of women's status after the invasion of Arabs and rise of Islam.

The Mughul invasion of Iran, starting in 1219, established new phenomena. The Islamic legal system was abandoned and instead the legal system was based on the code of honor, dignity and excellence of the Chingis Khan called the "Yasa of Chingis Khanj." According to the marriage codes, for example, every man

52 Leila Ahmed, Women, and Gender in Islam: Historical Roots of a Modern Debate 79-82 (Yale University Press 1992); Amīn, *supra* note 5, at 247.

53 Four Islamic school of thoughts were established: Mālikī, Ḥanafī, Shāfiʿī, and Ḥanbalī. Among these, Ḥanafī and Shāfiʿī became more influential in Iran. Amīn, *supra* note 5, at 210, 247.

should buy his bride. Women had to maintain and care for homes and could buy or sell as desired.[54]

Almost 900 years after the fall of the Sāsānīyān, the Ṣafavīyān Dynasty was established. They adopted Shīʿa Islam as the official religion of the country while the majority of Muslims in the world were Sunnī. One of the most important transformations was replacing hundreds of years of Sunnī rules with Shīʿa jurisprudence in their legal system. The establishment of a centralized government paved the way for creation of two separate jurisdictions. These were the religious jurisdiction and *urfī* (non-religious/state) jurisdictions, which endured until the establishment of the new legal system under the Pahlavī Monarchy in the first quarter of the 20th century.[55]

In general, after the Arab invasion, enormous harems of wives became the accepted practice for noble families.[56] Women had little power over their sexual, psychological and emotional lives.[57] A "woman" meant a purchasable object for a man's sexual desire.[58] Women's value and social position declined to that of "an object," causing them to lose all their relations to the outside world. They were treated as intellectually lower than men.[59]

Most of the documented information regarding the status of women during the Ṣafavīyān era is about royal or urban women. Historians are unable to identify much information about the status of rural or tribal women. Considering the fact that during the Ṣafavīyān time, Iran was a big rural society, not having a record of rural women's status is a clear statement about the neglected status of most women during that time. However, there are speculations about women's general duties in the rural areas. Women, for example, were expected to work at agriculture, taking care of animals in farms, baking bread, sewing, helping in constructing homes, and helping their husbands or fathers in family affairs. The above duties were in addition to women's duties at home to be obedient to their husbands and take care of their families, raise children, cook and clean. Jobs

54 AMĪN, *supra* note 5, at 299-303.

55 *Id.* at 333, 368.

56 AHMED, *supra* note 52, at 83.

57 *Id.* at 84.

58 *Id.* at 84-85.

59 TOQRANEGAR, *supra* note 16, at 65.

such as cloth weaving and carpet weaving were a common way for women to earn money.[60]

Upper class women's indirect role to empower their husbands to gain high political positions is a well-established tradition during Ṣafavīyān time.[61] During this time, Muslim women in Iran were wearing Islamic *ḥijāb* (proper Islamic cover)[62] in public that included a long *chādur* (a loose full body length outer garment) covering head to toe and *ruband* (face cover) that completely covered their faces other than their eyes.[63]

Even though, girls could marry as young as age ten, or in some cases even younger than ten years old, they could also re-marry after getting a divorce or after the death of their husband.[64] Temporary wives and slave girls were allowed during this time.[65] Pursuant to the Islamic traditions that resulted in gender segregation, it naturally created jobs specifically targeting women's affairs. The most important of these was dealing with women's medical problems, especially giving birth. As a result, there were women practicing women's medicine.[66] Gender segregation also created certain employment opportunities for some women in the service of the harem.[67] Urban women were active in jobs like nursing, teaching, calligraphy, painting, and taking notes from Qurān and other books.[68]

It has been speculated that women during the Sāsānīyān were on their path to move forward in improving their status and independence, and that the consequent victory of the Arabs and the fall of the Sāsānīyān practically reversed that trend and deprived women from participating in numerous social activities

---

60 Banafshih Ḥijāzī, Żaʿīfi: Barasīyi Jāygāhi Zani Irānī dar ʿṣri Ṣafavī [The Weak Sex: The Examination of Women's Status During the Ṣafavī Dynasty] 297, 298 (Qaṣīdi Sarā Publication 1992). (TA)

61 *Id.* at 189-196.

62 Ḥijāb, *infra* note 119, text. At this time, non-Muslim women did not wear ḥijāb and were free to communicate with men without covering their faces. However, the issue of women wearing ḥijāb was different in different parts of Iran. *Id.* at 270.

63 Ḥijāzī, *supra* note 60, at 269-280.

64 *Id.* at 89.

65 *Id.* at 105.

66 *Id.* at 300.

67 Women could be hair combers, bakers, reciters of the Quran, washerwomen, midwives, washers of the dead, mourners at funerals and female spies. Ahmed, *supra* note 52, at 84.

68 Ḥijāzī, *supra* note 60, at 300.

and roles. However, there are historians who have admired women's roles after rise of Islam in Iran and believe that there were independent women, for example, as religious leaders, poets and scientists during those times.[69]

Nonetheless, after the rise of Islam in Iran and despite some modest and limited achievements for women, because of falling apart from authentic Islamic rules, and prevalence of patriarchal traditions, and social, cultural and political trends, women were marginalized and continued to be controlled by men.[70]

69 *See* TOQRANEGAR, *supra* note 16, at 58-59.

70 *Id.* at 59.

Legal Status of Women during the Final Years of Qājār

a. Status of Women

The Qājār imperial political sovereignty ruled Iran from 1795 until its fall in 1925. The Qājār embedded two milestone political uprisings during the late 19th century and in the beginning of the 20th century. First, was the *Taḥrīmi Tanbāku* (Tobacco Revolt)[71] that climaxed in 1891. Second, was the Constitutional Revolution that took place in 1906-1907 that ultimately established a parliamentary system for the first time in the Iranian political history. It is critical to examine women's roles and challenges during this time because for the first time in Iranian history, and especially in the modern history of Iran, women played a prominent role not only by participating in political uprisings, but also by requesting legal, social and political reforms against them. Women, who for so long had been seen as objects, began to fight back against hundreds of years of patriarchal rules and customs that categorized them the same as criminals and the mindless. They fought against, for example, women's illiteracy and the legal ban on their enfranchisement. They confronted male dominant schools of thoughts by challenging them in newspapers and by forming women organizations.[72]

Since the beginning of the uprising against Qājār, women's political participation was divided into two major categories: women's movements that were based on following and supporting men's revolts in fighting back against Qājār tyranny; and independent women's movements. Women's roles, for example, in

71 Taḥrīmi Tanbāku (Tobacco Revolt), hereinafter Tobacco Revolt.

72 *See e.g.*, Niẓāmnāmiyi Intikhābāti Aṣnāfī Majlisi Shurāyi Millī 1285 [Election Law of the National Consultative Assembly 1906], arts. 3(1), 5(1), (Iran) (TA); Full Discussion of the National Consultative Assembly 2d Term-280 Session, May 12, 1947, at 1531, Library, Museum and Document Center of Iran Parliament.

establishing women's groups, schools, and women's newspapers were based on women's independent will to change and improve their status.[73]

Iran during the late 19th and early 20th centuries was predominantly an Shīʿa Islam country and patriarchal society.[74] Men were in complete control of every aspect of social, political and legal affairs; women's responsibilities were limited to their traditional family duties.[75] Even women's official dress identified them as a weaker sex unfit for anything but domestic roles and obedience to men's will.[76] Sexual segregation and wearing the veil were tools implementing a code of honor among Iranian women in the society. The veil was regarded as the symbol of the most oppressive institution, enforcing gender segregation and restricting women's physical mobility.[77]

Women were strictly prevented from entering the public domain, and their mobility was strictly controlled.[78] Even wealthy and elite women rarely left their homes; if they did, they had to be accompanied.[79] During this time, women were kept unaware of the social and political transformations taking place all over the world;[80] kings were used to their harems, which guaranteed the enjoyment of their lust and sexual appetite for women.[81] According to a few outspoken thinkers of that time, women were considered as objects; deprived from elementary

73 ʿbās Muḥamadī Aṣl, Mavāniʿi Mushārikati Sīyasīyi Zanān Dar Irān [Restriction Against Women's Political Participation in Iran], Scientific Information Database, at 108 (2004), *accessed at* http://www.sid.ir/fa/VEWSSID/J_pdf/62113831204.pdf. (TA)

74 Hamideh Sedghi, Women and Politics in Iran: Veiling, Unveiling, and Reveiling 26 (Cambridge University Press 2007).

75 Mihrangīz Kār, Mushārikati Sīyāsīyi Zanān [Women's Participation in Politics] 15 (Rushangarān va Muṭāliʿti Zanān Publication 2001). (TA)

76 Sedghi, *supra* note 74, at 26.

77 Janet Afary, Sexual Politics in Modern Iran 34 (Cambridge University Press 2009). *See also* Fatima Mernissi, Beyond the Veil: Male-Female Dynamics in Modern Iran 96 (2d ed., Indiana University Press 1987).

78 Sedghi, *supra* note 74, at 26.

79 *Id.*

80 Toqranegar, *supra* note 16, at 66.

81 *Id.*

education and involvement in sociopolitical affairs.[82] Women were socially segregated and imprisoned in their own homes.[83]

The practice of polygamy, which goes back to ancient times as early as the Hakhāmanishī Empire, was also commonly practiced during the Qājār for upper-class men. However, it rarely was practiced among rural or urban poor men.[84] During this time, men could legally marry four wives, and have an unlimited number of temporary wives and slave girls. Polygamy was also practiced among minority men such as Sunnīs and Armenians. For a man, having several wives was a sign of prestige confirming one's ties with the upper class, or a way of confirming one's improved economic status.[85]

b. Women's Role in the Tobacco Revolt

The 1891 Tobacco Revolt, during the last years of Qājār, was the first significant popular uprising in which, for the first time, women officially participated to establish the movement. This was aided by religious figures.[86] In a nutshell, the discontent of the people started with many privileges that were granted to foreign countries by the king, the most important of which was the Tobacco monopoly given to Britain in 1890.[87] As religious leaders and the people united, they demanded that the king void the privilege that was given to Britain. This

---

82 *See* SEDGHI, *supra* note 74, at 25.

83 *See* Full Discussion of the National Consultative Assembly 2d Term-280 Session, at 1531, LIBRARY, MUSEUM AND DOCUMENT CENTER OF IRAN PARLIAMENT.

84 JANET AFARY, SEXUAL POLITICS IN MODERN IRAN 33 (Cambridge University Press 2009).

85 *Id.* at 34.

86 AḤMAD KASRAVĪ, TĀRĪKHI MASHRUTIYI IRĀN [THE IRANIAN CONSTITUTIONAL REVOLUTION] 17 (Amīr Kabīr Publication 1999). (TA)

87 A British company obtained the monopoly over the production, sale, and export of tobacco from Iran. Granting these privileges brought many foreigners to the country, especially increasing the number of Europeans. As a result people and religious figures were disappointed, considered the privilege a big loss for the country and began to criticize the king. On the other hand it was very difficult for Iranians to accept the fact that they produced the tobacco, but had to sell it to the foreigners for a very low price, and then pay a higher price if they repurchased tobacco from them. Despite a merchants' letter to the king, demanding litigation in the matter, they did not get any reaction. Increasing numbers of companies and merchants in different cities, and the people and religious leader's disappointment, escalated to become one of the most important movements in the history of Modern Iran. Ultimately, the Tobacco Revolt caused Nāṣir Adīn Shāh to revoke the privilege. *Id.* at 15-17.

ultimately led to the Āyatullāh Mīrzā Shīrāzī'[88] famous *fatvā*--an Islamic legal decree issued by a leading Islamic jurist--to boycott tobacco. This was where women and men, young and old, rich and poor, were united, and closed down all tobacco stores and refused to buy and use tobacco in following the *fatvā*.[89] Boycotting tobacco shocked the foreign tobacco companies and the situation escalated to a bloody uprising that ultimately led to the king voiding the privilege.[90] Common people and women belonging to royal households, who never refused or even questioned the king's orders, participated in the creation of this event, broke their tobacco pipes, and refused to follow the king's order.[91] This set an unprecedented role of women in participating in request for social and political change.

c. Women's Rights Post-Constitutional Revolution

The existence of restrictive social practices against women during the early 20th century made it almost impossible for women to even bring up a discussion about sociopolitical rights and freedoms of women.[92] Nonetheless, women alongside men supported the Constitutional Revolution in 1906, hoping that the revolution would transform their private and social lives.[93]

Reformist women, for example, supported the Constitutional Revolution by publishing articles in newspapers to confront political and social discrimination against them imposed by men.[94] The main focus of those women was on acquiring social and political rights for women rather than dealing with women's status in the family, which was considered a private matter.[95]

---

88 Āyatullāh Mīrzā Shīrāzī was a famous Islamic scholar. He is widely known for his famous fatvā against the usage of tobacco in what became known as the Tobacco Revolt during the Qājār era.

89 Kasravī, *supra* note 86, at 15-17.

90 *Id.* at 17.

91 Toqranegar, *supra* note 16, at 66-67.

92 Kār, *supra* note 75, at 17.

93 Muḥammad Ḥusiyni Khusru Panāh, Hadafhā va Mubārizāti Zan dar Irān az Inqilābi Mashruṭi tā Salṭanati Pahlavī [Iranian Woman's Goals and Battles From the Constitutional Revolution until the Pahlavi Dynasty] 17 (Payāmi Imruz Publication 2002). (TA)

94 *Id.* at 44.

95 *Id.* at 47.

Pursuant to the triumph of the Constitutional Revolution in 1906, the first Constitution was adopted by the newly established first Majlis Millī (National Consultative Assembly)[96] in Iran. Later in 1907, additional supplementary laws were ratified and added to this Constitution.[97] This was the end of hundreds of years of the traditional style of autocratic governorship in Iran, in which the king was almost like a God, with unlimited legal and political power.[98] According to Article 2 of the newly adopted Constitution, the newly established National Consultative Assembly was the representative of all the people who could freely participate in the economic and political affairs of their county.[99] Following Article 8 of the Amendment to the Constitution, all Iranian people could enjoy "equal protection before the law."[100]

Despite women's deep involvement in establishing the parliamentary system that guaranteed the equal protection before the law for all,[101] women were explicitly barred from voting and being elected by the first election law for the assembly.[102] According to Article 3(1) of the *Niẓāmnāmiyi Intikhābāti Aṣnāfī Majlisi Shurāyi Millī* 1285 (Election Law of the National Consultative Assembly 1906), women were the first category among disfranchised groups of people. According to this law women were put under the same category as individuals under guardianships and the retarded.[103] Pursuant to Article 5(1) of this law, women were explicitly banned by the legislators from being elected to the National Consultative Assembly.[104]

One of the serious challenges faced by women after the establishment of the parliamentary system was fighting against deeply entrenched male schools of thought. The dominant patriarchal system still considered women intellectually mutilated, weak, foolish, and lazy, which was undoubtedly confirmed

96 Majlis Millī (National Consultative Assembly), hereinafter National Consultative Assembly.

97 *See* Qanun'i Assass'i Iran (Iranian Constitution) 1906; Mutamami Qānuni Āsāsī [Amendment to the Constitution] 1286 [1907].

98 Toqranegar, *supra* note 16, at 67.

99 *See* Qanun'i Assass'i Iran (Iranian Constitution) 1906, art. 2.

100 *See* Mutamami Qānuni Āsāsī [Amendment to the Constitution] 1286 [1907], art. 8.

101 *See id.*

102 *See* Niẓāmnāmiyi Intikhābāti Aṣnāfī Majlisi Shurāyi Millī 1285 [Election Law of the National Consultative Assembly 1906], arts. 3(1), 5(1) (Iran). (TA)

103 *See id.* at Art. 3(1).

104 *See id.* at Art. 5(1).

by the election laws. It was expected from women to fulfill the needs for their husbands.[105]

Women's supposed lack of awareness about the world, and their strictly controlled private and social status, were other hurdles in front of their political and public growth.[106] The government failed to provide any educational institution for Iranian women in the early 1900.[107] According to women advocates there was a critical need to educate women during those times.[108]

Later in 1907, the Law of the State and Provincial Associations explicitly banned women from voting and being elected to the National Consultative Assembly.[109] Pursuant to passage of the next election law in 1911, yet again women explicitly were put in the disfranchised categories along with retarded, bankrupts, robbers and murderers.[110] Article 7(2) of the same law also explicitly banned women from being elected.[111]

The aftermath of the First World War (1914-1918) created a new perspective for Iranian women. They became aware of the participation of European women during the war, working in factories, administration, and other jobs alongside men. European transformation served as a catalyst for Iranian women to reexamine their sociopolitical and legal status, and in questioning leaders of the county regarding their potential roles. The stirring of women's freedom continued. They were beginning to be educated and participate in public affairs, even if they were denied the basic legal right to vote and to be elected to the National Consultative Assembly and statewide elections. Despite women's progress in being able to criticize the country's governorship and analyze existing problems, women still lacked political, social and economic knowledge and expertise, which made them politically powerless.[112]

---

105 *See* Khusru Panāh, *supra* note 93, at 42.

106 *Id.* at 75.

107 Sedghi, *supra* note 74, at 53.

108 Khusru Panāh, *supra* note 93, at 75.

109 *See* Qānuni Anjumanhāyi Iyālatī va Vilāyatī 1286 [Law of the State and Provincial Associations 1907], arts. 7(4), 9(4) (Iran). (TA)

110 Qānuni Intikhābāti Majlisi Shurāyi Millī 1290 [Election Law of the National Consultative Assembly 1911], art. 4 (Iran), (TA)

111 *See id.* at Art. 7(2).

112 Khusru Panāh, *supra* note 93, at 181-184.

By the end of the House of Qājār in 1925, in spite of women's role in the demands for the rule of law and social justice, they still were battling to gain basic fundamental legal rights such as the equal political right to vote. The laws passed by the parliament since 1906 not only deprived women of their absolute political rights, it legally treated women the same as the mindless individuals and convicted criminals.

Legal Status of Women during the Pahlavī Monarchy

Concerning the advancement of the rights of women in modern Iranian history, the Pahlavī era is the most significant period. Riżā Pahlavī's[113] unprecedented and innovative, yet controversial, policies regarding women were the start of rapid removal of many social taboos and restrictions that had enslaved women for centuries. Half a century of Pahlavī reforms ultimately emancipated entrapped women from hundreds of years of severely restrictive patriarchal and Islamic customs. However, achieving these goals was not possible without simultaneously weakening the Islamic clerics who had previously been in charge of every aspect of people's lives.[114]

In the beginning of Riżā Pahlavī's rule in 1925, all the election laws, among other restrictions on women, stayed intact. These laws continued to treat women like mindless, criminals, and bankrupts; explicitly banned them from voting and being elected in the assembly and other government offices.[115] However there were unprecedented social and legal reforms during the reign of Riżā Pahlavī, and the next subsections will demonstrate the earliest and the most influential transformations for women.

a. Kashfi Ḥijāb (Unveiling)

Riżā Pahlavī's new unprecedented policies moved toward wiping out some centuries old Islamic traditions from the Iranian society; and replacing them

113 Riżā Pahlavī is the founder of the Pahlavī Monarchy in 1925 who served until 1941. In 1923, the National Consultative Assembly selected him as the Iran's Prime Minister. In 1925, he was appointed as the legal monarch of Iran by decision of Iran's constituent assembly. The assembly deposed Aḥmad Shāh Qājār, the last king of the Qājār and selected Riżā Pahlavī and Pahlavī Monarchy.

114 For example Kashfi Ḥijāb, marriage law, and educational reforms for women.

115 *See e.g.*, Qānuni Intikhābāti Majlisi Shurāyi Millī 1304 [Election Law of the National Consultative Assembly 1925], arts. 10(1), 13(2) (Iran). (TA)

with nationalism, secularism and modern policies.[116] His first innovative, yet bold, policy that directly affected women's public life was called *Kashfi Ḥijāb* (Unveiling).[117] Easy acceptance of such extreme deviation from restrictive Islamic traditions for women at that time was not possible. Those changes required him to reduce the Islamic clergy's authority not only in the political sphere but also in the legal, social, and economic affairs of the country.[118]

Ḥijāb is a generic term for the proper Islamic dress for women. In the traditional Islamic view, ḥijāb is a divinely ordered requirement that associates with men's unalterable weakness in resisting sexual temptations when facing any women (other than grandmothers, mothers, aunts, and sisters). Hijāb is a manifestation of chastity, dignity, and modesty. It is presented as something that always existed in Islam and always guaranteed women's presence in the public by liberating women to enter the social domain. It grants a woman human identity, allowing her to engage in social activities free from sexual attractions.[119]

Mandatory unveiling of women in public was a gradual process as wearing traditional women's clothes was not abolished overnight.[120] The unveiling decree officially was promulgated in the country in 1936.[121] At the first day of the execution of this decree, Riżā Pahlavī attended a graduation ceremony at Dānish Sarāyi Muqadamātīyi (Teachers' Training College) with his wife and daughters who were unveiled and appeared wearing European attire.[122] All women teachers and wives of government officials were also ordered to appear in European clothes and hats. This was the beginning of banning veiled women from appearing in public arenas. Riżā Pahlavī considered the *chādur* the enemy of progress and the development of women, and ordered uncovering for other such gatherings in the future so that the Iranian women could become accustomed to the

116 Afsāni Rushan, Masāʿili Kashfi Ḥijāb bi Rivāyati Asnādi Kitābkhāniyi Majlisi Shurāyi Millīyi Irān [Issues Surrounding Unveiling According to the Documents of the Library of the National Consultative Assembly], Institute for Humanities and Cultural Studies (Winter 2009), *accessed at* http://www.ensani.ir/storage/Files/20101205135852-Pages%20from%20payam6-54.pdf. (TA)

117 *See* Kār, *supra* note 75, at 25.

118 Rushan, *supra* note 116.

119 Reza Afshari, Human Rights in Iran: The Abuse of Cultural Relativism 262 (University of Pennsylvania Press 2001).

120 Sedghi, *supra* note 74, at 85.

121 Rushan, *supra* note 116.

122 *Id.*

new changes.[123] This was the beginning of removing a longstanding taboo that prevented women from socializing with men out in public without a proper Islamic ḥijāb as protection.

The implementation of the mandatory unveiling was the first direct attack against the Islamic beliefs of many people and Islamic clergy who considered wearing ḥijāb mandatory[124] for Muslim women in public. It also created much resentment among Islamic clergy.[125] The Islamic clergy was the strongest opposition group against the mandatory unveiling and considered it against Islam and the Qurān.[126] The clergy believed that unveiling was against hundreds of years of Islamic traditions, since the Prophet's time, and that unveiling was aimed at abolishing religion and eradicating Islamic roots in the Iranian society.[127]

b. Reforms in Family Law & Education

During the Riżā Pahlavī era the civil marriage law was ratified for the first time. It regulated marriages and divorces, which previously were solely within the jurisdiction of the Islamic clerics. This law required that marriage must be recorded with the government. It also outlined specific conditions for divorce. Even though the marriage law was progressive by the standards of that time, it did not target, for example, polygamy, temporary marriage, male guardianship, and exclusive rights of women and men in the event of divorce.[128]

It was not until 1967 that for the first time all family related laws and procedures were ratified and codified under one new law called the *Qānuni Ḥimāyati Khānivādi* 1346 (Family Protection Law 1967).[129] Article 8 of this law limited

---

123 SEDGHI, *supra* note 74, at 86, 87; 3 IMAM KHOMEINI, SAHIFEH-YE IMAM 309 (Majid Karimi & Mansoor Limba eds., the Institute for Compilation and Publication of Imam Khomeini's Work 2008).

124 *E.g., see* 3 IMAM KHOMEINI, SAHIFEH-YE IMAM 309 (Majid Karimi & Mansoor Limba eds., the Institute for Compilation and Publication of Imam Khomeini's Work 2008).

125 RUSHAN, *supra* note 116, at 2-4. *See also* CAMRON MICHAEL AMIN, THE MAKING OF THE MODERN IRANIAN WOMEN 112-113 (University Press of Florida, 2002).

126 RUSHAN, *supra* note 116.

127 *Id.*

128 CAMRON MICHAEL AMIN, THE MAKING OF THE MODERN IRANIAN WOMEN 13 (University Press of Florida, 2002).

129 This law was amended in 1975. *See* Qānuni Ḥimāyati Khānivādi 1346 [Family Protection Law 1967] (Iran); Qānuni Ḥimāyati Khānivādi 1353 [Family Protection Law 1975] (Iran), hereinafter FPL 1967, 1975. (TA)

man's exclusive right to divorce his wife without any court procedure.[130] This law also expanded the very limited right of a woman to divorce her husband.[131] It also limited a man's ability to have multiple wives by requiring a man to request judicial permission from the court to have a new wife. It also required that a man obtain permission from his first wife for his second marriage.[132] Later reform of the FPL in 1975 drastically expanded the rights of women to divorce,[133] and put even more restriction on men's right to have multiple wives.[134] It also raised the age of marriage for women from 15 years of age to 18 years.[135]

Concerning reforms in education, Riżā Pahlavī's rapid moves toward modernization included establishing a secular educational system that originally had been dominated by religious clerical authorities.[136] The most serious obstacle for women during that time was the high percentage of illiteracy among them.[137] Riżā Pahlavī invested more resources into reform and expansion of secondary and postsecondary education for women. Finally, it was in 1935 that women were officially permitted to get a higher education and be admitted to Tehran University.[138]

The combination of opening the educational system to women, reforming some family laws and abolishing restrictive ḥijāb in public were enormous state-run steps forward toward emancipation of women from hundreds of years of restrictive taboos.

c. Women's Suffrage

Despite Riżā Pahlavī's strict enforcement of the controversial mandatory unveiling policy, some reform of the marriage law, and progressive developments in women's education, the existence of de jure and de facto discrimination against

130 *See* Family Protection Law 1967, art. 8 (Iran).

131 *See id.* at Arts. 10, 11.

132 *See id.* at Art. 14.

133 *See* Family Protection Law 1975, art. 8 (Iran).

134 *See id.* at Arts. 16, 17.

135 *See id.* at Art. 23; See Qanuni-i- Madani [Civil Code] Tehran 1313 [1934], art. 1041.

136 SEDGHI, *supra* note 74, at 70.

137 TOQRANEGAR, *supra* note 16, at 120.

138 MICHAEL AMIN, *supra* note 128, at 154-159.

women barred the enjoyment of the most fundamental legal and political rights, such as voting and being elected to the National Consultative Assembly and other government offices for women.[139]

The opponents of women's suffrage in the National Consultative Assembly justified their views by asserting that women did not deserve to have the right to choose because, for example, they were under the "guardianship of men" under Islamic jurisprudence.[140] According to Āyatullāh Mudaris, one of the Islamic scholar members of the second National Consultative Assembly:

> I have had a very eventful life and I never was shaken by any of them, but today my body is shaking. The problem with this committee, first, is that the name of *women should never be mentioned as electors* because *women do not have the right to choose....* [T]oday the more I consider this matter, I realize that *God has not given women the capability and worth to have the right to choose... their brain lacks intelligence* and the reality is that according to our religion, *Islam, women* are *under the guardianships of men* and since they are under the guardianships of men, therefore *they will not acquire the right to choose. Others should protect women's rights,* likewise according to Qurān, God asserts that women are under the guardianships of men and will not have the right to choose.[141] [Emphasis Added]

Women's nearly fifty-eight year battle to win the equal right to vote since the establishment of the parliamentary system finally ended in 1964. Earlier, in 1962, the first attempt to reform the de jure election laws that discriminated against women had failed. According to the proposed bill three requirements -- being Muslim, being a man and swearing to Qurān for electorates and candidates -- were about to change. To be Muslim and swearing to Qurān was eliminated in order to include religious minorities such as the Bahā'ī faith. Additionally, it proposed the political enfranchisement of women. Initially, the government passed this bill. However, it was rejected strongly by the prominent religious

139 *See e.g.*, Election Law of the National Consultative Assembly 1925, arts. 10(1), 13(2) (Iran).

140 *See* Detailed Discussion of the NCA Term 2-Session 280, *supra* note 83.

141 *Id.*

leaders such as Imām Khumiynī.[142] Religious leaders contested and demanded repealing the bill because they considered the new changes nothing but a foreign conspiracy to destroy public modesty in Iran. They asserted that the changes were not to liberate women but to promote corruption and prostitution among them.[143] Ultimately, this newly passed election law was nullified later in 1962.[144]

It was in 1963 that Muḥammad Riżā Pahlavī held a national referendum and officially launched his most important series of progressive human rights reforms called the "White Revolution." The unprecedented "White Revolution" was based on equal rights and justice for all, and was approved by a majority vote of the Iranian people. Out of six principles, principle five of the "White Revolution"[145] was directly aimed at women, and demanded equal political rights for those who after all made up half the population. It requested that women no longer be legally treated as mindless and criminals in the 20th century.[146] Equal political rights for women, to vote and be elected to the National Consultative Assembly, the Senate of Iran, and the State and Provincial Associations became possible after the passage of the "White Revolution" by people, allowing ratification of new laws and amending older discriminatory election laws against women.[147]

The single Note of the *Qānuni Rājiʿ bi Shirkati Bānuvān Dar Intikhābāt* 1343 (Law on Women's Participation in Election)[148] was adopted by the National Consultative Assembly in 1964, stating:

"Articles 10(1) and 13(2) of the 1925 Election Law of the National Consultative Assembly that aims at the qualifications of the electors and candidates to be

142 *See Mukhālifat bā Lāyiḥiyi Anjumanhāyi Iyālatī va Vilāyatī [Opposition to the Bill of State And Provincial Associations]*, IMAM-KHOMEINI, *accessed at* http://www.imam-khomeini.ir/fa/c2688/زندگی_نامه/دوران_مبارزات/مخالفت_با_لایحه_انجمنهای_ایالتی_و_ولایتی. (TA).

143 *See Taṣvībi Lāyiḥiyi Anjumanhāyi Iyālatī va Vilāyatī Dar Dulati Asadullāhi Aʿlam [Passage of the Bill of State And Provincial Associations by the Government of Asadullāhi Aʿlam]*, ISLAMIC REVOLUTION DOCUMENT CENTER (1962), *accessed at* http://www.irdc.ir/fa/calendar/154/default.aspx. (TA)

144 *See* OPPOSITION TO THE BILL OF STATE AND PROVINCIAL ASSOCIATIONS, *supra* not 142.

145 MOHAMMAD REZA PAHLAVI, ANSWER TO HISTORY 117 (Stein & Day Publisher 1981).

146 *See* Full Discussion of the National Consultative Assembly Term 21-Session 1, LIBRARY, MUSEUM AND DOCUMENT CENTER OF IRAN PARLIAMENT.

147 PAHLAVI, *supra* note 145, at 117-118.

148 Qānuni Rājiʿ bi Shirkati Bānuvān Dar Intikhābāt 1343 [Law on Women's Participation in Election 1964] (Iran). (TA)

selected; in addition the word *z̲ukur* (men) in Articles 6 and 9 of the 1949 Election Law of the Senate, will be omitted."[149]

As a result, for the first time, not only did women participate as electors and candidates for the twenty-first National Consultative Assembly election; six women were elected as members of the twenty-first National Consultative Assembly.[150]

After the meaningful reforms of the "White Revolution," the clergy lost much of its previous power. They considered the "White Revolution" absolute violations of Islamic laws and fought back strongly, insisting Muḥammad Riżā Pahlavī reverse the changes.[151]

d. Women's Political Empowerment

During Riżā Pahlavī, considering the growth of social, political and legal status of women then, there were still no women holding any important political positions. The 1964 election law guaranteed the equal political right for women to hold public office, and it was the beginning of integration of women into decision-making public roles, such as members of the twenty-first National Consultative Assembly; members of cabinet; ambassadors and university professors.[152] It was in 1969 that for the first time a few women became judges.[153] The highest political position that was ever given to a woman during that time in the Middle East was given to Queen Faraḥ Pahlavī when she became the official Empress Regent in 1968.[154]

149 *Id. See also* Qānuni Ijāziyi Ijrāyi Niẓāmnāmiyi Intikhābāti Majlisi Sinā 1328 [Law Allowing the Enforcement of the Senate Election 1949] (Iran). (TA)

150 Detailed Discussion of the NCA Term 21-Session 1, *supra* note 146.

151 Riżā Āyirmilu, Zan dar Girdābi Sharī't 14, 15 [Women and the Islamic Fundamentalists], (Invand Publication, 2002) (TA). *See also e.g.*, 1 Imam Khomeini, Sahifeh-Ye Imam 272 (Majid Karimi & Mansoor Limba eds., the Institute for Compilation and Publication of Imam Khomeini's Work 2008).

152 *See* Pahlavi, *supra* note 145, at 118.

153 Noushin Ahmadi Khorasani, Iranian Women's Equality Calendar With Chronology of One Million Signatures Campaign Demanding Changes to Discriminatory Laws, (Sahar Mofakham & Mahsa Shekarloo & Leila Tavakoli trans., 2008), *accessed at* http://www.feministschool.com/english/IMG/pdf/Iranian_Women_s_equality_calendar-2.pdf. (TA)

154 After several unsuccessful attempts to assassinate Muḥammad Riżā Pahlavī, he named his wife as the official Empress Regent in case of his death or other problems such as incapacitation. Toqranegar, *supra* note 16, at 97. *See also* Marvin Zonis, Majestic Failure: The Fall of the Shah 280 (Esmail Zan, Batol Saidi trans., Noor Publication 1992).

It is ironic that even after all social, political, and legal improvements for women such as women's suffrage; the passage of the Family Protection Law; holding important political offices and presiding as judges; women still were not really seen as equal to men. The notion that women were still generally considered intellectually unequal to men, for example, is found in an interview with an American TV reporter, Barbara Walters, in 1977. Muḥammad Riżā Pahlavī was asked, "Do you think that your wife can govern as well as a man?"[155] Muḥammad Riżā Pahlavī refused to answer her question by responding "I prefer not to answer."[156]

Walters:
You think that women are equal to men?

Muḥammad Riżā Pahlavī:
In human rights, sure.

Walters:
You have given women in your country human rights; what about in intelligence?

Muḥammad Riżā Pahlavī:
You can always have some exceptions and find fantastic women.[157]

155 *Television Interview by Barbara Walters with Shāh of Iran*, YouTube (1977), *accessed at* https://www.youtube.com/watch?v=UDE4ZUcFR-I&list=FLHlAZQ_N2c1DM6_sOqoKZ3Q.

156 *Id.*

157 *Id.*

Systematic Discrimination against Women Post-Islamic Revolution

The Islamic Revolution of 1979 put an end to over half a century of the Pahlavī Monarchy, and introduced a new government known as the "Islamic Republic of Iran" with the leadership of Āyatullāh Khumiynī, under the principle of *Vilāyati Faqīh* (Guardianship of the Islamic Jurisprudence).[158] The Guardianship of the Islamic Jurisprudence strictly requires that all laws and regulations in the country must be in accordance with Islamic criteria. Article 12 of the Constitution declares the Twelve Jaʿfarī Shīʿa Islam as the official religion in the country that remains eternally immutable.[159] Pursuant to Article 4 of the Constitution, Article 72 explicitly asserts that the Islamic Consultative Assembly cannot enact laws contrary to the rules and principles of Islam or to the Constitution. It is the Constitutional responsibility of *fuqahā* (Islamic scholars)[160] in the Guardian Council to examine the compatibility of all legislation passed by the assembly to determine whether Islamic laws and principles have been implemented.[161] This guarantees the proper application of Islamic laws to all legislation in the country and prevents any divergence from Islamic rules and principles.

In the midst of the people's uprising against the monarchy, Āyatullāh Khumiynī not only requested women's political participation, but also

158 *See* Qanuni Assassi Jumhuri'i Islamai Iran [The Constitution of The Islamic Republic of Iran] 1358 [1980], Preamble, arts. 1, 2(5), 5, 107. *Vilāyati Faqīh* (Guardianship of the Islamic Jurisprudence), hereinafter Guardianship of the Islamic Jurisprudence.

159 *See* Qanuni Assassi Jumhuri'i Islamai Iran [The Constitution of The Islamic Republic of Iran] 1358 [1980], Preamble, arts. 4, 12.

160 Word fuqahā is a plural for word faqīh. Faqīh is someone who is knowledgeable of Islamic laws based on Qurān and customs and traditions of the Prophet and Infallible Imāms. He is able to construe based on a clear understanding of matters, and is able to render fatvā. 1 Siyid Muḥammad Hāshimī, Huquqi Asāsī Jumhurīyi Islāmiyi Iran (Constitution of Islamic Republic of Iran) 39 (Dādgustar Publication 1999).

161 *See* Qanuni Assassi Jumhuri'i Islamai Iran [The Constitution of The Islamic Republic of Iran] 1358 [1980], arts. 4, 72, 96, 97, 98.

emphasized the significance of women's roles and obligation to participate in the formation of the revolution against tyranny of Pahlavī.[162] In return, he promised freedom and gender equality for women in the future of the new government.[163] For example, a few months before the triumph of the Islamic revolution, in April 1978, Āyatullāh Khumiynī in his first interview with a foreign newspaper, the French daily "Le Monde," was asked:

> Lucien George:
>
> Please state your position and views on three basic issues concerning Iran: land reform, industrialization of the country and *women*? [Emphasis Added]
>
> Āyatullāh Khumiynī:
>
> With regard to the question of *women*, Islam has never been against their emancipation; on the contrary Islam has opposed the concept of a woman as a 'thing,' and has given them back their dignity and honor. *Women and men are equal. Women are as free as men in determining their destinies and spheres of activity.* However, by having them steeped in immorality, the Shah's regime attempts to keep them from being free. Islam is very much against such a state of affairs. The regime has of course trampled upon and deprived the women of their freedom as it has done in the case of the men. The women, just as the men, have filled the prisons of Iran. It is here that their freedom is threatened and imperiled. We wish to liberate them from the corruption that menaces them.[164] [Emphasis Added]

In a similar note Āyatullāh Khumiynī asserted,

"In an Islamic system, the women enjoy the same rights that men do, that is, right to education, right to work, right to property, and right to suffrage. Women enjoy the same rights that men do in all fields."[165] "The women are free in the Islamic government; their rights will be identical with those of men."[166]

162 TOQRANEGAR, *supra* note 16, at 159.

163 *See e.g.*, *infra* note 164; *infra* note 165.

164 Āyatullāh Khumiynī had this interview when he was in exile in Najaf (Iraq). 3 *Imam Khomeini, Sahifeh-Ye Imam* 380, 383-384 (Majid Karimi & Mansoor Limba eds., the Institute for Compilation and Publication of Imam Khomeini's Work 2008).

165 5 IMAM KHOMEINI, SAHIFEH-YE IMAM 185 (Majid Karimi & Mansoor Limba eds., the Institute for Compilation and Publication of Imam Khomeini's Work 2008).

166 *Id.* at 68.

Āyatullāh Khumiynī asserted that the concept of a plea for women's freedom by Pahlavī according to their standards distorted the issue of freedom for women and made them looked on as "objects," and "dolls."[167]

Establishment of an Islamic government based on gender equality, freedom and democracy was always on top of the promised future changes in Iran by Āyatullāh Khumiynī. This was promised in every interview and sermon regarding the future of women in the new government. In November 1978, for example, in an interview with Russell Kerr, a member of the British House of Commons and member of the Labor Party, when Āyatullāh Khumiynī was asked about the rights of women, once again he asserted:

> "The women are free in the Islamic government; their rights will be identical with those of men. Islam emancipated the women from the captivation of men and put them on an equal footing with men. The propaganda carried out against us aims to misguide the people. Islam has guaranteed all the human rights and issues."[168]

Consequently, one of the outstanding characteristics of the revolution was women's unprecedented presence to achieve the victory of overthrowing the Pahlavī monarch.[169] This overthrow was the beginning of polarizing women. It opened a new chapter in Iranian women's history that in one hand valued veiled religious women as powerful revolutionaries and on the other hand degraded secular women as westernized and monarchic.[170]

Islamic scholars like Sharīʿtī used the most respected Islamic female role figures like Fātimi and Ziynab, the daughters of the Prophet Muḥammad, to promote an ideal role model of Muslim womanhood who accomplished all their traditional duties, but were also aware of their social responsibilities.[171] They

167 *See* Iṭṭilāʿāt Newspaper (Iran), May 19, 1979, N. 15857, at 4 (TA). *See also* Imam Khomeini, *supra* note 165, at 287, 288.

168 Imam Khomeini, *supra* note 165, at 67, 68.

169 Toqranegar, *supra* note 16, at 158. *See also e.g.*, 4 Imam Khomeini, Sahifeh-Ye Imam 417 (Majid Karimi & Mansoor Limba eds., the Institute for Compilation and Publication of Imam Khomeini's Work 2008); Imam Khomeini, *supra* note 165, at 185, 235.

170 *See* Sedghi, *supra* note 74, at 200.

171 1 Hammed Shahidian, Women in Iran: Gender Politics in the Islamic Republic 109 (Greenwood Press 2002).

believed women's participation in politics should be used in favor of Islam by having women play an active role in bringing Islam to power.[172]

Despite the initial gender equality promises by Āyatullāh Khumiynī, women were among the first to sacrifice after the triumph of the Islamic revolution as they experienced their legal status and social positions dramatically decline. For instance, reinstatement of compulsory ḥijāb, repeal of the Family Protection Law, and dismissal and demotion of all existing women judges were among early attacks on women's fundamental rights and freedom.[173]

The following subsections will examine, first, the Constitution's view on the rights and freedoms of women as the primary framer of women's rights within the legal system of the Islamic Republic of Iran. It will then proceed to examine the systemic discriminatory legal system against women by demonstrating the earliest and most fundamental legal and social setbacks on women's rights after the 1979 revolution.

The express male gender requirement imposed by the 1982 Law on the Qualifications for Appointment of Judges that bans women from pursuing judgeships, exemplifies the discriminatory nature of the legal system against women, especially in key decision-making positions in the government of IRI. Another key decision-making position that in practice is prohibited for women is the position of a President. The judgeship and presidency positions demonstrate the imposition of a male gender qualification, among other requirements, by the Constitution and other relevant laws. There are other important decision-making positions created by the Constitution, such as the Supreme Leader and the Head of the Judiciary, which in practice make male gender one of the required qualifications, thereby discriminating against women. The analysis of the existence of de facto discrimination against women in all these key decision-making positions requires a keen study and analysis that requires a separate scholarly work and is beyond the scope of this book. This work will focus on the denial of judgeships to women as a critical example of this broader discrimination against women.

172 *Id.*

173 *See* Valentine M. Moghadam, Women in the Islamic Republic of Iran: Legal Status, Social Positions, and Collective Action, WILSONCENTER.ORG, at 1, 2 (2004), *accessed at* https://www.wilsoncenter.org/sites/default/files/ValentineMoghadamFinal.pdf.

a. Women's Constitutional Rights

Following approval of the Constitution of the Islamic Republic of Iran in 1979, its Preamble under the section called "Women in the Constitution," introduces the "family unit" as the basis of the Islamic society. It emphasizes the new restrictive gender agenda, and asserts that the Islamic revolution had transported women from the corruption and exploitation of capitalist imperialism by the previous regime.[174] The Preamble reads:

> "Women were drawn away from the family unit and (put into) the condition of 'being a mere thing,' or 'being a mere tool for work' in the service of consumerism and exploitation. Re-assumption of the task of bringing up *religiously-minded men and women,* ready to work and fight together in life's fields of activity is a serious and precious duty of *motherhood.*"[175] [Emphasis Added]

All the policies regarding women proceed from this fundamental principle. Assertion of the importance of "family" and the task of "motherhood" under "Women in the Constitution," considering that this is the first opportunity to address women, calls on women's momentous and precious role of motherhood in raising human beings in the family.[176] Motherhood is the focal point and the first Constitutional right for women intended to reform women's previous roles and require them to play a leading part in the family.[177]

The primacy of women's domestic role therefore affects women's role as citizens in their entire legal, social, economic, and political affairs.[178] Consequently, family rights will always prevail over women's other individual rights and

174 *See* Qanuni Assassi Jumhuri'i Islamai Iran [The Constitution of The Islamic Republic of Iran] 1358 [1980], Preamble; Special Rapporteur on Violence against Women, its Causes and Consequences, *Mission to the Islamic Republic of Iran,* ¶ 11 at 6, U.N. Doc. E/CN.4/2006/61/Add.3 (Jan. 27, 2006).

175 Qanuni Assassi Jumhuri'i Islamai Iran [The Constitution of The Islamic Republic of Iran] 1358 [1980], Preamble.

176 *See id.* at Preamble. *See also National Report,* ¶ 98 at 18, U.N. Doc. A/HRC/WG.6/7/IRN/1 (Nov. 18, 2009).

177 1 Shahidian, *supra* note 171, at 265; *See* U.N. Commission on the Status of Women, *Statement by Mrs. Maryam Mojtahedzadeh Advisor to the President and Head of the Center for Women and Family Affairs of the Islamic Republic of Iran before the 57th Session of CSW,* at 2 (March 5, 2013). *See also e.g.,* U.N. Commission of the Status of Women, *Statement by Elham Aminzadeh to the 53d Session of CSW,* at 3 (March 4, 2009).

178 1 Shahidian, *supra* note 171, at 118.

autonomy, making women's individual rights almost non-existent and dependent on a man and children's needs in the family.[179] It is a battle between the individual and collective rights of women.

Each individual is the "bearer of a multiple and complex identity", making her or him a unique human being that enables her or him to be part of communities. "Collective identities never encompass all the characteristics of any individual: they are formed on the basis of privileging certain parts of individual identities."[180] Women carry the burden to flourish both as an individual and a member of their families. Complete emphasis on the importance of women as mothers and wives in the family by the Preamble to the Constitution undermines women's individual rights as citizens and members of the broader community. In order to emphasize the equal rights of women and men, the Constitution should guarantee "personhood" for women first.[181] Articles 19, 20 and 21 of the Constitution more specifically address the rights of the people, each from different angles. Article 19 states:

> "All people of Iran, whatever the *ethnic group* or *tribe* to which they belong, enjoy *equal rights*; and *color, race, language*, and the *like*, do not bestow any privilege."[182] [Emphasis Added]

This article explicitly asserts its respect for equal rights for all Iranian people without discrimination only on the basis of their "ethnic" and "tribal" inherited status. It identifies equal rights for ethnic groups regardless of their shared "color," "race," "language," and "like." Clearly, this article does not protect "gender" equality.

However, Article 20 of the Constitution continues to aim at "equal rights of women and men" by stating:

179 *See e.g.*, Itṭilā'āt Newspaper (Iran), July 31, 1979, N. 15918, at 9. (TA)

180 Whenever people use the pronoun "we," referring to a collectivity, they select those markers of personal identity that highlight their link with a particular group of people. U.N. Secretary-General, *Transmit to the General Assembly the report of the Special Rapporteur in the field of cultural rights (Farida Shaheed-Cultural rights)*, ¶ 9 at 6, U.N. Doc. A/67/287 (Aug. 10, 2012).

181 *See id.* at ¶ 14 at 7.

182 Qanuni Assassi Jumhuri'i Islamai Iran [The Constitution of The Islamic Republic of Iran] 1358 [1980], art. 19.

> "All citizens of the country, *both men and women, equally* enjoy the protection of the law and enjoy *all* human, political, economic, social, and cultural rights, *in conformity* with *Islamic criteria.*"[183] [Emphasis Added]

Assertive language used by Article 20 guarantees gender equality before the law and enjoyment of human, socioeconomic and cultural rights on an equal footing for all. But the key imposed condition of this article, however, comes in the second part, which is "in conformity with Islamic criteria." This defines the extent of gender equality offered by the Constitution. Despite the encouraging language, "both men and women, equally enjoy the protection of the law and enjoy all...rights," the guaranteed gender equality is strictly limited, and is only according by what Islam prescribes for each sex.

Article 20 lays out the foundation for the subsequent article to define the rights of women. The first part of Article 21 reads:

> "The government must ensure the *rights of women in all respects,* in *conformity with Islamic criteria.*"[184] [Emphasis Added]

The Constitution establishes women's rights but recognizes Shīʿa Islamic jurisprudence as its fundamental measuring principle pertaining to women, which also is in conformity with Article 4 of the Constitution. It appears that the Constitution has taken an extra step to emphasize its belief in Shīʿa Islam as the determiner of gender equality and women's rights. Nonetheless, Articles 20 and 21 have failed to define or exemplify, with any specificity, these rights and freedoms. These issues are left completely to the Shīʿa interpretation of Islam.

Every dialogue about women's rights and freedoms in Iran must be understood in its religious context.[185] This justifies the different treatment of women from men by the entire legal system, because Islamic jurisprudence holds different but complementary rights and responsibilities for each sex. Accordingly, women and men due to their physical and psychological differences deserve different rights, responsibilities, and punishments.[186]

183 *Id.* at Art. 20.

184 *Id.* at Art. 21.

185 1 Shahidian, *supra* note 171, at 118.

186 *See* Murtiżā Muṭaharī, Niẓāmi Ḥuquqi Zan dar Islām [Women's Rights in Islam] 121, 122 (Ṣadrā Publication 2011).

The theological scrutiny imposed by the Constitution to measure women's rights and define gender equality requires examining the extent of Shīʿa jurisprudence in this regard. It is essential to identify Islam's approach regarding women's rights and understand what constitutes equal rights between sexes. Does Islam consider women equal to men? Does Islam recognize identical rights for both sexes?

According to Islam women and men are equal in respect to dignity and human rights. Islam certainly does not recognize identical rights, responsibilities and punishments for women and men due to their natural similarities and differences.[187] This does not mean that Islam is against the concept of equality between women and men; it is against similar rights.[188] According to Islam, existence of differences in their legal rights and responsibilities does not mean superiority of one gender to another. However it creates specific legal rights for women and men with regards to their specific roles in the family and society.[189]

However, by law and in practice, women have always been experiencing more exclusions and restrictions on their rights and freedoms in comparison to men. What constitutes discrimination against women has been enshrined in many human rights instruments, such as the Convention on the Elimination of all Forms of Discrimination Against Women (CEDAW), which explicitly defines discrimination against women as:

> "Any distinction, exclusion or restriction made on the basis of sex which has the effect or purpose of impairing or nullifying the recognition, enjoyment or exercise by women, irrespective of their marital status, on a basis of equality of men and women, of human rights and fundamental freedoms in the political, economic, social, cultural, civil or any other field."[190]

---

187 *Id.* at 121, 122; U.N. Commission of the Status of Women, *Statement to the General Discussion of the CSW 56th by Mr. Eshagh Al-Habib on behalf of Mrs. Maryam Mojtahedzadeh*, at 2 (Feb. 28, 2012). *See also* 1 Siyid Muḥammad Hashimī, Huquqi Asāsī Jumhurīyi Islāmiyi Iran (Constitution of Islamic Republic of Iran) 354 (Dādgustar Publication 1999). (TA)

188 Muṭahrī, *supra* note186, at 112.

189 Amīr Saʿīd Vakīlī *&* Purīyā Askarī, Qānuni Asāsī dar Zamāni Ḥuquqi Kununī [The Constitutional Law During Current times] 111, 112 (Mujd Publication).

190 CEDAW, art. 1. For more information on discrimination against women according to international human rights norms *see* Chapter 3.

The justified different treatment of women has resulted in de jure and de facto discrimination against women that violates the enjoyment and the exercise of their most fundamental rights and freedoms in Iran.[191] Restrictive clauses in the Constitution perpetuate different treatment between women and men by all laws and policies in the country, and justify discrimination against women.[192] These constitutional provisions authorize defining individuals' rights according to their personal characteristics such as "gender," judging them "unlike," and prescribing different rights for each sex. This interpretation of equal protection before the law serves to perpetuate actual inequality in its substantive sense.[193] This is used as a basis for treatment that in substance is discriminatory and always favors the male sex over women.[194]

b. Re-veiling & Setbacks in Family Law

After the triumph of the Islamic revolution, as the Islamization of the county began, once again the issue of women observing the Islamic dress code became the focal point of the new government. Unlike forty years earlier, when Rižā Pahlavī imposed a mandatory unveiling policy on women, this time the government imposed a compulsory policy to re-veil women. At the beginning, policies regarding proper ḥijāb for women were more lenient;[195] however, in less than a month after the triumph of Islamic revolution, and one day before International Women's Day, Āyatullāh Khumiynī in his speech at the Fiyżyhih Religious School, referred to unveiled women as "naked," and asserted:

---

191 *See e.g.*, G.A. Res. 65/226, *Situation of human rights in the Islamic Republic of Iran,* ¶ 2(f) at 1-2, U.N. Doc. A/RES/65/226 (Feb. 10, 2011); G.A. Third Committee, *Promotion and protection of human rights: Promotion and protection of human rights: Situation of human rights in the Islamic Republic of Iran,* ¶ 5(g) at 2, U.N. Doc. A/C.3/68/L.57 (Nov. 1, 2013); Special Rapporteur on Violence against Women, its Causes and Consequences, *Mission to the Islamic Republic of Iran,* ¶ 1-65 at 1-18, U.N. Doc. E/CN.4/2006/61/Add.3 (Jan. 27, 2006).

192 *See e.g.*, Commission on Human Rights, *Report on the situation of human rights in the Islamic Republic of Iran, prepared by the Special Representative,* ¶ 21 at 7, U.N. Doc. E/CN.4/1997/63 (Feb. 11, 1997); Committee on Economic, Social and Cultural Rights, *Concluding observations of the Committee on Economic, Social and Cultural Rights Iran,* ¶ 4 at 2, U.N. Doc. E/C.12/1993/7 (June 9, 1993).

193 *See* Commission on Human Rights, *Report on the situation of human rights in the Islamic Republic of Iran, prepared by the Special Representative,* ¶ 20 at 7, U.N. Doc. E/CN.4/1997/63 (Feb. 11, 1997).

194 *Id.* ¶ 21 at 7.

195 *See e.g.*, Iṭṭilāʿāt Newspaper (Iran), March 11, 1979, N. 15805, at 1; Iṭṭilāʿāt Newspaper (Iran), March 8, 1979, N. 15803, at 1. (TA)

> "Islamic women are not dolls. Islamic women must appear with Islamic ḥijāb in public, not with makeup.... Working at offices is not forbidden for women but they must wear Islamic ḥijāb.... I have been told that women in ministries are naked and this is against our religion. Women can participate in social affairs and workplaces so long as they observe Islamic ḥijāb."[196]

In the wake of Āyatullāh Khumiynī's public order for women to observe Islamic ḥijāb at workplaces, on International Women's Day thousands of women protested against compulsory ḥijāb, which continued for several days.[197] Ultimately, in 1982, the single Note of Article 102 of the *Qānuni Ta 'zīrāt* (punishment) stipulated punishment for failing to wear a ḥijāb by stating:

> "Women who appear without Islamic ḥijāb in the public sight and places will be punished up to seventy-four lashes."[198]

Later in 1996, according to the single Note of Article 638 of the Islamic Penal Code, the punishment was changed to imprisonment or fine.[199] Ḥijāb also became mandatory for all girls over the age of seven.[200] There is no explicit or written definition of what constitutes Islamic ḥijāb for women in Iranian law.[201] There are no specific rules and measures to implement these expected moral restrictions against women. Instead, its implementation has been left to the sole discretion of the disciplinary forces and the political atmosphere.[202]

---

196 Iṭṭilā'āt Newspaper (Iran), March 7, 1979, N. 15802, at 2. (TA)

197 *See e.g.*, Iṭṭilā'āt Newspaper (Iran), March 8, 1979, N. 15803, at 1, 2; Iṭṭilā'āt Newspaper (Iran), March 10, 1979, N. 15804, at 1 (TA). There were also pro-ḥijāb women who participated in these gatherings. *See e.g.*, Iṭṭilā'āt Newspaper (Iran), March 10, 1979, N. 15804, at 1; Iṭṭilā'āt Newspaper (Iran), March 14, 1979, N. 15808, at 1. (TA)

198 Qānuni Ta 'zīrāt 1362 [Punishment 1982], art. 102 (Iran). (TA)

199 Qānuni Mujāzāti Islamī 1375 [Islamic Penal Code 1996], art. 638 (Iran): "[w]omen, who appear in public places and roads without wearing an Islamic ḥijab, shall be sentenced to ten days to two months' imprisonment or a fine of fifty thousand to five hundred Rials." (TA)

200 The age of puberty for girls is nine years old under Shī'a Islam; however, since girls start going to school at the age of seven in Iran, therefore, the government of the IRI forces girls over seven years of age to observe full ḥijāb. Thirty-Five Years of Forced Hijab, Justice4Iran, at 4 (2014), *accessed at* http://justice4iran.org/wp-content/uploads/2014/03/Hejab-Report-JFI-English.pdf.

201 According to Shī'a Islam, ḥijāb is covering hair and the entire body with the exception of below the wrists.

202 Thirty-Five Years of Forced Hijab, Justice4Iran, at 4 (2014), *accessed at* http://justice4iran.org/wp-content/uploads/2014/03/Hejab-Report-JFI-English.pdf.

Despite absence of direct language in the Constitution regarding women's appearance in public with Islamic ḥijāb', Article 21 of the Constitution makes mandatory ḥijāb justified, reaffirming the paradoxical status of women in Iran. On one hand, the Constitution guarantees equal rights of women and men, but on the other hand limits such equality as found in religious principles that underlie its establishment. Under such principles women are severely restricted compared to men. Women are respected as mothers, for example, but cannot choose their dress while appearing in public.[203]

In October 2014, the Plan to Protect Ḥijāb and Modesty was submitted by thirty-six members of the Parliament. The Bill calls for more restrictions on women's right to work at certain jobs and for gender segregation. It also attempts to regulate workplace dress codes. It mandates that employees in public or private sectors that do not meet Islamic standards for proper clothing could be penalized by paycheck cuts up to a third of their salary, for a minimum period of one month and a maximum of one year.[204] This bill imposes strict and discriminatory rules on women and girls' dress across the country.[205]

The passage of the Family Protection Law[206] during the Pahlavī era initially was criticized strongly by Islamic scholars because it curtailed polygamy and the unilateral right to divorce for men. It expanded women's rights, for example, in divorce and child custody. However, Islamic scholars and jurists considered this against Islamic rules.[207] A few months after the revolution, the office of the Āyatullāh Khumiynī sent an official letter that asserted the nullification of Family Protection Law because it was in conflict with Islamic laws.[208]

Iran now, for example, recognizes the validity of two forms of marriage: permanent and temporary marriages. Temporary marriages, referred to as *s̱īghih*,

203 *See* Report of the Special Rapporteur on Violence against Women, its Causes and Consequences, *Mission to the Islamic Republic of Iran*, ¶ 25, 62 at 8, 18, U.N. Doc. E/CN.4/2006/61/Add.3 (Jan. 27, 2006).

204 Human Rights Council, *Special Rapporteur on the Situation of Human Rights in the Islamic Republic of Iran (Ahmed Shaheed)*, ¶ 57 at 16, U.N. Doc. A/HRC/28/70 (March 12, 2015).

205 Interim Report of the U.N. Secretary-General to the HRC at its 31st Session, *Secretary-General on the Situation of Human Rights in Iran Note by the Secretary-General*, ¶ 36 at 11, U.N. Doc. A/HRC/31/26 (March 3, 2016).

206 *See* Family Protection Law, *Supra* note 129.

207 *See e.g.*, Iṭṭilāʿāt Newspaper (Iran), Feb. 26, 1979, N. 15794, at 2 (TA); Hossein Mehrpour, Mabāḥisī az Ḥuquqi Zan (Certain Issues on Women's Rights) 151 (Ettela'at Publications 2000) (TA).

208 *See* Iṭṭilāʿāt Newspaper (Iran), Feb. 26, 1979, N. 15794, at 2. (TA)

between Muslim men and women are contractual arrangements that legally unite them for a designated amount of time and for which the temporary wife is paid.[209] According to Islam a man can have up to four permanent wives, and unlimited temporary wives, meaning as many as the husband desires and can afford.[210]

c. Women in Key Decision-making Positions

The Guardianship of the Islamic Jurisprudence requires the Supreme Leader to be the highest official in the country.[211] After the position of the Supreme Leader, the President is the highest official in Iran.[212] As the head of the executive branch, the most important duty of the President is to implement the Constitution. There are, however, a few exceptions that are within the exclusive duties of the Supreme Leader.[213] In addition to the President's responsibility to the people, the Leader and the Islamic Consultative Assembly, his other important duties include signing legislation approved by the assembly, signing treaties, protocols, contracts, and agreements concluded by the Iranian government with other governments.[214]

A good example of discrimination against women in key decision-making positions is Article 115 of the Constitution. Article 115 of the Constitution sets the qualifications for a President as:

> "The President must be elected from among religious and political *rijāl* possessing the following qualifications: Iranian origin; Iranian nationality; administrative capacity and resourcefulness; a good past-record; trustworthiness and

---

209 Hossein Mehrpour, Mabāḥisī az Ḥuquqi Zan (Certain Issues on Women's Rights) 97 (Ettela'at Publications 2000). *See also* Tamilla F. Ghodsi, *Tying a Slipknot: Temporary Marriages in Iran,* 15 Mich. J. Int'l L. 645, 645 (1994).

210 Hossein Mehrpour, Mabāḥisī az Ḥuquqi Zan (Certain Issues on Women's Rights) 97-107 (Ettela'at Publications 2000).

211 *See* 1 Siyid Muḥammad Hāshimī, Huquqi Asāsī Jumhurīyi Islāmiyi Iran (Constitution of Islamic Republic of Iran) 117 (Dādgustar Publication 1999). *See also* Ali Vafādār, Huquqi Asāsī vaTaḥavulāti Sīyāsī (Constitutional Law and Political Evolutions) 461 (Shirvīn Publication 1995).

212 *See* Qanuni Assassi Jumhuri'i Islamai Iran [The Constitution of The Islamic Republic of Iran] 1358 [1980], art. 113.

213 *See id.* at Art. 113.

214 *See id.* at Arts. 122, 123, 125.

piety; convinced belief in the fundamental principles of the Islamic Republic of Iran and the official religion of the country."[215] [Emphasis Added]

The key word used by the lawmaker is the explicit yet equivocal Arabic word, "*rijāl*," in this article: the President must be elected from among religious and political *rijāl*. According to a prominent Persian encyclopedic dictionary, Farhangi Fārsīyi Muʿīn, the first and prevailing definition of the word "*rijāl*" means "men" in Farsi.[216] If the intention of the lawmaker by asserting "*rijāl*" is to require "male gender" as one of the qualifications for a President, this requires a President be elected only among "religious and political men." As a result, the article in question excludes women as a group from becoming a President and nullifies the equal right to exercise their political rights as citizens to become a President. The gender based qualification makes any qualified woman who meets all other required qualifications, by default "unqualified" because of their sex. This constitutes discrimination against women according to international human rights.

Nevertheless, it has been speculated that the lawmaker did not intend to exclude women from being elected as a President by using the word *rijāl*. For example, right before the presidential election of 2013, the spokesperson of the Guardian Council, Dr. Kadkhudāī in an interview with Mehr News Agency was asked, "There are ambiguities surrounding the definition of political *rijāl*, what are the criteria for political *rijāl*?"[217] Dr. Kadkhudāī said:

> It is possible that it is ambiguous but the lawmaker has created an authority called the Guardian Council and it depends on the assessment and judgment of this Council to determine; whatever the decision of the Council is, that is correct. Political *rijāl* is someone who is well opinioned in the political sphere, with political background, reputation and the ability to serve in the highest

215 *Id.* at Art. 115.

216 *See* 2 MUHAMMAD MO'IN, FARHANGE FARSI [PERSIAN ENCYCLOPEDIC DICTIONARY] 1639 (Amirkabir Publication 1963). (TA)

217 *Bāzbīnī Dar Aṣli 115 Barāyi Salāmatīyi Intikhābāt [Review of Article 115 for a Fair Election]*, GUARDIAN COUNCIL, *accessed at* http://www.shora-gc.ir, http://www.shora-gc.ir/Portal/Home/ShowPage.aspx?Object=News&CategoryID=1649831b-f60a-44a8-ac21-51d63e34cdb9&WebPartID=bffcf800-40b2-46a5-931c-4a56db364e44&ID=b9895649-6051-40fb-b09e-7c18b60d44cc.

political office; the same thing is applicable to the religious *rijāl*... having just a higher education is not a factor.[218]

The response of the spokesperson of the Guardian Council did not either clarify or deny the gender ambiguity arisen from the word *rijāl* in the Constitution. This response suggests that the lawmaker did not anticipate excluding women by using the word *rijāl* in Article 115. However, the Guardian Council has failed to explicitly reject the male gender interpretation of the word *rijāl*. Article 98 of the Constitution has empowered the Guardian Council to interpret the Constitution.

In the June 2013 presidential election, for example, all thirty women who registered their candidacy were found "disqualified."[219] According to the government all female candidates were unqualified because of their lack of "executive and political experience" and that "gender" was not a consideration.[220] Once again, this indicates that the government is "officially" rejecting the prevailing meaning of the word *rijāl* as men; instead it takes a gender-neutral position in the application of Article 115 of the Constitution.

In practice, however, since the establishment of the Islamic Republic in 1979, despite women's participation as potential candidates in the presidential elections of 2001, 2005, 2009, and 2013 no women has ever been found to be "qualified" by the Guardian Council for this position.[221]

In 2011, for example, when the Human Rights Committee asked, "Why no woman may serve as president of the country,"[222] the government asserted that the "Guardian Council has not made any interpretation of Article 115 of the Constitution."[223] This answer neither rejects nor confirms if *rijāl* means men. If *rijāl* does not mean men, and male gender is not one of the qualifications

218 *Id.*

219 *See* U.N. Secretary-General Transmits the Report of the Special Rapporteur of HRC to the General Assembly at its 68th Session, *Situation of human rights in the Islamic Republic of Iran Note by the Secretary-General*, ¶ 34 at 10, U.N. Doc. A/68/503 (Oct. 4, 2013).

220 *See id.* ¶ 35 at 10.

221 Women, Power and Politics in 21st Century Iran 123 (Tara Povery & Elaheh Rostami Povery eds., Ashgate Publishing 2012).

222 Human Rights Committee, *List of issues to be taken up in connection with the consideration of the third periodic report of the Islamic Republic of Iran*, ¶ 2 at 1, CCPR/C/IRN/Q/3 (May 17, 2011).

223 Human Rights Committee, *Consideration of reports submitted by States parties under article 40 of the Covenant: Islamic Republic of Iran*, ¶ 7 at 3, CCPR/C/IRN/Q/3/Add.1 (Sept. 12, 2011).

for a President, why for almost thirty-five years has the Guardian Council not fulfilled its Constitutional obligation to clarify the continuous ambiguity surrounding Article 115 regarding the meaning of *rijāl* as it pertains to women's presidency? Why has the Guardian Council failed to reject the definition of *rijāl* as meaning men through all these years?

Contrary to this response by the government, earlier in 2004 the then spokesperson of the Guardian Council, Ghulām Ḥusaīni Ilhām, asserted that "there has not been any new position taken by the Guardian Council in changing the interpretation of '*rijāl*' in the context of presidential candidates, and this word is not applicable to women."[224] The 2011 statement by the government contradicts the 2004 statement of the spokesperson of the Guardian Council, which limited the word *rijāl* to meaning men.

This equivocal language of Article 115 has produced several vague and contradictory responses by the government. Some say the Guardian Council has not construed Article 115 of the Constitution; others, like in 2004, assert that *rijāl* is not applicable to women. The careful Arabic word choice in the Constitution of a country, whose official language is Farsi, is concerning when it pertains to women's rights. Certainly, even if the lawmaker did not intend to exclude women, in practice women have been completely excluded since the first time they attempted to be presidential candidates.

The lawmaker used the Arabic word in the Constitution whose prevailing meaning is men, but it can also be interpreted, according to some, as religious and political figures. In the absence of any official clarification or interpretation to remove the ambiguities by the Guardian Council, as the Constitution requires, the clear consistency in practice is that women have been allowed to "register" to be considered for presidential candidacy, but they have always been found unqualified. Pragmatically, women can register to be considered for this position without being discriminated against, but in practice they are excluded from moving forward and becoming a presidential candidate. Regardless of the legislators' intent, the undeniable fact is that in practice the interpretation of the word *rijāl* as "men" has prevailed. This exclusion on the basis of women's sex constitutes discrimination against women.

---

224 The spokesman of the Guardian Council asserted "in case of deciding whether women candidates are qualified in the presidential election, the Guardian Council has the ultimate duty according to Article 115 of the Constitution to make a decision. Ilhām: *Tafsīri Shurāyi Nigahbān az Vāzhiyi Rijāli Sīyāsī Tagyīrī Nakardi Ast [Elham: the Guardian Council's Interpretation of the Term "Rijāl" has not Changed]*, JAMEJAM ONLINE (Jan. 22, 2005), *accessed at* http://www1.jamejamonline.ir/newstext.aspx?newsnum=100004167229. (TA)

If the true intention of the lawmaker was to seek out all influential figures, and not just men, why has the Guardian Council not taken any proactive role to either amend or interpret Article 115 for the last thirty-five years? Why are all the government and Guardian Council's responses contradictory? Why is it still ambiguous what *rijāl* really means? Why have all women candidates been found unqualified and never allowed to go further than just being registered?

This is another compelling example of discrimination against women in practice, especially as part of denying their equal political rights in pursuing key decision-making positions.[225]

Another example of discrimination against women is the *Qānuni Sharāyiti Intikhābi Qużāti Dādgustarī* 1361 (Law on the Qualifications for Appointment of Judges in the Ministry of Justice 1982). This law exemplifies the express gender requirement for judges, which once again results in an exclusion of women in a key government decision-making position.[226] Article 163 of the Constitution sets general rules for judgeships by stating:

"The conditions and qualifications to be fulfilled by a judge will be determined by law, in accordance with the criteria of *fiqh*."[227]

To implement Article 163, the Law on the Qualifications for Appointment of Judges in the Ministry of Justice was ratified in 1982.[228] According to the single Note of this law, an explicit male gender requirement was asserted at the beginning of this law. Its direct language requires that all judges must be selected among qualified men.[229] This law explicitly excludes women from pursuing judgeships in Iran. The direct assertive language of this law leaves no room for any speculation similar to Article 115 of the Constitution. This direct male gender requirement is a de jure discrimination against women banning them from pursuing another key decision-making position in the government. This compelling issue of de jure discrimination against women pursuing judgeships will be analyzed in great detail in Chapter 2.

225 *See e.g.*, Committee on Economic, Social and Cultural Rights, *General Comment No. 20: Non-discrimination in economic, social and cultural rights*, ¶ 10(b) at 4, U.N. Doc. E/C.12/GC/20 (July 2, 2009).

226 *See* Qānuni Sharāyiti Intikhābi Qużāti Dādgustarī 1361 [Law on the Qualifications for Appointment of Judges in the Ministry of Justice 1982], (Iran). (TA)

227 Qanuni Assassi Jumhuri'i Islamai Iran [The Constitution of The Islamic Republic of Iran] 1358 [1980], art. 163.

228 *See* 1982 Law on the Qualifications for Appointment of Judges in the Ministry of Justice 1982 (Iran).

229 *See id.*

Conclusion

In the first part of the 20th century, in the process of establishing a parliamentary system in Iran, women found the chance to finally challenge longstanding taboos against them. However, despite women's unprecedented participation in the formation of the 1906 Constitutional Revolution that adopted the first Constitution and established the first Parliament, in the end it was rather disappointing for women. By the end of the first quarter of the 20th century, women still were discriminated against in serious ways, such as by election laws, and were denied the right to equal fundamental political rights to vote or run for office. This was simply because they were women, under the guardianship of men, and men had the right to protect them, according to Islamic traditions.

After fifty years, the Pahlavī monarchy had granted Iranian women the most legal, political, and social rights they had enjoyed for more than two thousand years. The empowerment and advancement of the rights of women were accomplished by abandoning the strict patriarchal and Islamic traditions that extremely restricted all aspects of women's lives. During the reign of the first Pahlavī, despite innovative policies that aggressively transformed Iran and its legal system, his progressive yet controversial state policies did not go far enough to transform and solidify women's political and legal rights. Laws such as the election laws stayed intact; laws still discriminated against women.

The second period of Pahlavī, ruled by Muḥammad Rižā Pahlavī, counts especially as the most significant and progressive period in the 20th century for women in Iran. Unprecedented legal reforms to empower women were rapidly granted. For example, the enfranchisement of women, holding key government decision-making positions, presiding as judges, and the protections of the Family Protection Law were granted. Women had more rights than most countries in the Islamic world. Nonetheless, substantive discrimination against women still continued, and women were often counted as unequal to men by laws and societal traditions and norms.

The Islamic Revolution of 1979 put an end to the progressive path of legal reforms that aimed to improve women's roles in key decision-making positions. For the 20th century modern Iranian women, who had previously fought just a few decades earlier for the removal of social and religious taboos left from much of the long history of patriarchal and Islamic traditions, the past returned with a vengeance.

Women's status was constitutionally redefined after Islamization of the country to reaffirm the government's belief in women's domestic role of "motherhood," rather than women's autonomous rights. Out of 177 articles in the Constitution, the two articles that aim at gender equality and women are both scrutinized by application of Islamic jurisprudence.

Whether it is the equivocal language used by the Constitution in Article 115, complementarianism[230] approaches regarding sexes, or direct discrimination against women on the basis of sex imposed by a statute to exclude women from judgeships, Iranian women continue to face systemic inequalities and discrimination, both in law and in practice, and in all areas of their lives.[231]

230 According to Islam women and men have different but complementary roles and responsibilities in various fields. *See supra* note 187-189.

231 *See* U.N. General Assembly, *Situation of Human Rights in the Islamic Republic of Iran*, ¶ 31 at 10, U.N. Doc. A/70/352 (Aug. 31, 2015).

Chapter 2

Barring Women from Judgeships in Iran: A Legal Analysis

Introduction

Today, the Guardianship of the Islamic Jurisprudence strictly requires that all laws and regulations in Iran must be in accordance with the Twelve Ja'farī Shīʿa, school of thought confirmed in the Constitution.[1]

This also is a reaffirmation of centuries old Islamic traditions and authorities in Iran.[2] The qualifications required to be a judge, according to the Constitution, are determined by law according to Islamic jurisprudence.[3] This chapter will examine the statutory qualifications for judgeship positions in Iran, and in particular it will demonstrate and analyze gender roles in securing this position. The core analysis of women as judges also requires examining the "decision-making" authority of a judge, and whether women have the legal authority and power to make an independent decision and render the court verdict. Can a qualified woman become a judge today in Iran? Can a woman become a judge with authority to render the final decision of a court today in Iran?

To have a clear understanding of this complex issue this chapter will include six sections. First, it will present the modern legal history and laws of employment of judges ever since the ratification of the first law in Iran. This section consists of four sub-sections that will analyze this issue during four critical historical times, starting with the final years of Qājār Dynasty[4] until the 1979 Islamic Revolution. Second will be the analysis of the status of women judges post-Islamic revolution. Third will demonstrate and analyze the de jure discrimination against women pursuing judgeships in Iran imposed by statutes. Fourth will demonstrate what constitutes "gender equality" under Islamic juris-

1 *See* Qanuni Assassi Jumhuri'i Islamai Iran [The Constitution of The Islamic Republic of Iran] 1358 [1980], Preamble, arts. 4, 12.

2 For more details regarding the history of Islam in Iran *see* Chapter 1.

3 *See* Qanuni Assassi Jumhuri'i Islamai Iran [The Constitution of The Islamic Republic of Iran] 1358 [1980], art. 163.

4 The Qājār Dynasty ruled Iran from 1795 until 1925.

prudence. Fifth the gender requirement for judges according to *fiqh* (Islamic jurisprudence) will be presented. Finally will be a discussion illustrating the reasoning of the Shīʿa jurist and scholars that calls for banning women from judgeships.

Modern Legal History and Laws on Employment of Judges in Iran

a. Legal System during the Final Years of the Qājār

The significance of the early 20th century events during the final years of the Qājār Dynasty lays in the unprecedented establishment of the parliamentary system and abolition of the arbitrary power of the monarchy in Iran. The Constitutional Revolution (1905-1907) served as a catalyst to adopt the first Constitution in Iran that counts as the beginning of new political changes in the history of modern Iran.

The Qājār kings, for well over 130 years, had absolute power over the country. There was no other parallel power or codified laws against the kings to limit their power.[5] Occasionally, however, the religious leaders could influence the kings.[6] Before adoption of the first Constitution, in addition to the king's absolute power, and non-existent separate branches of government, the heads of the local government and religious leaders were in charge of settling the people's claims.[7] The absence of an independent judicial branch, in addition to the king's absolute power and the erratic power of the local leaders and clergy, resulted in an unjust, decentralized and chaotic system of settling people's claims.[8]

---

5 *See* Siyid Jaʿfar Hāshimī Bājgānī, Barasīyi Taṭbīqīi Uṣuli Muḥākimāti Madanī [The Comparative review of the principles of civil trials] 60 (1st ed., The Islamic Documentation Center Publication 1999). Translated by author, hereinafter TA.

6 *Id.* at 56, 57.

7 *See* Siyid Ḥasan Amīn, Tārīkhi Ḥuquqi Irān [The History of Law in Iran] 387, 464 (3d ed., Dā'ratulmaʿārifi Irān Shināsī Publication 2012). (TA)

8 *See id.*

The Qājār's legal system was based on what was practiced previously during the Ṣafavī Dynasty,[9] which was based on the dual court system that required separation of the *Maḥākimi Sharʿī* (religious tribunals) from the *Marājiʿi Urfī* (state tribunals).[10] During the Qājār, claims and disputes also were divided into two major categories: *Sharʿī* (religious) and the *Urfī* (state).[11] The "state tribunals" were the ultimate destination for hearing cases related to criminal and other public matters. Everything that was related to public safety, property and honor was within the jurisdiction of the state tribunals, judged by the Qājār king and the heads of the local government.[12]

On the other hand, the vast majority of the civil and private claims were judged by the *mujtahidīn* (Islamic jurisprudents)[13] who considered themselves as the ultimate authority to judge in the "religious tribunals."[14] Ordinary claims such as marriage, divorce, inheritance, private non-commercial transactions, and money and property matters were among religious jurisdiction cases.[15] It was a well-established practice that the religious tribunals were specifically banned from interfering with criminal cases especially homicide, *hatki nāmus* (insulting his honor) and robbery cases.[16]

---

9 *See* Chapter 1. The Ṣafavī Dynasty was one of the important ruling powers in Iran because for the first time it established the Shīʿā Islam as its official religion and as the basis for its legal system. This significantly separated Iran both politically and culturally from the rest of the Muslim world, which were Sunnī Muslims. *Id.* at 333.

10 Amīn, *supra* note 7, at 388.

11 *Id.* In addition to the official religious and state tribunals, during the Qājār, there were the "*Marājiʿi* Dādrasī Ikhteṣāsī" (exclusive procedural tribunals). *Id.* at 408.

12 Amīn, *supra* note 7, at 389, 390, 404.

13 Mujtahidīn is the plural of Mujtahid, who is a competent clergyman with authority on divine law who is entitled to give an independent judgment on a point of theology or law. 4 Imam Khomeini, Sahifeh-Ye Imam 276 (Majid Karimi & Mansoor Limba eds., The Institute for Compilation and Publication of Imam Khomeini's Work 2008). *See also* 1 Siyid Muḥammad Hāshimī, Huquqi Asāsī Jumhurīyi Islāmiyi Iran (Constitution of Islamic Republic of Iran) 113 (Dādgustar Publication 1999). (TA)

14 Amīn, *supra* note 7, at 388.

15 *Id.* at 404.

16 Hāshimī Bājgānī, *supra* note 5, at 67, 68.

The chief judges[17] in religious tribunal were selected by the direct order of the king.[18] In the absence of the rule of law, elements such as raw power and politics were sometimes decisive factors in determining the jurisdiction of each tribunal, which led to conflicts between the dual court systems.[19] Even though there were efforts made to reform and establish a more centralized legal system during different times of the Qājār, the legal structure stayed chaotic and without much improvement before the Constitutional revolution.[20]

Up to the establishment of the constitutional system beginning in 1906, the state tribunals were found unreliable by the people. This was due to the dependency of the state judiciary on executive power, primarily the king and heads of the local government as the ultimate decision makers, and on the account of the absence of either a central justice system or codified laws. In contrast, the religious tribunals became more popular and authoritative because of their coherence and foreseeability in their judgments. The religious tribunals based their judgments on the well-developed and predictable Shīʿā Islamic jurisprudence that was familiar and trusted by the people for centuries.[21]

Ultimately, the fragmentary and chaotic legal system during the Qājār compelled reformists and revolutionaries to demand the establishment of the *ʿdālatkhāni* (House of Justice) as an official destination for the public redress and elimination of ongoing injustice. This request, however, was merged with a bigger request which was changing the entire political system in Iran. It was believed that the establishment of the House of Justice would mend the broken legal system and that the establishment of separate government powers through the parliamentary system would guarantee the prevalence of the judicial justice in Iran.[22]

Ultimately in August 5, 1906, after a yearlong series of popular uprisings and demonstrations, Muẓaffaradīn Shāh[23] issued a royal proclamation that called for

17 Usually they were called, for example, the "Shaīkhul Islām" and "Amīnul Sharʿ." AMĪN, *supra* note 7, at 404.

18 AMĪN, *supra* note 7, at 404.

19 *See id.* at 406.

20 *Id.* at 460-462.

21 *Id.* at 391, 464.

22 *See id.* at 463.

23 Muẓaffaradīn Shāh Qājār (1896-1907) was the last king of the Qājār Dynasty in Iran.

the formation of the first National Consultative Assembly and the drafting of the first Constitution.[24]

b. Legal System Post-Constitutional Revolution

Pursuant to the victory of the 1906 Constitutional Revolution, the first Iranian Constitution was ratified and promulgated in 1906,[25] and the Supplementary Fundamental Laws were added to the Constitution later in 1907.[26] The Constitution was the first officially written affirmation of the newly created centers of government powers such as the National Consultative Assembly[27] and the Senate;[28] creating their duties and functions while limiting the king's authority.[29] Fifty-one articles of the Constitution emphasized the authority of the newly shaped legislative branch, and expressed the vital role of the newly formed National Consultative Assembly and the Senate. Yet, the Constitution failed to create or even address a new judiciary branch.[30] In spite of a request to establish the "House of Justice" by the constitutional revolutionaries as their most fundamental demand for public justice, this failure of the Constitution was disappointing.[31]

Similarly, the Constitution was silent in addressing and creating fundamental rights, such as the rights and freedoms of the people and imposing limits on the authorities of the monarchy.[32] The shortcomings of the Constitution called for the adoption of new sets of laws[33] to the Constitution.[34] As a result, provisions

24 Amīn, *supra* note 7, at 465.

25 *See* Qanun'i Assass'i Iran (Iranian Constitution) 1906.

26 *See* Mutamami Qānuni Āsāsī [Amendment to the Constitution] 1286 [1907].

27 *See* Qanun'i Assass'i Iran (Iranian Constitution) 1906, arts. 1-42.

28 *See id.* at Arts. 43-48.

29 *See id.* at Arts. 2, 15-19, 21-26.

30 Amīn, *supra* note 7, at 465.

31 Hāshimī Bājgānī, *supra* note 5, at 185.

32 *Id.* at 74.

33 Mutamami Qānuni Āsāsī [Amendment to the Constitution] 1286 [1907].

34 Hāshimī Bājgānī, *supra* note 5, at 185.

such as the "Rights of the Persian Nation,"[35] "Powers of the Realm,"[36] "Rights of the Monarchy,"[37] and "Powers of the Tribunal of Justice" were created.[38] Article 27 of the Amendment to the Constitution, for example, explicitly established the independent judicial branch,[39] in addition to the newly formed legislative and executive government branches.[40]

In the wake of the creation of the parliamentary system, the most important step taken by the new government to improve the failed judiciary was carefully separating the religious jurisdiction from the state jurisdiction.[41] Once again, the principal of the separate state and religious tribunals was affirmed by provisions of the Amendment to the Constitution,[42] which had been a long standing tradition since the Ṣafavī era in Iran.[43] Articles 27 and 71, however, restricted the authority of the religious tribunals only to the religious matters, judged only by just and qualified *mujtahidīn* (Islamic jurisprudents).[44]

In the light of establishment of a lawful society created by the new Constitution, the power of religious authorities to guarantee the implementation of the Islamic laws in the legislature was nonetheless re-affirmed by the Constitution.[45] Article 2 of Amendment to the Constitution explicitly asserted that all the laws must be in accordance with Islamic jurisprudence, approved by the *mujtahidīn* (Islamic jurisprudents) and qualified *fuqahā* (Islamic scholars)[46]

35 *See* Mutamami Qānuni Āsāsī [Amendment to the Constitution] 1286 [1907], arts. 8-25.

36 *See id.* at Arts. 26-29.

37 *See id.* at Arts. 35-57.

38 *See id.* at Arts. 71-89.

39 *See id.* at Art. 28.

40 *See id.* at Art. 27.

41 Amīn, *supra* note 7, at 471.

42 *See* Mutamami Qānuni Āsāsī [Amendment to the Constitution] 1286 [1907], arts. 27, 71. *See also id.*

43 For more information about the Ṣafavī Dynasty *see supra* note 9, and Chapter 1.

44 The *"dīvāni ʿdālati ʿẓmī"* (Ministry of Justice) and the *"maḥākimi ʿdlīyi"* (Justice Tribunals) were established by the supreme law of the land, separate and independent of religious tribunals. *See* Mutamami Qānuni Āsāsī [Amendment to the Constitution] 1286 [1907], arts. 27, 71.

45 *See* Mutamami Qānuni Āsāsī [Amendment to the Constitution] 1286 [1907], art. 2.

46 The word Fuqahā (Islamic scholars) is a plural for word faqīh. Faqīh is someone who is knowledgeable of Islamic laws based on Qurān and Sunnat (customs and traditions of the Prophet and infallible Imāms), who is able to construe religious statement or proclamation or decree based on a clear understanding of matters. 2 Siyid Muḥammad Hāshimī, Huqūqi Asāsī Jumhurīyi Islāmiyi Iran (Constitution of Islamic Republic of Iran) 39 (Dādgustar Publication 1999). (TA)

members of the newly formed National Consultative Assembly.[47] Although, the new legislative branch consisted of the king, the National Consultative Assembly, and the Senate,[48] the ultimate power to confirm the passage of any law was given to the religious members of the parliament to examine and approve all the proposed laws in order to guarantee the proper application of Islamic jurisprudence.[49]

Article 80 of the Amendment to the Constitution established the selection of the chiefs and members of the Justice Tribunals according to the newly ratified law, and left their appointments to the direct order of the king.[50]

The constitutional affirmation of principles such as the separation of the government powers in the end meant little. In practice, the goal of establishing an autonomous judiciary branch failed. The failure to obtain this goal had its deep roots in battles between dissimilar schools of thoughts that originated in the constitutional establishment in Iran: the clergy versus reformists and constitutionalists. For the clergy, establishing the constitutional rule of law meant losing their religious authority that would limit the expansion of the Islamic rule of law. For the constitutionalists and reformists, on the other hand, it was the school of thought that focused on the rule of law, the recognition and following the secular European constitutions and legal systems, and the separation of church and state.[51]

Despite newly formed systems, however, the laws substantially and procedurally stayed intact and judges were adjudicating cases and issuing verdicts based on the Islamic jurisprudence.[52] For instance, criminal law and punishment was still based on the traditional Islamic jurisprudence.[53] Throughout the Qājar, both before and after the Constitutional Revolution, until the crowning of Riżā Pahlavī in 1925, judgeships and judicial procedures remained decentralized. Religious leaders had an exclusive jurisdiction over religious matters.[54]

47 *See* Mutamami Qānuni Āsāsī [Amendment to the Constitution] 1286 [1907], art. 2.

48 *See id.* at Art. 27.

49 *See id.* at Art. 2.

50 *See id.* at Art. 80.

51 *See* Amīn, *supra* note 7, at 526-527.

52 *See id.* at 490.

53 *Id.* at 493.

54 *See e.g.*, Mutamami Qānuni Āsāsī [Amendment to the Constitution] 1286 [1907], arts. 27, 71.

Gradually, during the reign of Rižā Pahlavī, when the entire justice system underwent drastic transformation, together with enactment of new laws, pragmatically the power of the religious tribunals virtually ended.[55]

It is noteworthy that even a few years after the 1906 revolution, the appointed state tribunal judges lacked the confidence to call their court decisions the "final decision of the court." This was due to their fears of the religious judges who still considered themselves the final word on judgments. It was in 1911 that the bill to finally change the entire legal system was proposed to the parliament. It was strongly opposed, however, by the religious members of the parliament such as Āyatullāh Mudaris.[56]

The law of Principles Governing Justice Department, Religious Offices and Peace Courts[57] was passed by the National Consultative Assembly in 1911, setting the groundwork of the modern Iranian legal system. This was a comprehensive legislation that in practice covered the loopholes within the Iranian legal system during that time; it included areas such as the organization of the courts and the employment of judges and lawyers.[58]

According to Article 1 of this law, the justice tribunal system was divided into two main categories: "public" and "exclusive" tribunals.[59] According to this law, the jurisdiction of "public tribunals" included all disputes unless restricted explicitly by a specific law.[60] Likewise, the jurisdiction of "exclusive tribunals" was defined and limited only to specific disputes set by specific law, such as commerce courts.[61] This law, however, did not explicitly categorize the religious tribunals as part of an exclusive court system. The 1911 Rules of Legal Procedure[62] explicitly defined the jurisdiction of each court, including the religious tribunals.[63] Article 145 explicitly specified eight categories of disputes under jurisdic-

55 Hāshimī Bājgānī, *supra* note 5, at 187, 188.

56 Amīn, *supra* note 7, at 496.

57 *See* Qānuni Uşuli Tashkīlāti ʿdlīyi va Maḥāżiri Sharʿīyi va Āḥkāmi Ṣulḥīyi 1290 [Law of Principles Governing Justice Department, Religious Offices and Peace Courts 1911] (Iran). (TA)

58 *See* Amīn, *supra* note 7, at 497-498.

59 *See* Law of Principles Governing Justice Department, Religious Offices and Peace Courts 1911, art. 1 (Iran).

60 *See id.* at Art. 2.

61 *See id.* at Art. 4.

62 Uṣuli Muḥākimāti Ḥuquqī 1290 [Rules of Legal Procedure 1911] (Iran). (TA)

63 *See id.* at Arts. 144, 145.

tion of the religious tribunals, judged by the *mujtahidīn*.[64] The subject matter of religious courts was exclusively related to religious matters judged based on Islamic jurisprudence such as marriage, divorce, and legal guardianship.[65]

Article 147 of the 1911 Law of Principles Governing Justice Department, Religious Offices and Peace Courts explicitly specified required qualifications for various positions in the Justice Department. Required qualifications, accordingly, included: Iranian nationality, Islam, minimum age (varying according to the positions), and taking the required exams (scientific and practical).[66]

Article 148 exclusively banned seven groups of individuals from being employed in the Justice Department; women were not explicitly included. Amongst them, for example, were criminals and bankrupts.[67] Article 148(4) stated, "people who are under the Islamic or legal guardianships of others;"[68] this, however, implicitly included women.[69] It was well established that women were considered under the "guardianship" of men at that time according to Islam. For instance this view was reflected in the argument of a prominent Islamic member of the National Consultative Assembly, Āyatullāh Mudaris, during his speech in the parliament rejecting the political enfranchisement of women. The view of Āyatullāh Mudaris, as the ultimate defender of Islamic jurisprudence, was the predominant religious interpretation regarding the status and rights of women during those days. Despite the absence of the word "women" by the lawmakers in Article 148(4), a more general phrase was used: people who are under the Islamic or legal guardianships of others. As a result, according to prevailing Islamic laws, women were amongst people under the guardianships of others and needed to be protected by men. Accordingly, this resulted in banning women from being employed in all possible positions available in the Justice Department, including judgeships.[70]

---

64 *See id.* at Art. 145.

65 *See id.*

66 *See* Law of Principles Governing Justice Department, Religious Offices and Peace Courts 1911, art. 147 (Iran).

67 *See id.* at Art. 148.

68 *See id.* at Art. 148(4).

69 *See infra* note 70.

70 *See* Full Discussion of the National Consultative Assembly 2d Term-280 Session, at 1531, Library, Museum and Document Center of Iran Parliament. *See also* Chapter 1.

The first statute that exclusively set the required qualifications for the appointment of judges in the justice tribunals, which then were called the "*Ḥukāmi Maḥākimi ʿdlīyi,*" was passed in 1923.[71] According to the first part of Article 1 of the Employment Law of the Justice Tribunals' Judges and the Officers of the Public Prosecutor Office, four required qualifications were stipulated for judges: Iranian nationality, Islam, minimum age of thirty, and taking the exam according to the law.[72]

Article 1 of this law also contained the second section called "Mentioned Individuals Cannot Enter in the Judicial Service."[73] This part explicitly banned five specific groups of individuals from judicial service as follows: criminals, infamous and morally corrupt, opium addicts, and individuals with contagious diseases.[74] This law unlike the previous law[75] did not include the individuals under the guardianships of others among the prohibited groups. For women this meant that they were neither explicitly nor implicitly banned from becoming judges.[76]

c. Legal Transformation during the Reign of Riżā Pahlavī

In 1927, it was during the reign of Riżā Pahlavī, the new head of the Ministry of Justice, Alī Akbar Dāvar, proposed a bill to nullify the entire justice system. Among many goals of the new reformed justice system was the selection of new qualified judges. After the establishment of the new justice system, the Civil Procedure Codes were amended. It was during the inaugural ceremony of the newly formed justice system, pursuant to the order of Riżā Pahlavī, that those new judges of the Supreme Court, appellate courts, and other province courts were appointed.[77]

---

71 *See* Qānuni Istikhdāmi Ḥukāmi Maḥākimi ʿdlīyi va Ṣāḥibmanṣabāni Pārki 1302 [Employment Law of the Justice Tribunals' Judges and the Officers of the Public Prosecutor Office 1923], (Iran). (TA)

72 *See id* at Art. 1.

73 *See id.*

74 *See id.*

75 Law of Principles Governing Justice Department, Religious Offices and Peace Courts 1911, (Iran).

76 *See supra* note 70.

77 Amīn, *supra* note 7, at 530-532.

The process of creation of a more modern secular system was on its fast path by establishing new judiciary bodies and ratifying new codified laws.[78] Meanwhile, Dāvar insisted on employing the new judges from amongst the law school, political science and religious studies graduates, and graduates from foreign universities. Yet, he rarely selected from among previously serving judges. Consequently, the newly ratified laws and judicial appointments weakened the religious authority that was considered by some to be the ultimate authority--to judge in Islamic society by clergy. As a result, the religious authorities strongly opposed the newly formed justice system, calling it illegitimate.[79]

In 1928, the Employment Law of the Judges and Officials of the Public Prosecutor's Office and Registration Office[80] was ratified, which explicitly used the new term "*qużāt*" (judges) for the first time in its heading. The term "*qużāt*" is still used in the statutes today.

Article 1 of this law explicitly identifies two groups of judges: the *Ḥukami Maḥākimi ʿdlīiyi* (Justice Tribunals' Judges) and the *Ḥukāmi Maḥākimi Sharʿ* (Religious Tribunals' Judges). This law included the required qualifications for each one of these positions.[81] This statute nullified the previous employment law of the Justice Tribunals' Judges (1923).[82] According to Article 1, the judges of the "justice tribunals" had to meet three qualifications: Iranian nationality;

78 Ratification of laws such as the Qānuni Madanī (Civil Code), Qānuni Āīni Dādrasī Madanī (Civil Procedure), Qānuni Mujāzāti Umumī (General Penal Code), Qānuni Uṣuli Muḥākemāt va Mujāzāti Neẓāmi (Military Civil Procedure), Qānuni Uṣuli Tashkīlāti Jadīdi Vizārati ʿdlīyi (Law of the Principles of the New Organizations in the Justice Ministry) and the abolition of the Law of Capitulation. *Id.* at 541.

79 Amīn, *supra* note 7, at 534-538.

80 Qununi Istikhdāmi Quẓāt va Ṣāḥibmanṣabāni Pārki va Mubāshirini S̱abti Asnād 1306 [Employment Law of the Judges and Officials of the Public Prosecutor's Office and Registration Office 1928] (Iran). (TA)

81 *See id.* at Art. 1.

82 *See id.* at Art. 48. *See also* Ruznamehi Rasmi Jumhuri Islami Iran [The Official Gazette of the Islamic Republic of Iran], *Fihristi Qavānini Mansukh Ṣarīḥ 1285-1335 [List of Nullified Laws from 1906-1956]*, 465 (Iran, 2012), *accessed at* http://www.rooznamehrasmi.ir/Laws/ShowLaw.aspx?Code=666. (TA)

minimum age of twenty-five; and be knowledgeable in *fiqh*,[83] logic, and various laws, and successful passage of oral and written exams.[84]

Likewise, the judges of the "religious tribunals" also had to meet specific qualifications according to this law as follows: being a Islamic scholar who had reached the "*ijtihād*"[85] level with the written approval of two *marjaʿi taqlīd*-- a grand Islamic scholar with the authority to make legal decisions within the Islamic law for Muslims.[86]

Pursuant to Article 1 setting the required qualifications for judges, it continues to the section that explicitly bans specific groups of individuals from judgeships. This includes criminals, infamous and morally corrupt, and opium addicts.[87] Once again women, neither explicitly nor implicitly, were banned from pursuing judgeships.

Even though the religious tribunals still were the legitimate destination for disputes within their jurisdiction, as guaranteed by the Constitution and related laws, the passage of the Law of the 1931 Religious Tribunals[88] strictly reduced their jurisdiction, from eight[89] to four categories, compare to the previous law.[90] According to Article 1 of 1931 Religious Tribunals, religious tribunals were now

---

83 Fiqh generally includes rules and requirements regarding all aspects of a human's life. The general rules come directly from Qurān and Sunnat. Hard works of Islamic scholars discovers detailed rules. 1 SIYID MUḤAMMAD HĀSHIMĪ, HUQUQI ASĀSĪ JUMHURĪYI ISLĀMIYI IRAN (CONSTITUTION OF ISLAMIC REPUBLIC OF IRAN) 113 (Dādgustar Publication 1999).

84 *See* Employment Law of the Judges and Officials of the Public Prosecutor's Office and Registration Office 1928, art. 1 (Iran).

85 The word "ijtihād" is the synonyms of "fiqh," meaning the ultimate effort to a meticulous and scholarly understanding and discovering of new Islamic rules based on its main sources (Qurān and Sunnat). Ijtihād is the main instrument of interpreting the divine laws, relating it to the changing conditions of the Muslim community in its objectives to attain justice, salvation and truth. MOHAMMAD HASHIM KAMALI, PRINCIPLES OF ISLAMIC JURISPRUDENCE, 468 (3d ed., The Islamic Texts Society 2003).

86 *See* Employment Law of the Judges and Officials of the Public Prosecutor's Office and Registration Office 1928, art. 1 (Iran).

87 *See id.* at Art. 1.

88 Qānuni Maḥākimi Sharʿ1310 [Law of the Religious Tribunals 1931] (Iran). (TA)

89 *See* Rules of Legal Procedure 1911, art. 145 (Iran).

90 *See* Law of the Religious Tribunals of 1931, art. 7 (Iran). Law of the Religious Tribunals of 1931 nullified the Law of Principles Governing Justice Department, Religious Offices and Peace Courts. Fatḥullāh Yāvarī, *Dādgāhi Madanīyi Khāṣ dar Niẓāmi Jumhurīyi Islāmīyi Iran [The Special Civil Courts in the Islamic Republic of Iran]*, GHAVANIN (1991), *accessed at* http://www.ghavanin.ir/PaperDetail.asp?id=664. (TA)

categorized as exclusive tribunals.[91] Article 3 asserted that the religious tribunals still were presided over by a qualified *mujtahid* (Islamic jurist).[92] Article 7 limited the scope of the religious jurisdiction to claims such as marriage and divorce, appointing guardianship and will executor.[93] Later in 1940, the Law of Non-Litigious Matters[94] was passed, which restricted the religious authority even more, and limited their jurisdiction only to marriage and divorce cases. As a result, all matters with the exception of marriage and divorce were handled in a newly formed justice system that either paid little attention to Islamic laws or completely ignored it. This approach continued in large part until the late 1960s.[95]

The law of the employment of judges[96] was amended in 1936.[97] According to Article 18 of the Law Amending Parts of the Principals Governing the Justice Department and the Employment of Judges, the required qualifications for judges were amended as: Iranian nationality, minimum age of twenty-five, and a bachelor's or higher degree from either domestic or foreign law and political science degrees.[98]

According to this law, specific groups of individuals were banned from serving as judges: criminals, infamous and morally corrupt, and opium addicts.[99] Even though, the required qualifications were amended slightly, banned groups of individuals stayed the same as the previous law. Yet again, according to this new law, gender was not mentioned. Women were neither explicitly nor implicitly barred from judgeships.

---

91 *See* Religious Tribunals of 1931, art. 1 (Iran).

92 *See id.* at Art. 3.

93 *See id.* at Art. 7.

94 Qānuni Umuri Ḥisbī 1319 [Law of Non-Litigious Matters 1940] (Iran). (TA)

95 Fatḥullāh Yāvarī, *Dādgāhi Madanīyi Khāṣ dar Niẓāmi Jumhurīyi Islāmīyi Iran [The Special Civil Courts in the Islamic Republic of Iran]*, Ghavanin (1991), *accessed at* http://www.ghavanin.ir/PaperDetail.asp?id=664. (TA)

96 *See* Employment Law of the Judges and Officials of the Public Prosecutor's Office and Registration Office 1928 (Iran).

97 *See* Qānuni Iṣlāḥi Qismatī az Qāuni Uṣuli Tashkīlāti ʿdlīyi va Istikhdāmi Qużāt 1315 [Law Amending Parts of the Principals Governing the Justice Department and the Employment of Judges 1936] (Iran). (TA)

98 *See id.* at Art. 18.

99 *See id.*

Sixteen years of Riżā Pahlavī rule made the legal system centralized for the first time in modern history. New legislation and substantial reforms in the justice system moved toward secularizing the legal system. One of the most hostile opposition groups against Riżā Pahlavī's reforms was the religious leader whose traditional jurisdiction was substantially restricted and therefore threatened by the ongoing legal reforms.[100] Regardless of the hostility of the religious leaders, the powers and numbers of the *non-mujtahid* secular judges were rapidly increasing. The increasing numbers of new secular laws throughout the Pahlavī legislature from its beginning to its end in 1979 were insensitive to the religious authority that originally was confirmed by Article 2 of the Amendment to the Constitution.[101] Creation of the new Ministry of Justice during this period put enormous restrictions on the scope of religious jurisdiction, resulting in decreasing their judicial power and disregarding their Constitutional rights.[102]

The absence of any language, explicit or implicit, to ban women from pursuing judgeships ever since the ratification of the first law pertaining to qualifications of judges, is a significant point during the first quarter of the 20th century. During that time women were otherwise treated as second-class citizens by de jure and de facto discriminatory laws. Although all the laws regarding qualifications of judges were gender neutral as written, it still did not mean that in practice women had the opportunity to pursue important decision-making positions such as judgeships, and in fact in practice they were discriminated against.[103]

During the Qājār, for example, one of the most important challenges for women was fighting the patriarchal school of thought that considered women "intellectually mutilated," "weak," "foolish," and "lazy."[104] Women were "under the religious guardianships and protection of men;"[105] even participation in the most basic social and legal matters was nothing but a taboo for women.[106] Women's

100 Amīn, *supra* note 7, at 550.

101 *See id.* at 553.

102 In some cases the new ratified laws went even against the Islamic laws; good examples were the unveiling policies, provisions of new Penal Codes, Marriage Laws and passage of the Family Protection Laws. *E.g., id.* at 553.

103 *See* Chapter 1.

104 *See* Muḥammad Ḥusiyni Khusru Panāh, Hadafhā va Mubārizāti Zan dar Irān az Inqilābi Mashruṭi tā Salṭanati Pahlavī [Iranian Woman's Goals and Battles From the Constitutional Revolution until the Pahlavi Dynasty] 42 (Payāmi Imruz Publication 2002). (TA)

105 *See supra* note 70.

106 *See* Chapter 1.

role was restricted only to traditional family duties;[107] and even their attire in the public introduced them as a weaker sex.[108] According to a few thinkers during the Qājār, women were victims of a social and political system that deprived them of their natural rights.[109] Other social restrictions such as prohibiting women from the public domain[110] made it almost impossible for women to even consider key decision-making positions such as judgeships during those days.

In the absence of statutory gender-based qualification for judgeships, however, in practice the exclusion of women from pursuing judgeships was implied by the patriarchal rules and traditions and women were discriminated against in practice from even pursuing key positions. For example, one of the requirements for becoming judges in 1920s was to be knowledgeable in variety of skillful areas such as laws and *fiqh* (principles of Islamic jurisprudence), and to pass the judgeships' oral and written exams successfully.[111] In reality this was impossible for almost all women since it was not until 1907 that the first women's elementary school was opened in Iran.[112] The most serious hurdle for women to participate in basic political and legal affairs was the excess of female illiteracy in the total population. Even for a very limited percentage of literate women, working and participating in social affairs was rare due to other social restrictions imposed by patriarchal traditions.[113] Pursuing judgeship positions that required attaining skillful and higher education became almost impossible for women during those times.

Unprecedented policies such as mandatory unveiling of women in public and endorsing women to get higher education for the first time[114] were amongst

107 Mihrangīz Kār, Mushārikati Sīyāsī Zanān (Women's Participation in Politics) 15 (Rushangarān va Muṭāliʿti Zanān Publication 2001). (TA)

108 Hamideh Sedghi, Women and Politics in Iran: Veiling, Unveiling, and Reveiling 26 (Cambridge University Press 2007).

109 Camron Michael Amin, The Making of the Modern Iranian Women 27, 28 (University Press of Florida 2002).

110 Sedghi, *supra* note 108.

111 *See e.g.*, Employment Law of the Judges and Officials of the Public Prosecutor's Office and Registration Office 1928, art. 1 (Iran); Employment Law of the Justice Tribunals' Judges and the Officers of the Public Prosecutor Office 1923, art. 1 (Iran).

112 Sedghi, *supra* note 108, at 53.

113 *See* Hassan Toqranegar, Ḥuquqi Sīyāsī va Ijtimāʿyi Zanān Qabl va Baʿd az Pīruzīyi Inqilābi Islāmīyi Irān [Political and Social Rights of Women, before and after the Islamic Revolution of Iran] 120 (The Center for Islamic Revolution Documents, 2010). (TA)

114 Michael Amin, *supra* note 109, at 154-159.

the most important women's emancipation policies during the Riżā Pahlavī.[115] However, despite all these unprecedented and innovative policies to remove hundreds of years of social taboos and patriarchal restrictions against women in some areas, the political disenfranchisement of women made women's chances to pursue decision-making positions next to none.

Since ratification of the first election law in 1906,[116] women were explicitly banned from voting and being elected to the parliament and the Senate until 1964. It was only then for the first time that woman got the equal political right to vote for the first time.[117] The election laws were the reflection of the patriarchal traditions and views of the society about women and their share in the society. Women were directly discriminated against by all elections laws and deprived from their most fundamental political rights.[118]

It was believed that women did not have the capacity to choose their representative in the government. How could a woman compete for independent decision-making positions like judgeships, while by every election law, for example, she was prohibited from voting, and put in the same category as mentally ill individuals who lacked mental and legal capacity to choose? Therefore, chances of being even considered for judgeships, even in the presence of neutral laws regarding qualifications for judges, were remote for women.

d. Women's Empowerment: Decision-making Positions during the Reign of Muḥammad Riżā Pahlavī

Meaningful women's rights reforms, subsequent to the "White Revolution,"[119] proposed by Muḥammad Riżā Pahlavī, finally granted women political enfran-

115 *See* Chapter 1.

116 *See* Niẓāmnāmiyi Intikhābāti Aṣnāfī Majlisi Shurāyi Millī 1285 [Election Law of the National Consultative Assembly 1906], (Iran). (TA)

117 *See* Qānuni Rājiʿ bi Shirkati Bānuvān Dar Intikhābāt 1343 [Law on Women's Participation in Election 1964] (Iran). (TA)

118 *See e.g.*, Election Law of the National Consultative Assembly 1906, arts. 3(1), 5(1) (Iran); Law of the State and Provincial Associations 1907, arts. 7(4), 9(4) (Iran); Election Law Two Degree 1909, art. 5(1) (Iran); Election Law of the National Consultative Assembly 1911, art. 4(1) (Iran); Election Law of the National Consultative Assembly 1925, arts. 10(1), 13(2) (Iran).

119 The "White Revolution" was series of reforms in Iran launched by Muḥammad Riżā Pahlavī in 1963. It included, for example, land reforms and abolishing Feudalism; nationalization of forests; profit sharing; privatization of the government owned enterprises; formation of the health and literacy corps and free and compulsory education.

chisement and the right to be elected in 1964.[120] This was the beginning of Iranian women's legal and political participation in key decision-making positions.[121] As a result, for the first time, not only did women participat as voters and candidates for the twenty-first National Consultative Assembly elections, but also six women were elected as members of the twenty-first National Consultative Assembly.[122] Women instantly were integrated into important public roles, such as ministers, members of the cabinet, ambassadors, and university professors.[123] The removal of these de jure discriminatory laws counted as a turning point for modern Iranian women to pursue key decision-making positions in the government.

The required qualifications for serving in the judiciary were revised once again in 1964.[124] According to Article 1 of the Employment Law of the Judges and the Internship of 1964,[125] the amended qualifications for judges were: Iranian Nationality, Bachelor's Degree from Law School (domestic or foreign schools), Muslim and considered of good moral character, completion of the internship, and at least twenty-five years of age. The same groups of individuals such as criminals and morally corrupt were amongst the banned groups from judgeships.[126] Nonetheless, this law stayed gender neutral and neither implicitly nor explicitly excluded women from pursuing judgeships; later in 1969 it was amended[127] another time without making any references to gender qualification.

Almost sixty-three years since adoption of the first 1906 Constitution that explicitly guaranteed equality before the law for all Iranian people, and now with the absence of a statutory gender requirement, ultimately a few women

120 *See* Law on Women's Participation in Election 1964, Single Note (Iran). *See also* Chapter 1.

121 *See* Chapter 1.

122 *See* Full Discussion of the National Consultative Assembly 21st Term-1st Session, Library, Museum and Document Center of Iran Parliament. (TA)

123 Mohammad Reza Pahlavi, Answer to History 118 (Stein & Day publisher 1981).

124 *See* Qānuni Rāji' bi Istikhdāmi Qużāt va Sharāyiti Kārāmuzī 1343 [Employment Law of the Judges and the Internship 1964] (Iran). (TA)

125 *Id.* at Art. 1.

126 *Id.*

127 *See* Qānuni Iṣlāhi Qānuni Istikhdāmi Qużāt va Sharāyiti Karāmuzī of 1343 (1347) [Amendment to the Law of the Employment of Judges and Internship of 1964 (1969)] (Iran). (TA)

were appointed as judges in 1969.[128] Subsequently, every year before the 1979 Islamic revolution, the number of women judges increased until there were more than 100 women judges.[129] Many factors, such as international efforts on gender equality; domestic pressure coming from women's organizations and women's rights advocates; increasing numbers of female law students; increased women's applications for the judicial and judgeship internships, and the absence of a gender-based legal prohibition, finally forced the judiciary branch to review their conduct and accept women's applications for judgeships.[130]

Considering the long history of Iran, more specifically since the invasion of Arabs in the mid-seventh century until today, women officially have presided as judges for only ten years—from 1969 until 1979. After the triumph of the Islamic revolution, existing women judges were immediately dismissed or demoted. Later, in 1982, women were statutorily excluded from holding judgeships.

---

128 In June 4, 1969 few women sat as judges for the first time in Iran. Noushin Ahmadi Khorasani, Iranian Women's Equality Calendar With Chronology of One Million Signatures Campaign Demanding Changes to Discriminatory Laws 25 (Sahar Mofakham & Mahsa Shekarloo & Leila Tavakoli trans., 2008), *accessed at* http://www.feministschool.com/english/IMG/pdf/Iranian_Women_s_equality_calendar-2.pdf; *See* Amendment to the Constitution 1907, art. 8.

129 Alī Muḥammad Jahāngīrī, *Niẓāmi Jumhurīyi Islāmī va Ḥaqi Qiżāvati Zanān [The Islamic Republic of Iran and the Rights of Women Judges]*, ASRE-NOU.NET (Dec. 11, 2012), *accessed at* http://asre-nou.net/php/view.php?objnr=24459. (TA)

130 HOSSEIN MEHRPOUR, MABĀḤIS̱Ī AZ ḤUQUQI ZAN [CERTAIN ISSUES ON WOMEN'S RIGHTS] 315 (Ettela'at Publications 2000). (TA)

Step Down, You are a Woman: Women Judges Post-Islamic Revolution

The triumph of the Islamic Revolution put an end to more than half a century of the Pahlavī Monarchy, and introduced its new government as the Islamic Republic of Iran in 1979.[131] Establishing an explicitly Shīʿa Islamic country required changing the Constitution so that it was strictly based on Islamic jurisprudence; to lay out the Islamic foundation for every aspect of the country's affairs. As a result, a few months after the victory, the Assembly of Experts of the Constitution,[132] consisting of seventy-five representatives, was formed.[133] The representatives were selected from among the most well established scholars of Islamic jurisprudence to implement Āyatullāh Khumiynī's order to write a new Islamic Constitution. The Constitution of the IRI was approved by the affirmative vote of a majority of 98.2% of people voting in the referendum of 1979.[134] The principle of the "*Vilāyati Faqīh*" (Guardianship of the Islamic Jurisprudence) was approved under the leadership of Āyatullāh Khumiynī.[135] The Guardianship of the Islamic Jurisprudence requires the government to conform to Islamic laws, interpreted by a selected group of qualified religious scholars.[136] Passing an Islamic Constitution was the beginning of Islamization of the country, and

---

131 *See* Qanuni Assassi Jumhuri'i Islamai Iran [The Constitution of The Islamic Republic of Iran] 1358 [1980], art. 1. Islamic Republic of Iran, hereinafter IRI.

132 Majlisi Khubrigāni Qānuni Asāsī (Assembly of Experts of the Constitution).

133 *See Rasmīyat Yāftani Qānuni Asāsīyi Jumhurīyi Islāmīyi Irān [Finalized Constitution of the Islamic Republic of Iran]*, The Center for Islamic Documentations 1979, *available at* http://www.irdc.ir/fa/calendar/65/default.aspx. (TA)

134 *See* Qanuni Assassi Jumhuri'i Islamai Iran [The Constitution of The Islamic Republic of Iran] 1358 [1980], art. 1. *See also id.*

135 *See id.* at Arts. 2, 5.

136 *See id.* at Arts. 2, 4, 5. *See also* Arezoo Osanloo, Politics of Women's Rights in Iran, (Princeton University Press 2009).

the rejection of so-called un-Islamic laws practiced by previous regime.[137] This resulted in a drastic transformation of the country that touched every aspect of the people's lives, particularly women.

Despite women's immense role in the victory of the revolution and the referendum approving the constitution and all gender equality promises made by Āyatullāh Khumiynī over an extended period of time, existing women judges were dismissed from their positions almost immediately. This was just one among many legal setbacks against women soon after the victory of Islamic revolution, all of which significantly repressed the role and status of women in a wide range of both public and private arenas.[138]

Banning women from the judgeships did not become an instant law; rather it appeared piecemeal through different announcements and legislative processes. Meanwhile women lawyers, judges, and law students in protest against discrimination against women, courageously and openly fought back for equal rights to work as judges.[139] But in a relatively short time, the struggle was lost. Women were barred from judgeships.

A few days before the victory of the Islamic revolution, Āyatullāh Sharīʿtmadārī[140] in an interview with the "Voice of America" and "Reuters," expressed his views about the future of the Islamic Iran. In his response to the question "Isn't it true that women cannot become judges?"[141] He asserted,

> "A judgeship is not an easy task and there are qualifications for judges to meet, especially in an Islamic society it even has a more important role. In my opinion this position is *not suitable* for *women*; they *do not meet all the required qualifications* for this post."[142] [Emphasis Added]

Āyatullāh Sharīʿtmadārī continued, "Becoming judges for women goes *against their psychological* and *physical nature*, because of their *tenderness in hearts*,

137 *See e.g.*, Iṭṭilāʿāt Newspaper (Iran), June 19, 1979, N. 15883, at 1, 12. (TA)

138 Toqranegar, *supra* note 113, at 158; *see e.g.*, Iṭṭilāʿāt Newspaper (Iran), March 31, 1979, N. 15883., at 4 (TA). *See also* Chapter 1.

139 *See e.g.*, Iṭṭilāʿāt Newspaper (Iran), June 11, 1979, N. 15876, at 2 (TA); Iṭṭilāʿāt Newspaper (Iran), July 28, 1979, N. 15915, at 3 (TA); Iṭṭilāʿāt Newspaper (Iran), Oct. 12, 1979, N. 15928, at 9 (TA).

140 Āyatullāh Sharīʿtmadārī was one of the prominent Islamic jurists.

141 Iṭṭilāʿāt Newspaper (Iran), Feb. 1, 1979, N. 15774. (TA)

142 *Id.*

and their *physical* and *psychological delicacy*."[143] [Emphasis Added] And further, "This is a very clear matter that women by *their nature* are *delicate* and *quickly influenced*; not only should they not become judges but in other social positions this problem also exists."[144] [Emphasis Added]

In another important newspaper after establishment of the new government, "being a man" was explicitly asserted as one of the required qualifications for judges, which was based on the consensus of opinion of the Islamic scholars.[145]

As a result of Islamization, a few months after the Islamic revolution the entire judicial system was dissolved including the court system.[146] Meanwhile, Āyatullāh Khumiynī emphasized the massive need for new Islamic judges, as he considered most of the existing judges from the Pahlavī era un-Islamic or disqualified.[147] Āyatullāh Khumiynī in his "Eight Articled Directive" in particular emphasized the importance and urgency of Islamization of all the government organizations and the judiciary and its judges.[148]

Āyatullāh Khumiynī also emphasized the significance of pronouncing judgments in Islam and how this perilous duty lies on judges to administer justice, eradicate injustice, settle disputes, and differentiate between the oppressor and the oppressed. According to Āyatullāh Khumiynī, a judgeship is "adjudicating among people to end disputes; this position is amongst the most important positions given by God to the Prophet Muḥammad, and on his behalf to the infallible Imāms, and on their behalf to the qualified *fuqahā*."[149] He continued, "Judging among people is forbidden for unqualified individuals...and

143 *Id.*

144 *Id.*

145 *See* Inqilābi Islāmī Newspaper (Iran), Oct. 25, 1980, N. 384, at 3. (TA)

146 *See* Iṭṭilāʿāt Newspaper (Iran), Aug. 4, 1979, N. 15921, at 1, 2 (TA); Iṭṭilāʿāt Newspaper (Iran), Aug. 6, 1979, N. 15922, at 1, 2 (TA).

147 *See e.g.*, 13 Imam Khomeini, Sahifeh-Ye Imam 45-46 (Majid Karimi & Mansoor Limba eds., the Institute for Compilation and Publication of Imam Khomeini's Work 2008); 14 Imam Khomeini, Sahifeh-Ye Imam 232, 291-292 (Majid Karimi & Mansoor Limba eds., the Institute for Compilation and Publication of Imam Khomeini's Work 2008).

148 *See* 17 Imam Khomeini, Sahifeh-Ye Imam 132 (Majid Karimi & Mansoor Limba eds., the Institute for Compilation and Publication of Imam Khomeini's Work 2008).

149 4 Āyatullāh Khumiynī, Taḥrīr Alvasīli 241 (4th ed., Dāralʿlam Publication 2007). (TA)

for individuals who are qualified it is a *vājibi kafā'ī*."[150] According to Āyatullāh Khumiynī "The responsibility (of the office) is extremely heavy.... Those who fulfill all the requirements and are 'mujtahids' [Islamic jurist] must take the office and if there are not enough of them, those appointed by the mujtahids must fill the ranks."[151]

In less than a month after the revolution, in March 1979, and before the adoption of the new Constitution, the Law Amending the Ministry of Justice and the Employment of the Judges[152] was passed by the provisional Islamic Revolution Council.[153] Article 1 of this law formed the "Correction Board" to purify the Ministry of Justice for the duration of six months.[154] The board had the discretionary power to eliminate any court and judicial positions if necessary.[155] Among other authority, the Correction Board had the power to change the "existing judges" once they believed their service was no longer necessary in the Ministry of Justice.[156] Demotion; stripping judges' judicial authority; conversion to administrative roles, or temporary or permanent dismissals were amongst the speculated changes for existing judges.[157]

The first sign of banning women from judgeships appeared when the first Minister of Justice of the provisional government was reluctant to issue work permission to the women judicial trainees who had successfully completed their training term.[158] This was the beginning of women's unrest and continuous protests in the next few months against the discriminatory policies and speculation

150 *Id.* at 162, 242. According to the consensus of opinion of Shī'a scholars, judgeships in Islam are a "*vājibi kafā'ī*." (collective duty). Meaning if there is a need for judgeships, qualified individuals have a religious obligation to judge, and in a case of refusal, it counts as a sin. As a result, in case of need for judges, it becomes the duty of the religious leader to find judges. Bājgānī, *supra* note 5, at 43.

151 13 Imam Khomeini, Sahifeh-Ye Imam 97 (Majid Karimi & Mansoor Limba eds., the Institute for Compilation and Publication of Imam Khomeini's Work 2008).

152 lāyiḥiyi Qānunīyi Iṣlāḥi Sāzmāni Dādgustarī va Qānuni Istikhdāmi Quẓāt 1357 [Law Amending the Ministry of Justice and the Law of Employment of the Judges] (Iran). (TA)

153 *See id.*

154 *See id.* at Art. 1.

155 *See id.* at Art. 2.

156 *See id.* at Art. 3.

157 *See id.*

158 Jahāngīrī, *supra* note 129.

of banning women from becoming judges in the near future.[159] For months, women judges, lawyers, and law students sought to gain gender equality at work.[160] The women activists protested by writing letters and sending telegrams to different government personnel, making sure that their voice was heard against the violations of their fundamental human rights.[161] Finally after a few months unrest, during the oath ceremony of the judicial trainees, women judicial trainees were prevented from entering the ceremony. Meanwhile, during the oath ceremony, the Minister of Justice declared that lower positions were being considered for existing women judicial trainees without affecting their judicial salary.[162] This increased the protest against this policy, among other discriminatory strategies such as refusal to register women in the upcoming judicial training, differentiating between women and men's judiciary oath, and the dismissing of women judges in the provinces; the protesters called it disregarding the human rights of women.[163] According to a prominent Iranian newspaper, the Women Judges' League in an official notice stated:

> Unfortunately the Ministry of Justice, which should be the ultimate destination for justice, now is turning to a cruel system by nullifying women's human rights and limiting women's rights to choose their work. Allocating the *exclusive right to become judges only to men* and depriving women from judgeship positions despite all the gender equality promises in the Constitution of the Islamic Republic of Iran; several promises made by Āyatullāh Khumiynī stating that women can even become president; refusal of the registration of women in the judicial training; differentiating between the judicial oath for women and men, and dismissal of women judges in the province courtrooms are among acts that will create nothing but discontent.[164] [Emphasis Added]

159 *See e.g.*, Āyandigān Newspaper (Iran), June 13, 1979, N. 3374, at 2 (TA); Iṭṭilā'āt Newspaper (Iran), June 11, 1979, N. 15786, at 2 (TA); Iṭṭilā'āt Newspaper (Iran), July 28, 1979, N. 15915, at 3 (TA); Iṭṭilā'āt Newspaper (Iran), Oct. 12, 1979, N. 15928, at 2 (TA).

160 Jahāngīrī, *supra* note 129. *See also e.g.*, Iṭṭilā'āt Newspaper (Iran), Oct. 12, 1979, N. 15928, at 2 (TA).

161 Jahāngīrī, *supra* note 129. *See also e.g.*, Āyandigān Newspaper (Iran), June 13, 1979, N. 3374, at 2 (TA).

162 Jahāngīrī, *supra* note 129.

163 *See* Āyandigān Newspaper (Iran), June 13, 1979, N. 3374 at 1, 2 (TA).

164 *Id* at 2.

In a separate notice the Association of Graduates of the Educational Complex of Qum declared:

> As part of the recent attacks on all democrat organizations and individual and social freedoms, this time we are witnessing the attack on one of the most fundamental individual rights, which is the right to choose a work. They *do not issue diplomas for women judicial trainees* only because of their *gender* (being a woman), who successfully completed their terms just like men. It is regretful that at this time when talk of equality between women and men is more than ever...instead of taking advantage of the skillful work force in the society, boldly they are invading not only women's rights, but rights of the society as a whole."[165] [Emphasis Added]

As other women's rights organizations joined the protest against the possibility of banning women from the judgeships in the future of the Islamic Republic government, the Minister of Justice stressed Āyatullāh Khumiynī's view that believed in strict implementation of Islam in every aspects of the nation's affairs; and that under the Islamic laws "judgeships" and "guardianships" are, however, banned for women.[166]

Yet in an open letter to the Minister of Justice, the League of Iranian Women Judges, called the dismissal of women judges in various provinces, and the refusal of registration of women in the judicial training "outrageous."[167] They declared, "Dismissal of women judges for the crime of a gender is insulting to the humans' nobility."[168] Also, a group of Iranian women graduates from Tehran University Law School, through their protest, requested gender equality in all respects by relying on few Qurānic verses to reject the new discriminatory actions, by stating:

"In Islam the most qualified people become judges, not men or women. There is no relation between gender and qualification."[169]

---

165 *Id.*

166 *See* Jahāngīrī, *supra* note 129.

167 League of the Iranian Women Judges' Protest against the Board of Correction of the Ministry of Justice. *See* Itṭilāʿāt Newspaper (Iran), July 28, 1979, N. 15915, at 3 (TA).

168 *Id.*

169 Itṭilāʿāt Newspaper (Iran), Oct. 12, 1979, N. 15928, at 9 (TA).

Nine months after the revolution in November 1979, the provisional Board of Ministers ratified a new law, which was called Transferring Women with Judicial Titles from the Ministry of Justice to other Ministries and Conversion of their Judicial Titles to Administrative.[170] As its title suggests, it aimed only at "existing women judges."[171] According to this law, existing women judges with a judicial title were transferred to other government organizations and their judicial titles were changed to administrative ones. Meanwhile, in the process of changing women judges' judicial titles to administrative, this law guaranteed the salary for the demoted judges as if they kept their judicial titles.[172]

Despite counting women's votes in the referendum, which was an indication of strong desire by women to participate in the future of the new Islamic Republic government,[173] dismissal of the existing women judges even before ratification of the new constitution imposed a severe limitation on women's ability to participate in key decision-making positions like judgeships. This was the beginning of serious setbacks on women's authority in key government decision-making positions.

---

170 *See* Intiqāli Bānuvān bā Rutbiyi Qażāī az Vizārati Dādgustarī bi Sāyiri Vizāratkhānihā va Tabdīli Rutbiyi Qażāīyi Ānhā bi Idārī 1358 [Transferring Women with Judicial Titles from the Ministry of Justice to other Ministries and Conversion of their Judicial Titles to Administrative 1979] (Iran). (TA)

171 *See id.*

172 *See id.*

173 *See e.g.*, Iṭṭilāʿāt Newspaper (Iran), May 19, 1979, N. 15857, at 2 (TA).

De Jure Discrimination against Women Pursuing Judgeships

After adoption of the Constitution of the Islamic Republic of Iran, considering the Twelve Ja'farī Shīʿa Islam to be the official religion of the country,[174] Article 4 of the Constitution states that all legal, political, and social affairs to be in accordance with the Islamic jurisprudence.[175]

Concerning the qualifications for judges, Article 163 of the Constitution states:

> "The conditions and *qualifications* to be fulfilled by a *judge* will be determined by law, *in accordance* with the criteria of *fiqh*."[176] [Emphasis Added]

To implement Article 163 of the Constitution, the first Islamic Consultative Assembly ratified the Law on the Qualifications for Appointment of Judges in the Ministry of Justice in 1982, setting the required qualifications for judges. The Single Article reads:

Judges will be selected among qualified *men* who meet these requirements:

1. Piety, justice, and practical commitment to the Islamic principles and laws, and loyalty to the government of the Islamic Republic of Iran
2. Legitimate child
3. Iranian nationality as well as military service or holding legal exemption
4. Good health and ability to work and free from any narcotic dependency

174 *See* Qanuni Assassi Jumhuri'i Islamai Iran [The Constitution of The Islamic Republic of Iran] 1358 [1980], art. 12.

175 *See id.* at Art. 4.

176 *Id.* at Art. 163.

5. Reached the ability to *ijtihād*[177] with the approval of the Supreme Judicial Council; or attained the right to judge from the Supreme Judicial Council with the Judicial Bachelor degree, Bachelor in Theology, or Bachelor's degree from the University of Judicial Science and Administrative affiliated with the Ministry of Justice, or a Judicial Degree from the Qum University or theologian who accomplished... as long as there is not enough qualified *mujtahid* in the Supreme Council.[178] [Emphasis Added]

This existing law is as clear as it reads; judges will be selected among qualified men. Only "men" can pursue judgeships in Iran. The male gender is the key qualification for judges. Even in the case of a qualified woman, she will be found unqualified for the sole reason of her sex. If she were a man, the law in question would not deprive her of a judgeship. The intentional distinction has been made on the ground of "sex" of the applicant to carefully exclude women as a group from pursuing judgeships. The direct male gender qualification imposed by this law intentionally nullifies women's right to have equal access to judgeships and choose this post as their profession.

According to Single Article (5), the lawmakers, however, give the primary right of judgeships to a qualified *mujtahid* by stating, "as long as there is not enough qualified *mujtahid* available in the Supreme Judicial Council" at the end of this section.[179] The concept of *mujtahid* as the ultimate authority to judge is not a foreign concept within the Iranian legal system. Since the adoption of the first Constitution in 1906 the legal system gave the exclusive right to judge to the qualified *mujtahidīn* (religious tribunals), and once again it is repeating itself. However, this time it is in all courts, and in 21st century Iran.

Despite legislators' assertive language to prefer qualified male *mujtahids* as judges, the burden to train Islamic judges was imposed on the Minister of Justice considering the time and circumstances of the country and the absence of sufficient qualified *mujtahids* in the country. According to the lawmakers, one of the most undisputed qualifications for judges in Islam is "being a man," and women can neither become judges nor guardians of the Islamic jurisprudence.

177 Ijtihād, *supra* note 85.

178 *See* Qānuni Sharāyiti Intikhābi Qużāti Dādgustarī 1361 [Law on the Qualifications for Appointment of Judges in the Ministry of Justice 1982], (Iran).

179 *See id.* at Single Article (5).

A judgeship in Islam is one of the branches of *imāmat* (religious leadership),[180] and prophecy[181] that exclusively belongs to men.[182]

During the first Islamic Consultative Assembly, the lawmakers in the process of determining the required qualifications for judges according to Islam, referred to the undisputed Islamic principle that believes a woman cannot become a judge, but she can become an "investigative judge." A woman can start preparing, investigating, and reading the case but she can never "render the final decision" of the court. Rendering the final decision of the court and ending the dispute is the most important responsibility of a judge, and according to the Shīʿa interpretation of Islam, women do not have the capacity to fulfill this serious obligation and it belongs only to men.[183] In essence, for example, women may be a law clerk for a judge, but never a judge.

Article 167 of the Constitution stipulates the decision-making authority of a judge by stating a "judge is bound to render the final decision of the court" even in the absence of law, a deficiency of law or law's contradictory nature. The judges "cannot refrain from delivering his judgment."[184] In addition, other laws have confirmed a similar or identical principal of rendering a final decision of the court by the judge.[185]

The statutory direct exclusion of women as a group from pursuing judgeships based on their "sex" is a de jure discrimination against them. This affirms the gender inequality between women and men before the law and denies women equal access to be employed as judges. By default women are found "unqualified" regardless of their ability, skills, or training on the basis of their sex.

---

180 Imāmat is a true continuous leadership of human society in Shīʿa Islam, which originally was the Prophet's responsibility. 1 Siyid Muḥammad Hāshimī, Huquqi Asāsī Jumhurīyi Islāmiyi Iran (Constitution of Islamic Republic of Iran) 96 (Dādgustar Publication 1999). (TA)

181 *See* Full Discussion of the Islamic Consultative Assembly 1st Term-Session 252, n. 10735, Dec. 22, 1981, at 32, Library, Museum and Document Center of Iran Parliament. (TA)

182 *See* Full Discussion of the Islamic Consultative Assembly 1st Term-Session 227, n.10689, Oct. 22, 1981, at 21, Library, Museum and Document Center of Iran Parliament (TA). *See also id.* at 32.

183 *See* Full Discussion of the Islamic Consultative Assembly 1st Term-Session 227, n.10689, Oct. 22, 1981, at 21, Library, Museum and Document Center of Iran Parliament. (TA)

184 *See* Qanuni Assassi Jumhuri Islamai Iran [The Constitution of The Islamic Republic of Iran] 1358 [1980], art. 167.

185 *See* Qānuni Āʿīni Dādrisīyi Dādgāhhāyi Umumī va Inqilāb dar Muridi Umuri Madanī 1379 [Codes of Civil Procedure in the Public and Revolutionary Courts 2000], art. 3 (Iran) (TA); Qānuni Iṣlāḥi Qānuni Tashkīli Dādgāhhāyi ʿumumī va Inqilāb 1381 [Law Amending the Law of Public and Revolutionary Courts 2002], Single Note (7) (Iran). (TA)

The second part of the 1982 statute consists of a Single Note that confirms the application of the aforementioned qualifications to the "existing working judges," including almost 100 working women judges.[186] Measuring and deciding whether the mentioned qualifications were met among the existing judges was within the authority of the Supreme Judicial Council.[187] As a result, first women judges were found "disqualified" solely because they failed to meet the male gender qualification according to this statute.[188] The Council in the case of finding existing judges disqualified, then had the authority to make them forcefully retire, demote them to consultant positions, or transfer them to administrative posts.[189]

In order to "Islamitize" [sic] the new justice system, the lawmakers made sure that the principles of Islam were strictly implemented in every aspect of the newly transformed justice system.[190] Everything that lacked an Islamic foundation had to be flushed out of the system including working women judges.[191] In order to filter the justice system from its un-Islamic judges, who were left from the Pahlavī era, the remedy was to force them out. Therefore, by passing this Single Note, the previously working judges were first found "disqualified"; then they were forced to retire or work in lower positions.[192]

The term "disqualified judges" was carefully used in this Single Note, expressing the intent of the lawmakers. The remedy, therefore, was simply finding existing women judges "disqualified" first, because they did not meet the male gender qualification anymore. By finding women "disqualified," the lawmaker

186 *See* Law on the Qualifications for Appointment of Judges in the Ministry of Justice 1982, Single Note (Iran).

187 *See id.*

188 *See* Full Discussion of ICA-1st Term Session 227, *supra* note 183, at 22.

189 *See* Law on the Qualifications for Appointment of Judges in the Ministry of Justice 1982, Single Note (Iran).

190 *See* Full Discussion of ICA-1st Term Session 252, *supra* note 181; Full Discussion of the Islamic Consultative Assembly 1st Term-Session 253, n. 10736, Dec. 23, 1981, at 26, Library, Museum and Document Center of Iran Parliament. (TA)

191 *See* Full Discussion of the Islamic Consultative Assembly 1st Term-Session 253, n. 10736, Dec. 23, 1981, at 32, Library, Museum and Document Center of Iran Parliament (TA). *See also* Full Discussion of ICA-1st Term Session 252, *supra* note 181, at 32, 33.

192 *See* Full Discussion of the ICA-1st Term Session 252, *supra* note 181, at 32. *See also* Full Discussion of the Islamic Consultative Assembly 2d Term-Session 69, n. 11635, Dec. 25, 1984, at 32, Library, Museum and Document Center of Iran Parliament. (TA)

foresaw an easy way to force them out because they failed to meet the statutory requirements.

In 1985, during the second term of the Islamic Consultative Assembly, five additional Notes were affixed to the 1982 Law on the Qualifications for Appointment of Judges, of which Note 5 explicitly addressed the situation of women with the judicial titles.[193] According to Note 5 of this law, women who meet the requirements for judgeships according to the previous law[194] could work as "consultants," keeping their "judicial titles," but only in the Special Civil Courts, and the Office of the Guardianship of Minors.[195]

This law applies to women who meet all the qualifications according to the 1982 Law on the Qualifications for Appointment of Judges, except the male gender requirement. Earlier, when disqualified women judges were demoted to consultant roles, the lawmakers did not initially stipulate any specific judicial titles or specific work destinations for them. However, the 1985 statute guaranteed to the female "consultants" with the judicial titles the salary as if they still kept their judgeship positions.[196]

The legislators made it clear that since the majority of the clientele in the Special Civil Courts and the Office of the Guardianship of Minors were women, it made a perfect fit for the now disqualified women judges to work in these places, but only as consultants. Certainly they no longer were judges. The lawmakers emphasized that women clientele could more easily talk to these judges, now called "consultants," because they were women. The consultant women judges were allowed to keep their "judicial titles," in order to receive the same salary as judges.[197]

193 *See* Qānuni Alḥāqi Panj Tabṣari bi Qānuni Sharāyiti Intikhābi Qużāt Dādgustarī 1363 [Five Notes Affixed to the Law on the Qualifications for Appointment of Judges in the Ministry of Justice 1985] (Iran). (TA)

194 Law on the Qualifications for Appointment of Judges in the Ministry of Justice 1982. (Iran).

195 *See* Five Notes Affixed to the Law on the Qualifications for Appointment of Judges in the Ministry of Justice 1985, Note 5 (Iran).

196 *See* Full Discussion of the Islamic Consultative Assembly 2d Term-Session 69, n. 11635, Dec. 25, 1984, at 32-33, Library, Museum and Document Center of Iran Parliament. (TA)

197 *See id* at 33. *See also infra* note 201.

Later, the Nation's Exigency Council[198] passed the Law Amending the Law of Divorce in 1992.[199] According to Note 5 of this law, in the Special Civil Courts "if necessary," qualified women, who meet all the required qualifications mentioned in the 1982 statute, can work as "female consultants."[200] The lawmakers, even though foresaw the position of female consultants in the Special Courts, nonetheless, by using the careful language "if necessary," they made sure that the presence of a female consultant would not financially in any way burden the government and would not be mandatory.[201]

According to the open discussion in the assembly, one of the representatives stated that the purpose of having a female consultant judge in the Family Courts is to assist the women clientele, who are under tremendous pressure of family, divorce, and child custody disputes. They can enjoy "guidance," "support," and "sympathy" from someone of the same sex. She asserted that women in these courts can "share their secrets" and as the result the female consultant judge can defend them.[202]

In 1995, the Five Notes Affixed to the Law on the Qualifications for Appointment of Judges (1982) was amended by the fourth Islamic Consultative Assembly due to its shortcomings.[203] According to the Single Note, qualified women who meet the required qualifications set by the 1982 statute can be employed with the "judicial titles," by the Chief of the judiciary, in newly created positions, for example, "consultation" or as "investigative judges."[204] The

198 Majmaʿi Tashkhīṣi Maṣlaḥati Niẓām hereinafter Nation's Exigency Council.

199 Qānuni Iṣlāḥi Muqararāti Marbut bi Ṭalāq 1371 [Law Amending the Law of Divorce 1992] (Iran). (TA)

200 *See id.* at Note 5.

201 *See* Full Discussion of the Islamic Consultative Assembly 3d Term-Session 471, n.13774, March 11, 1992, at 27-28, Library, Museum and Document Center of Iran Parliament. (TA)

202 *See id.* at 27.

203 *See* Qānuni Iṣlāḥi Tabṣiriyi Panji Qānuni Alḥāqi Panj Tabṣiri bi Qānuni Sharāyiti Intikhābi Qużāti Dādgustarī Muṣavabi 1363 [Law Amending the Note Five of the Five Notes Affixed to the Law on the Qualifications for Appointment of Judges of 1985 (1995)] (Iran) (TA); *See* Full Discussion of the Islamic Consultative Assembly 4th Term-Session 322, n.14624, April 18, 1995, at 25, Library, Museum and Document Center of Iran Parliament (TA).

204 Newly created positions such as consultant to the Court of Administrative Justice and the Special Civil Courts; investigative judges; drafting laws for the Minister of Justice, and administration of Guardianship of Juveniles. *See* Law Amending the Note Five of the Five Notes Affixed to the Law on the Qualifications for Appointment of Judges of 1985 (1995), Single Note (Iran). *See also* Full Discussion of the Islamic Consultative Assembly 4th Term-Session 322, n.14624, April 18, 1995, at 26, Library, Museum and Document Center of Iran Parliament. (TA)

lawmakers also required possession of "judicial title" for the purpose of these newly created positions; nonetheless, they made it crystal clear that these positions did not mean "judging" the case. They explicitly asserted, "Certainly what women should never enter into is rendering the final decision of a court."[205]

An "investigative judge" works under the supervision of a judge (male), in matters that are referred to them such as prosecuting and conducting an inquest.[206] For instance in Public Courts, the court should proceed with the presence of a judge or an investigative judge. Accordingly, the investigative judge can do preliminary work and investigation of the case according to the Codes of Civil Procedure.[207] Certainly, the investigative judge does not have the right to render the final decision of the court. The (male) judge assigned to the case is the sole authority to render the final decision of the court and end dispute.[208]

More specific to women consultant judges in the Family Courts, the court should proceed at least with the presence of a female consultant who possesses a judicial title, and that her "advisory opinion" should be taken into account by the judge who has the sole authority to render the final decision of the court according to the constitution.[209]

According to the lawmakers, to give legal advice a consultant requires possession of a "judicial title"; otherwise it is forbidden even for a qualified woman who meets all the required qualifications for judgeships according to the 1982 statute but who fails to have a judicial title.[210] Nonetheless, the lawmakers stipulated that women consultants and investigative judges, even with the judicial titles, would not act as decision-making judges according to the Constitution with the authority to render the final decision of the court.[211] Women can advise and consult; men will always decide and render the verdicts.

---

205 *See* Full Discussion of the Islamic Consultative Assembly 4th Term-Session 322, n.14624, April 18, 1995, at 26, Library, Museum and Document Center of Iran Parliament. (TA)

206 *See* Qānuni Tashkīli Dādgāhhāyi Umumī va Inqilāb 1373 [Law of Establishing Public and Revolutionary Courts 1994], art. 15 (Iran). (TA)

207 *See* Full Discussion of the ICA-1st Term Session 227, *supra* note 183, at 21; *See* Law Amending the Law of Public and Revolutionary Courts 2002, at N. 7 (Article 14-a) (Iran). (TA)

208 *See* Law of Establishing Public and Revolutionary Courts 1994, arts. 8, 14, 17 (Iran); Law Amending the Law of Public and Revolutionary Courts 2002, at N. 3 (Article 8), N. 7 (Article 14-c) (Iran).

209 *See* Law Amending the Law of Public and Revolutionary Courts 2002, at N. 7 (Article 14-b) (Iran).

210 *See* Full Discussion of the ICA-4th Term Session 322, *supra* note 205, at 26.

211 *See id.*

The only purpose of keeping women's judicial titles was to guarantee their salary as judges, and not for the purpose of rendering the final decision of the court or otherwise fulfilling actual judicial functions.[212] In 1997, the assembly made a modest improvement with regards to women consultant judges and passed the law called Allocating the Number of Existing Courts to the Family Courts.[213] According to Note 3 of Single Article:

> "Every Family Court starts its obligations to the *extent possible* with the presence of a female consultant judge, and the final decision of the court will be rendered *after consultation* with the *female consultant judge*."[214] [Emphasis Added]

One of the goals behind the ratification of this law was to address women's increased need to be heard in the Family Courts, more than half of whose clientele were women. The lawmakers believed that women ending up in the Family Courts had a greater need and desire to be heard by the female consultant judges. They believed that women do not feel comfortable openly discussing their family disputes with men in the public courts, and that in the absence of women consultant judges, issues will not get solved. The lawmakers also believed that since the position of women consultant judges already existed, requiring their mandatory presence in every family dispute will strengthen the Family Courts system as a whole and that it will gradually decrease family disputes. They also believed that to preserve the women's dignity in the Family Courts, it is necessary to allocate women as neutral person to hear women's stories first, so that with their legal language and skills they can convey the raised issues to the judge.[215] Similarly, the lawmakers considered the women consultant judges to be the most beneficial when they are working in family related disputes; more beneficial than in places such as Public Courts, where

212 *See id.*

213 *See* Qānuni Ikhtiṣāṣi Tiʿdādī az Dādgāhāyi Mujud bi Dādgāhāyi Mużuʿi Aṣli (21) Qānuni Asāsī (Dādgāhi Khānivādi) 1376 [Allocating the Number of Existing Courts to the Family Courts 1997] (Iran). (TA)

214 The subject matter of the Family Courts jurisdiction according to this law is strictly family/marriage dispute related: permanent and temporary marriages; divorce; dowry; trousseau; alimony; visitation and custody of children; re-marriage; guardianship; terms and conditions of marriage. *See id* at Single Article.

215 *See* Full Discussion of the Islamic Consultative Assembly 5th Term-Session 111, n.15428, July 30, 1997, at 25, Library, Museum and Document Center of Iran Parliament. (TA)

most disputes are not family centered.[216] The presence of a woman consultant judge, therefore, in each Family Court became an important concern, but only to the extent of making her an advisor to women litigants.

Meanwhile, the possibility of financial burden on the government by mandating the presence of a female consultant judge in each case was foreseen by the lawmakers. By using the term "to the extent possible," which means "if possible," the lawmakers prevented the chances of a financial burden on the government. The lawmakers insisted that only if there are already available female consultant judges in the Family Courts, should the court take advantage of their presence. Otherwise if getting them is financially "burdensome" to the court, this law does not require women consultant judges' presence.[217]

It is, however, essential to examine the authority of women consultant judges to see whether they ever have the authority to render the final decision of the court according to the Constitution. The clear language used in the 1997 statute stipulates that the final decision of the court will be rendered after consultation with a female consultant judge, without giving further details. This law fails to specify what constitutes "consultation" and to what extent the judge is obligated to implement her opinion in his verdict.

However, for example, a later statute in 2002, similar to the 1997 law, expands its language by asserting:

> "In Family Courts...and the *advisory opinion* of the female consultant judges *will be taken into account* by the head of the court (judge) *before rendering* his *verdict*."[218] [Emphasis Added]

This makes the opinion of a female consultant judge an "advisory opinion," and the judge is obligated to consider her advisory opinion before issuing his verdict. Accordingly, it also reaffirms the judge's authority to render the final decision of the court without obligating the judge to follow the advisory opinion of the female consultant judges.

The latest addition to these laws concerning women consultant judges is the ratification of the Family Protection Law in 2012.[219] Article 2 states:

---

216 *See id.* at 24.

217 *See id.* at 25.

218 *See* Law Amending the Law of Public and Revolutionary Courts 2002, No. 7 (Article 14-b), (Iran).

219 *See* Qānuni Ḥimāyati Khānivādi 1391 [Family Law Protection 2012] (Iran). (TA)

> Family Court is formed with the presence of a chief or prosecutor and a *female consultant judge*. A consultant judge is obligated to submit her written and well-reasoned opinion about the case within three days after closing hearing. The *judge with the authority to render the final decision of the court* in his judgment should *refer* to the female consultant judge's *opinion*, and in the case of *disagreement* with her opinion, *he can reject* it by stating his reasoning.[220] [Emphasis Added]

This law makes the legitimacy of the Family Court dependent on the presence of a consultant female judge. It also requires a female consultant judge to submit her well-reasoned written opinion to the court. However, once again the full and ultimate authority to end the dispute is explicitly left to the judge who has the power to render the final decision of the court. Clearly, in the case of disagreement with the opinion of the female consultant judge, he can simply reject her opinion with stated reasoning.[221]

All previous laws that directly addressed the position of female consultant judges emphasized only the "presence" and "consultation" aspects that are more procedural rules. These statutes, however, failed to authorize women consultant judges any decision-making power. The decision-making power of a judge is explicitly enshrined in the Constitution, which is rendering the final decision of the court and ending the disputes. Details such as "judge who renders the final decision of the court with the authority to write a verdict," or "female consultant judges with advisory opinion," explicitly un-authorizes the female consultant from issuing a verdict.

None of the laws previous to this 2012 law, however, required submission of a written advisory opinion by a female consultant judge to the judge. Even though this law offers more details on the procedural aspect of the advisory opinion of female consultant judges, the decision-making authority for them is still non-existent. It guarantees that the male judge will read the female consultant judge's advisory opinion before rendering his verdict, but it does not require him either to accept or implement her opinion in his verdict.[222] Accordingly,

220 *See id.* at Art. 2.

221 *See id.*

222 *See id.*

rejecting the consulting judges' views takes merely a brief written statement of his legal reasoning.[223]

The passage of the Family Protection Law increased the need to have female consultant judges in the judiciary. For example, in late 2014 out of almost 25,000 applicants, there were well over 9,000 registered women (35%) for the judiciary exam.[224] In an interview the spokesperson of the Judicial and Legal Commission of the Parliament stated that in 2013 there were a "substantial number of women judges working in the Ministry of Justice, Public Prosecutor Office, and Assistant to the Public Prosecutor."[225] He also indicated that the presence of a consultant judge ultimately "will help the judges of the Family Courts to consider all aspects that are necessary to preserves the family units."[226] He also stated, "even though following the female consultant judge's advisory opinion is not necessary for the judge of the court, her presence may influence his verdict."[227] He also expressed his hopes for the Family Courts to offer higher quality service while dealing with a high volume of divorce cases and the need for a more careful hearing when dealing with divorce. He also indicated "we have had female consultant judges in the Public Prosecutor Offices and in the penal system that were dealing with issues such as children without guardians, and selecting guardians."[228] In 2013, the IRI government, in response to the report of the Human Rights Council Special Rapporteur that indicated "women appear to be permitted to serve only as female advisory judges and issue advisory opinions in family courts,"[229] stated

223 Mobin Edalat, *Ilzāmī Budani Ḥużuri Qāżīyi Mushāviri Zan dar Daʿāvīyi Khānivādi [Necessity of the Presence of a Female Consultant Judge]*, Hedayatmobin (Aug. 16, 2014), *accessed at* http://hedayatmobin.com/%D8%A7%D9%84%D8%B2%D8%A7%D9%85%DB%8C-%D8%A8%D9%88%D8%AF%D9%86-%D8%AD%D8%B6%D9%88%D8%B1-%D9%82%D8%A7%D8%B6%DB%8C-%D9%85%D8%B4%D8%A7%D9%88%D8%B1-%D8%B2%D9%86-%D8%AF%D8%B1-%D8%AF%D8%B9%D8%A7%D9%88%DB%8C/. (TA)

224 Dar Āzmuni *Qāżī* 93 [*In the Judiciary Exam 93*], Ekhtebar, (Sep. 29, 2014), *accessed at* http://www.ekhtebar.com/در-آزمون-قضاوت-93-،-348-رای‌داد-مرد-و-64-رای‌داد-زن/. (TA)

225 Islamic Consultative Assembly News Agency, *Bā Ishāri bi Ilzāmi Qānun Barāyi Jazbi Zanān dar Dādgāhāyi Khānivādi [According to The Legal Necessity of Attracting Women in Family Law Courts]*, ICANA (Nov. 2, 2013), *accessed at* http://icana.ir/Fa/News/240234. (TA)

226 *Id.*

227 *Id.*

228 *Id.*

229 U.N. Secretary-General, *Situation of human rights in the Islamic Republic of Iran Note by the Secretary-General*, G.A., ¶ 69 at 19, U.N. Doc. A/69/356 (Aug. 27, 2014).

"there are currently 670 women judges" in Iran.[230] This report avoids the issue raised by the Special Rapporteur that women's only opportunity to become judges is "consultant judges" in the Family Courts. This will be analyzed closely in the next chapter. Calling an "assistant" or "consultant" a judge does not make them judges according to the Iranian Constitution.

Regarding the decision-making authority of a judge, the Constitution, in addition to other relevant laws, has made it clear that the most paramount responsibility of a judge is to end disputes by rendering the final decision of the court. A final decision of the court will result in adjudication of individual rights, and expanding of public justice in the society.[231]

In a nutshell, despite women's unprecedented participation in creation of the Islamic revolution, and all gender equality promises, existing women judges were found "disqualified" solely because of their gender. They were forced into retirement or demotion. This was the ultimate betrayal of women who requested change and participated in protesting against Pahlavī in the creation of the new Islamic Republic government that promised gender equality in its future. Later in 1982, the discriminatory statute on the qualification of judges was passed that directly imposed a male gender as the key qualification for judges. To this day, upholding this law for almost 34 years has resulted in excluding and preventing women from pursuing judgeships in Iran.

Since then, despite a few legal reforms, which resulted in the creation of new positions such as female consultant judges, women carry on the misleading title of the "judge" without having the Constitutional decision-making authority of a judge. The purposeful statutory exclusion of women as a group from pursuing judgeships solely on the basis of their gender constitutes a de jure discrimination against women in Iran today.

230 Response of the Islamic Republic of Iran to Draft Report of Special Rapporteur for Submission to the 69th Session of the UN General Assembly, SHAHEEONIRAN.ORG, at 28, 29 (2014), *accessed at* http://shaheedoniran.org/wp-content/uploads/2014/10/Response-of-the-Islamic-Republic-of-Iran-to-Draft-Report-of-Special.pdf.

231 *See* Qanuni Assassi Jumhuri'i Islamai Iran [The Constitution of The Islamic Republic of Iran] 1358 [1980], art. 167. *See also* 2 SIYID MUḤAMMAD HĀSHIMĪ, HUQUQI ASĀSĪ JUMHURĪYI ISLĀMIYI IRAN (CONSTITUTION OF ISLAMIC REPUBLIC OF IRAN) 403 (Dādgustar Publication 1999).

Gender Equality According to Islam

Articles 20 and 21 of the Constitution explicitly limit gender equality and women's rights according to Islamic jurisprudence. Article 163 of the Constitution also sets the qualifications to be fulfilled by a judge according to Islam. Therefore, it becomes essential to examine Islamic views about "gender equality." The most fundamental Islamic principle that defines gender equality is based on the existence of "physical and psychological differences" between women and men. This requires that women and men have different rights, responsibilities, and punishments according to their "natural differences." This view, for example, has been continuously and unequivocally asserted by the delegations of the IRI government in many State reports regarding women and gender equality under Islamic views. It becomes important to examine whether women are considered equal to men under the Shīʿa interpretation of Islamic jurisprudence. Doe gender equality constitute identical rights under Shīʿa Islam? In particular, what does Shīʿa Islam say regarding gender equality in employment, particularly government decision-making positions like judgeships?

In order to understand women and men's natural capabilities, Islam requires examining all different characteristic traits, inclinations, instincts, capacities, and physical and psychological differences between women and men. Subsequently, it determines their rights and responsibilities according to these God-given disparities.[232] The existence of these dissimilarities does not make one gender superior or defective. The differences are created by nature to strengthen ties between women and men in the family unit, and accordingly create different rights and responsibilities for each one of them in the family.[233] Based on these inevitable physical and psychological differences, the foundation of a "family"

232 *See* Ṣāliḥī Najaf Ābādī, Qiżāvati Zan dar Fiqhi Islāmī (Women's Judgeships in the Islamic Fiqh) 18 (Umīdi Fardā Publication 2005). (TA)

233 *See* Murtiżā Muṭahrī, Niẓāmi Ḥuquqi Zan dar Islām [Women's Rights in Islam] 159, 160 (Ṣadrā Publication 2011). (TA)

is shaped and continues to strengthen.[234] This chart demonstrates some of the physical and psychological differences always attributed to women and men by Islamic scholars:[235]

Women	**Men**
Be protected by men Beautiful and graceful Become emotional faster Emotionally less stable Housewives and mothers Incapable of analyzing and understanding serious intellectual issues Inclined toward art, literature, and detailed works Inclined toward embellishment and luxury unlike men Kind and affectionate Less sexual Need to conquer men's heart Overall undeniable physical and psychological difference compare to men Physically and emotionally delicate Puberty in a younger age/ Younger menopausal age Quiet Secretive Soft voice Sympathetic and compassionate Tenderhearted / crying more /prone to faint Timid, careful and talkative	Brave Conquer the world Driven and hard workers Fierce Inclined toward intellectual, scientific and sport fields Intellectual and rational Less emotional Loud and coarse voice Men's brain size is bigger than a woman Older menopausal age Older puberty age Physically larger, taller, heartbeats are different Rough Sexually lustful

234 Najaf Ābādī, *supra* note 232, at 18-19. *See also id.* at 160.

235 *See e.g.*, Najaf Ābādī, *supra* note 232, at 18-19. *See also* Muṭaharī, *supra* note 233, at 164.

Based on these natural differences between women and men, Islam certainly does not recognize identical rights, responsibilities, and punishments for them.[236] According to this principle "identical rights" are different from "equal rights."[237] The principle of gender based equal rights, without considering natural differences between women and men, is considered an undoubtedly western perspective and this is where it becomes fundamentally different from the Islamic view.[238] " Equal rights" does not mean, " identical rights" from the Islamic point of view.[239] Importantly, Islam is not against "equality" between women and men; but it is against "identical" rights between women and men.[240] According to Islam, women and men do not have identical rights; likewise they do not have identical responsibilities, or punishments.[241] Based on these physical and psychological differences, the principle of Islamic justice requires that each gender must have responsibilities suitable and tolerable according to their physical and psychological nature.[242] As a result, application of this principle helps the prosperity of a family unit and moving the society forward in a right direction.[243] Justice is not served if the responsibilities given to women and men mismatch their abilities and tolerance level.[244]

236 Muṭaharī, *supra* note 233, at 122-123.

237 *Id.* at 115.

238 *Id.* at 122.

239 *Id.* at 115.

240 *Id.* at 112.

241 *Id.* at 116.

242 *See* Najaf Ābādī, *supra* note 232, at 20.

243 Muṭaharī, *supra* note 233, at 124.

244 Najaf Ābādī, *supra* note 232, at 20.

Gender Requirement for Judges According to Fiqh

Article 163 of the Constitution requires that the selection of judges must be according to *fiqh* (Islamic jurisprudence). This makes it critical to examine the Islamic jurisprudence's view regarding key qualifications for judges. Since the core aspect of this paper is to analyze the mandatory male gender qualification for judges, this section will only demonstrate the prominent Islamic Shīʿa scholars' view on whether a male gender is required for judges. Analyzing the *fiqh* aspect of this matter is a complex religious matter that goes beyond the scope of this book.

Islamic jurists and scholars according to the constitution are the ultimate authority to extract the full content of the recognized sources of Islamic law and fit them for practical use according to time and place. According to Islam, in the absence of the Muḥammad and infallible Imāms, Islamic jurists have the sole authority for the discovery, understanding, and formulation of a law, which already exists by the law of God.[245] However, analyzing their approaches and examining of the credibility and accuracy of their sources in this regard is beyond the scope of this book.

The issue of women's judgeships post-Islamic Revolution has been tense and at the same time controversial. The majority of Islamic scholars believe that women cannot become judges, as reflected in laws, because they are emotional; they use women's sensitive and emotional traits against them to prove their weakness in judgment and that women are unable to fulfill the serious responsibilities of a judge.[246]

245 For Islamic jurist *see* Tony Weir, An Introduction to Comparative Law 304 (K. Zweigert & H. Kotz trans., 3d ed., Oxford University Press 1998).

246 Dukhti Iran, *Farāz va Furudi Qiżāvati Zanān dar Iran* [*Ups and Downs of the Women's Judgeships in Iran*], Dokhtiran (July 8, 2013), *accessed at* http://www.dokhtiran.com/interview/1392_04/001375.php. (TA)

The most famous Islamic scholars such as Shaīkhi Ṭusī, Shahīd Avval,[247] Shahīd S̱ānī,[248] ʿllāmi Ḥillī, Muḥaqiq Ḥillī, Shaykhi Mufīd, and Ibni Idrīs are among the most prominent S̱hīʿa jurists that analyzed the qualifications for judges.

Shaīkhi Ṭusī and Shahīd S̱ānī are among the most famous Shīʿa scholars whose writings assert women are banned from judgeships. Their books are considered the main sources to discover Islamic rules.[249] Shaīkhi Ṭusī was the first Shīʿa jurist who discussed the gender requirement for judgeship in the fourth century.[250] He explicitly prohibits women from becoming judges.[251] Both ʿllāmi Ḥillī and Muḥaqiq Ḥillī, in their books, explicitly require male gender as one of the required qualifications for judges.[252]

Other famous Islamic scholars such as Shahīd Avval and Shahīd S̱ānī both stated that being a man is one of the essential qualifications for judges.[253] Other famous Shīʿa scholars, such as Ṣāḥibi Javāhir and Ibni Qadāmi Ḥanbalī, also require a male gender qualification.[254]

Famous contemporary Islamic scholars such as Āyatullāh Khumiynī also indicated that male gender is one of the essential qualifications for judges.[255] There are, however, other famous Shīʿa scholars such as Shikhi Mufīd[256] and Ibni

---

247 Shahīd Avval was one of the most famous Shīʿa Islamic jurisprudent. Lumʿi is one of his famous books that s been teaching for centuries. 1 Shahīd Avval, Lumʿi Damshaqīyi 12 (Asad Allāh Lutfī trans., 2d ed., Khursandī Publication 2011). (TA)

248 Shahīd S̱ānī was one of the most well respected Islamic jurists from the 10th Century. One of his books has been used for teaching in different Islamic universities for the last four hundred years. Shahīd S̱ānī, Sharḥi Lumʿi 7 (Assad Allah Lotfi trans., 7th ed., Mujd Publication 2010). (TA)

249 1 Siyid Muḥammad Hāshimī, Huquqi Asāsī Jumhurīyi Islāmiyi Iran (Constitution of Islamic Republic of Iran) 111 (Dādgustar Publication 1999). (TA)

250 Women, Power and Politics in 21st Century Iran 110 (Tara Povery & Elaheh Rostami Povery eds., Ashgate Publishing 2012).

251 Najaf Ābādī, *supra* note 232, at 26.

252 *See* ʿllāmi Ḥillī, Tabṣaraʾl Mutiʿalimīn, 696 (ʿllāmi Shiʿrānī trans., 6th ed., Islāmīyi Publication 2006) (TA); Muḥaqiq Ḥillī, Sharāyiʿ Alislām, 1624-1632, (Abul Qāsim Ibni Aḥmad Yazdī trans., 6th ed., Tehran University Publication 1996). (TA)

253 *See* Shahīd S̱ānī, Sharḥi Lumʿi 9 (Assad Allah Lotfi trans., 7th ed., Mujd Publication 2010) (TA); 1 Shahīd Avval, Lumʿi Damshaqīyi 156 (Asad Allāh Lutfī trans., 2d ed., Khursandī Publication 2011). (TA)

254 2 Āyatullāh Ḥusiīn Alī Muntaẓirī, Official Website of Montazeri 101, *accessed at* https://amontazeri.com/book/mabani/volume-2/101#cref-3.

255 Khumiynī, *supra* note 149, at 245.

256 Shikhi Mufīd was a prominent Twelve Shīʿa Islam.

Idrīs[257] who do not prohibit women from judgeships.[258] Among other famous contemporary Shīʿa scholars, Āyatullāh Yusif Ṣāniʿī, Ṣāliḥī explicitly had announced that women can become judges and gender should not be a requirement.[259]

257 Ibn Edrīs is a well know Islamic jurist.

258 MEHRPOUR *supra* note 130, at 321.

259 *Id.* at 322.

Reasoning of the Shīʿa Jurists to Ban Women from Judgeships

The Shīʿa jurists and scholars have used original Islamic sources such as the Qurān, *rivāyāt*[260] and *ijmāʿ*[261] in their arguments to justify that women cannot become judges in Islam.[262] There is no explicit use of language in the Qurān suggesting that only men can become judges.[263] Despite the absence of an explicit or direct male gender requirement in the Qurān, there are, however, four Qurānic verses[264] that have been interpreted by predominant Islamic scholars as prohibiting women from becoming judges.[265]

There are number of *rivāyāt* (narratives)[266] that have been quoted by some of the Shīʿa scholars and interpreted as a justification to ban women from judgeships. Some of these narratives explicitly ban woman from judgeships. There are other suggestive narratives that have been interpreted as a justification to ban women form judgeships.[267] These narratives explicitly ban women's *vilāyat* (guardianship).[268] These narratives strictly prohibit others from consulting and

---

260 Rivāyāt is the narratives that tell us about speeches, actions, and written documents by the Prophet Muḥammad and infallible Imāms. Rushanʿalī Shikārī, Uṣuli Fiqh [The Foundation of Islamic Jurisprudence] 18-19 (Ṭarḥi Nuvīn Andīshi Publication 2008). (TA)

261 Ijmāʿ is reached when there is a unanimous agreement of mujtahidīn of the Muslim community of any period following the demise of the Prophet Muḥammad on any matter. Muḥamad Hāshim Kamālī, Principles of Islamic Jurisprudence 230 (3d ed., The Islamic Texts Society 2003).

262 Mehrpour *supra* note 130, at 324-325.

263 *Id.* at 324.

264 Verse 34 Suriyi Nisāʿ; Verse 228, Suriyi Baqarih; Verse 18, Suriyi Zukhruf; Verse 33, Suriyi Aḥzāb.

265 Mehrpour *supra* note 130, at 324-329.

266 Rivāyāt, hereinafter narratives.

267 Mehrpour *supra* note 130, at 329.

268 Najaf Ābādī, *supra* note 232, at 30. *See also* Full Discussion of ICA-1st Term Session 227, *supra* note 183, at 21.

following women's decisions.[269] Accordingly, *zimāmdārī* (statesmanship/governorship) also is prohibited for women. Because a judgeship is one of the key government positions that require making decisions, and since women are banned from governorship, therefore, they are banned from becoming judges.[270]

In the open discussion of the Islamic Consultative Assembly, during the discussion of the passage of the Law on the Qualifications of Judges, the lawmakers explicitly stated that the judgeship is a ramification of the *imāmat* (Islamic leadership)[271] and prophecy.[272] Concerning a male gender requirement, the lawmakers explicitly stated that since the judgeship is one branch of the *vilāyati faqīh* (Islamic guardianship) and women are prohibited from Islamic guardianship, women, therefore, could not become judges.[273]

Additionally, there are narratives that explicitly address women's supposed intellectual and cognitive inability and physical and emotional weakness, such as words used in Nahjul Balāghi.[274] It has been construed that because of women's intellectual disabilities and emotional instability, consultation with women regarding political affairs can lead to an unhealthy society with unpleasant results. Therefore, consultation and following their decisions are prohibited for others; even in the case of a woman giving good ideas and guidance.[275] For example, Nahjul Balāghi confirms the existence of physical and psychological differences between women and men, and that based on the intellectual differences between the sexes, a woman's testimony is worth half that of a man's testimony, or a woman is entitle to half the share of inheritance available to a man; confirming the supremacy of a male gender.[276]

Based on a few narratives, it has been construed that women should be strictly controlled so that they will be unable to associate with others, and that

---

269 Mehrpour *supra* note 130, at 329.

270 *Id.* at 333-334.

271 Imāmat is a true continuous leadership of human society in Shīʿa Islam, which originally was the Prophet's responsibility. 1 Hāshimī, *supra* note 249, at 96.

272 *See* Full Discussion of ICA-1st Term Session 252, *supra* note 181, at 32.

273 *See* Full Discussion of ICA-1st-Term Session 227, *supra* note 183, at 21. *See also* Inqilābi Islāmī Newspaper, *supra* note 158.

274 *See* Imām Alī, Nahjul Balāghi 91, 383 (Muhammad Dashtī trans., Tehran Badr Publication 2011) (TA). *See also* Mehrpour *supra* note 130, 334.

275 Mehrpour *supra* note 130, at 334, 335.

276 *See* Imā Alī, Nahjul Balāghi 91 (Muhammad Dashtī trans., Tehran Badr Publication 2011). (TA)

they should be in charge of nothing; if possible, they should never associate with anyone other than their husbands.[277]

Many of the Shīʿa scholars in their written documents have referred to women's deficiency in comparison with men. Some explicitly indicate that women are defective, foolish, and weak-minded by nature. Others blame women's emotional status for their inability and that women's unstable emotional status prevails over their intellect.[278] Since the judgeships require intellect and competency according to these narratives, therefore women cannot become judges.[279]

Even though, there have been some narratives that either explicitly or implicitly prohibit women from judgeships, most Shīʿa scholars rely on *ijmāʿ*, which is the unanimous and undisputed opinion of all Shīʿa scholars on one matter, to ban women from becoming judges.[280]

The language used by the Shīʿa scholars, after referring to *ijmāʿ* and narratives to justify banning women form the judgeships, indicates there has been clear reference to other old Islamic traditions. For example, the tradition of maximum physical coverage of women in the presence of men and preventing women from associating with men; the tradition that the Prophet Muḥammad and infallible Imāms did not honor women in judgeships, and the continuous usage of word *rijāl* (men) referring to judges, which is an indication of the common tradition of the Prophet Muḥammad and other infallible Imāms in their appointment of judges.[281]

Today, the lawmakers and religious leaders have refrained from using explicit terms such as women are "flawed," or "unable to choose" as they were used earlier in the century; rather these views are used cleverly and carefully in concealed ways. The legislature uses careful language in presenting their justifications to ban women from key decision-making positions such as judgeships. They openly refer to general and well-established Islamic principles, for example, women are banned from *Imāmat* and *vilāyat*, to justify the further exclusion pertaining to women in various fields. However, they fail to present detailed reasoning to exclude women from these positions.

277 Mehrpour *supra* note 130, at 335.

278 *Id.* at 342.

279 *See id.* at 329.

280 *Id.* at 336.

281 *See id.* at 348, 351.

For instance, in 2011 when for the first time the judiciary announced that women could participate in the judgeship exam, one of the members of the Judicial and Legal Commission of the Parliament,[282] in an interview with the Islamic Consultative Assembly News agency, declared that the "recruitment of women judges (consultant women judges) is not in the best interest of the judiciary."[283] He emphasized "the presence of women as judges neither in the Family Courts nor elsewhere is compatible with their nature."[284] Furthermore, he stated "women in addition to work in the judiciary have responsibilities such as housekeeping, taking care of their husbands and children."[285] He concluded "women have more tenderness in their hearts than men and it is possible that they can be influenced by their emotions; therefore becoming judges is not suitable for them."[286]

In a different interview after the announcement of accepting women for the judiciary exam, one of the members of the Judicial and Legal Commission of the Eighth Parliament[287] warned the judiciary and declared "selection and appointment of women in judgeship positions, according to the explicit order of Islam, is not appropriate."[288] He also concluded that "Islam put the logical and reasonable judgment in the man's way of thinking and since women are tenderhearted compare to men and it is possible that they be influenced by their feelings and emotions, therefore, Islam has put a judgeship within the territory of men."[289]

282 Abulfażl Abuturābī.

283 Khāniyi Millat, *Qiżāvat bā Ruḥīyiyi Zanān Sāzigār Nīst [A Judgeship is not Compatible with Women's Nature]*, Islamic Consultative Assembly News Agency (July 9, 2012), *accessed at* http://www.icana.ir/Fa/News/200733. (TA)

284 *Id.*

285 *Id.*

286 *Id.*

287 Hujatul Islām Muḥammad Taqī Rāhbar.

288 Bāshgāhi Khabarnigārān, *Ḥujatul Islām Rahbar Hushdār Dād [Ayatullāh Rahbar Warned]*, Khabarnigārān (June 22, 2012), *accessed at* http://www.yjc.ir/fa/news/3996965/YJC.IR. (TA)

289 *Id.*

Chapter 3

Gender and Judgeships in Iran: an Analysis of International Human Rights Laws and Mechanisms

INTRODUCTION

Iran, despite being the land of the world's first Declaration of Human Rights,[1] and the host of the first International Conference on Human Rights,[2] proclaiming the elimination of discrimination against women,[3] is today among the top nations with myriad violations of the most fundamental human rights and freedoms.[4]

Today, despite the passage of almost seventy years since the formation of the United Nations and the adoption of the equality doctrines and elimination of gender-based discrimination as UN jurisprudence, women still continue to experience violations of their human rights and fundamental freedoms all over the world.[5] For centuries women's gender has been a catalyst to deny and restrict

1 The Cyrus Cylinder has been declared the world's first Declaration of Human Rights, promoting peace in ancient times. *See* The Iran Heritage Foundation (America), *IHF AmericaWhat is the Cyrus Cylinder?* IHF AMERICA (Oct. 12, 2012), *accessed at* http://cyruscylinder2013.com/2012/10/what-is-the-cyrus-cylinder/.

2 The first International Conference on Human Rights was held in Tehran from April 22 to May 13, 1968 to review the progress made in the twenty years since the adoption of the Universal Declaration of Human Rights and formulate an agenda for the future. It required the member States to fulfill their obligations to promote and encourage respect for human rights and fundamental freedoms for all without any kinds of discrimination. Proclamation of Tehran, Final Act of the International Conference on Human Rights, Teheran, 22 April to 13 May 1968, art. 1 at 1, U.N. Doc. A/CONF. 32/41 (1968).

3 Proclamation of Tehran, Final Act of the International Conference on Human Rights, Teheran, 22 April to 13 May 1968, art. 15 at 3, U.N. Doc. A/CONF. 32/41 (1968).

4 *See* UN Special Rapporteur on the Situation of Human Rights in the Islamic Republic of Iran, Video: *Dr. Shaheed Addresses United Nations Press Corps-a press conference to preview his 2014 report,* SHAHEEDONIRAN.ORG (Oct. 28, 2014), *accessed at* http://shaheedoniran.org/english/english/dr-shaheeds-addresses-united-nations-press-corps/.

5 *See* G.A. Res. S-23/3, *Further actions and initiatives to implement the Beijing Declaration and Platform for Action,* ¶ 27 at 10, U.N. Doc. A/RES/S-23/3 (Nov. 16, 2000). *See also* SUSAN DELLER ROSS, WOMEN'S HUMAN RIGHTS 1 (University of Pennsylvania Press 2008); Fareda Banda, Project on a Mechanism to Address Laws that Discriminate Against Women, OFFICE OF THE HIGH COMMISSIONER FOR HUMAN RIGHTS AND GENDER UNIT, at 115 (March 6, 2008), *accessed at* http://www.ohchr.org/Documents/Publications/laws_that_discriminate_against_women.pdf.

their civil, political, economic, social and cultural rights. Even today, women are still considered inferior, intellectually deficient, and physically and emotionally submissive to men in many countries.[6] One critical example is the 1982 Law on the Qualifications for Appointment of Judges in the Ministry of Justice[7] in Iran that explicitly requires male gender as the core qualifications for judges. Because a woman is considered incompetent due to her sensitive and emotional nature, lacking the logic and reasonable judgment that the brain of a man has to pass judgment.[8]

Today, protecting and empowering women are more possible than ever before due to the existence of international human rights mechanism for women. States, for example, by incorporating different international human rights laws and principles in their domestic legal systems, can take steps to improve the legal status of women and guarantee women equal enjoyment of civil, political, economic, social and cultural rights regardless of their gender.[9]

This chapter will demonstrate and analyze different human rights monitoring mechanisms under the United Nations system as they relate to the protection and promotion of universal human rights of women in Iran, more specifically to women pursuing judgeships. This will include the analysis of Iran's legal obligations under international human rights mechanisms such as various UN charter-based and treaty-based bodies.

The key domestic legislation to be analyzed is the existing 1982 Law on the Qualifications for Appointment of Judges in the Ministry of Justice that explicitly requires male gender as one of the core qualifications for granting judgeships in Iran today. According to this law, the differential treatment of imposed exclusion of women by the legislature bans women from becoming judges based solely on their sex. The key question to be analyzed, first, is whether this gender-based exclusion constitutes discrimination against women under international human rights jurisprudence? Do women have any universally guaranteed

---

6 Javaid Rehman, International Human Rights Law: A Practical Approach 345 (Pearson 2003).

7 Qānuni Sharāyiti Intikhābi Qużāti Dādgustarī 1361 [Law on the Qualifications for Appointment of Judges in the Ministry of Justice 1982] (Iran). (Translated by Author, hereinafter TA). For more detail about his law *see* Chapter 2.

8 *See id. See also* Intiqāli Bānuvān bā Rutbiyi Qażāī az Vizārati Dādgustarī bi Sāyiri Vizāratkhānihā va Tabdīli Rutbiyi Qażāīyi Ānhā bi Idārī 1358 [Transferring Women with Judicial Titles from the Ministry of Justice to other Ministries and Conversion of their Judicial Titles to Administrative 1979] (Iran) (TA); Chapter 2.

9 Susan Deller Ross, Women's Human Rights 1 (University of Pennsylvania Press 2008).

human rights? Does this exclusion make women victims of possible violations of their human rights by Iran under international law? Can universally accepted human rights doctrines penetrate the Iranian legal system to promote and protect the Iranian women's rights?

It is also essential to examine State's obligations under international law; further, what are Iran's legal obligations to protect and promote the human rights of Iranian women? What does the passage and upholding of the existing 1982 statute mean as it pertains to Iran's obligations under international law?

The current statutory ban on women pursuing judgeships in Iran is only one compelling example of a pervasive discrimination against Iranian women that has its deep roots in the existence of de jure[10] and de facto[11] discrimination against women. This was reaffirmed by the latest report of the Secretary-General to the General Assembly's seventieth session in August 2015 that women continue to face systemic inequalities and discrimination, both in law and in practice, and in all areas of their lives.[12]

This chapter will first explain what constitutes "human rights" and "women's human rights" and examine whether women's rights are considered human rights. The next section will illustrate sources of international law, and a State's responsibilities as a legal actor to protect women's guaranteed human rights under international law. This will be followed by a discussion of women's rights under the Charter of the United Nations and Universal Declaration of Human Rights. The chapter will then discuss the human rights enforcement mechanisms under two subsections: Charter-based bodies and Treaty-based bodies. Each one of these operates under various instruments to pressure States into complying with their human rights obligations.

Each mechanism will also provide detailed official fact-finding documents on the issue of banning women pursuing judgeships in Iran and various Committees' views and recommendations on this issue. This will include in depth analysis of human rights and principles as they relate to protection

10 De jure discrimination means discrimination exists in law. ABC of Women Workers' Right and Gender Equality, International Labour Office, at 50 (2d ed., Geneva 2007), *accessed at* http://www.ilo.org/wcmsp5/groups/public/---dgreports/---gender/documents/publication/wcms_087314.pdf.

11 De facto discrimination means it exists in reality or in practice. ABC of Women Workers' Right and Gender Equality, International Labour Office, at 50 (2d ed., Geneva 2007), *accessed at* http://www.ilo.org/wcmsp5/groups/public/---dgreports/---gender/documents/publication/wcms_087314.pdf.

12 *See* U.N. General Assembly, *Situation of Human Rights in the Islamic Republic of Iran*, ¶ 31 at 10, U.N. Doc. A/70/352 (Aug. 31, 2015)

and promotion of women's rights in Iran. Iran's legal obligations under each official body will be examined. The last sections will analyze the issue under the International Labour Organization[13] as one of the Conventions adopted under the United Nations special agencies that drafts and supervises State's compliance with international labour standards, followed by the summary of the violations of women's rights pursuing judgeships in Iran under international law.

13 International Labour Organization, hereinafter ILO. *See* text *infra* note 377-383.

Development of Universal Human Rights & Women's Human Rights

1. Definition of Human Rights

It is essential to examine, first, what constitutes universal "human rights" under international law and whether a concept of protection and promotion of "women's rights" exists under the international human rights instruments.

The term "human rights" has been used more in common usage and has not been authoritatively defined.[14] Rules concerning the basic rights of the human person are *erga omnes* obligations,[15] meaning every human possesses and is entitled to enjoy human rights by virtue of being human.[16] According to Donnelly, a Western political scientist, a person's moral nature is the source of human rights, which is associated with the human nature.[17] According to him, "human rights are needed not for life but for a life of dignity."[18]

14 Lori F. Damrosch, Louis Henkin, Sean D. Murphy, Hans Smit, International Law: Cases and Materials 959 (5th ed., West Publishing 2009).

15 The Latin phrase "erga omnes" means "towards everyone" or "towards all." Human Rights Committee, *General Comment No. 31 [80]: The Nature of the General Legal Obligation Imposed on States Parties to the Covenant*, ¶ 2 at 1, U.N. Doc. CCPR/C/21/Rev.1/Add.13 (May 26, 2004).

16 Women, Law & Development International; Human Rights Watch Women's Rights Project, Women's Human Rights Step by Step: A Practical Guide to Using International Human Rights Law and Mechanisms to Defend Women's Human Rights 8 (Margaret A. Schuler & Dorothy Q. Thomas, eds., Women, Law & Development International and Human Rights Watch 1997).

17 Jack Donnelly, Universal Human Rights in Theory and Practice 14 (2d ed., Cornell University Press 2003).

18 *Id.*

Human rights are universally accepted norms of individual entitlements that have been incorporated in the post United Nations[19] human rights documents.[20] Despite several references to human rights in the Charter of United Nations,[21] the birthplace of human rights, it fails to define what constitutes human rights.[22] Nevertheless, the comprehensive Universal Declaration of Human Rights,[23] adopted in 1948, states in the Preamble:

> "Recognition of the inherent dignity and of the equal and inalienable rights of all members of the human family is the foundation of freedom, justice and peace in the world."[24]

The UDHR declares human rights as a common standard of achievement for all people in the world irrespective of their gender, religion, race, and language. The UDHR uses words such as "all human beings," "everyone," and "all," relating them to all enumerated human rights in its provisions.[25]

According to a number of scholars, including Donnelly, the origin of the "concept of human rights," is derived from modern Western civilization.[26] Donnelly states, "[m]ost non-western cultural and political traditions lack not only the practice of human rights but the very concept. The concept of human rights is an artifact of modern Western civilization."[27]

---

19 United Nations, hereinafter UN. *See* text *infra* not 75-80.

20 Shaheen Sardar Ali, Gender and Human Rights in Islam and International Law: Equal Before Allah, Unequal Before Man? 198 (Kluwer Law International 2000).

21 Charter of the United Nations, June 26, 1945, 59 Stat. 1031, T.S. 993, 3 Bevans 1153, *entered into force* Oct. 24, 1945. Hereinafter the Charter.

22 Rehman, *supra* note 6, at 53.

23 Universal Declaration of Human Rights, G.A. Res. 217A, U.N. Doc. A/810 at 71 (1948). Hereinafter UDHR.

24 *Id.* at Preamble.

25 International Human Rights Law, Six Decades after the UDHR and Beyond 49 (Mashood A. Baderin & Manisuli Ssenyonjo eds., Ashgate Publishing 2010).

26 Sardar Ali, *supra* note 20, at 18.

27 Jack Donnelly, Human Rights and Dignity: An Analytic Critique of Non-Western Human Rights Conception 303 (1982).

2. WOMEN'S RIGHTS ARE HUMAN RIGHTS

Since the adoption of the Charter in 1945 two principles of "equality" and "non-discrimination"[28] were born as UN jurisprudence. Since then they have been developed and enshrined in all international human rights texts. Focusing on women, the twin UN concepts of "gender equality" and prohibition of "gender-based discrimination" have been enshrined by almost all human rights treaties.

Since the historical birth of the United Nations from the ashes of the Second World War, the universal commitment to advance women's equal human rights has gone through dramatic evolution.[29] Fighting against various forms of discrimination has been one of the long-standing principals of the international human rights mechanism from its outset.[30] However, since the creation of the United Nations, it took almost thirty-five years for the UN to adopt a treaty that exclusively aims at women. A Convention on the Elimination of All Forms of Discrimination against Women[31] was adopted by the General Assembly in 1979 as a landmark international agreement that affirms the elimination of gender-based discrimination and explicitly defines what constitutes discrimination against women.[32]

Nonetheless, before adoption of the CEDAW, similar principles such as "equal rights of women and men" and "elimination of all kinds of discrimination" were broadly addressed by all core international human rights documents, such as the International Bill of Rights.[33] The International Bill of Rights collectively consists of the International Covenant on Civil and Political Rights,[34] the International

28 *See e.g.*, U.N. Charter Preamble, arts. 1(2), 1(3), 8, 55, 55(c).

29 Human Rights: Concept and Standards 231 (Janusz Symonides ed., Ashgate Publishing 2000). *See also* International Human Rights Law, Six Decades, *supra* note 25, at 4.

30 Expanding The Horizons of Human Rights Law 80 (Ineta Ziemele ed., Martinus Nijhoff Publishers 2005).

31 Convention on the Elimination of All Forms of Discrimination against Women, G.A. res. 34/180, 34 U.N. GAOR Supp. (No. 46) at 193, U.N. Doc. A/34/46, *entered into force* Sept. 3, 1981. Hereinafter CEDAW.

32 CEDAW, art. 1.

33 Deller Ross, *supra* note 9, at 12, 54.

34 International Covenant on Civil and Political Rights, G.A. res. 2200A (XXI), 21 U.N. GAOR Supp. (No. 16) at 52, U.N. Doc. A/6316 (1966), 999 U.N.T.S. 171, *entered into force* Mar. 23, 1976. Hereinafter ICCPR.

Covenant on Economic, Social and Cultural Rights,[35] and the UDHR, which also guarantees equal protection before the law to all.[36]

Contrary to the complete consensus on the prohibition of "racial discrimination" as *jus congens*;[37] the importance of discrimination on the basis of sex is more controversial. Very few authors have argued that the same idea—a norm from which no derogation is permitted—should be applied for "gender discrimination," even considering the fact that such discrimination affects half of the world's population.[38]

Most national, regional and universal human rights systems concerning the human rights of women have been developed and implemented with a male perspective.[39] Before the World Conference on Human Rights in 1993,[40] the express protection of women's rights was clearly absent from all international human rights instruments.[41] The Vienna Declaration and Programme of Action[42] was adopted during the 1993 World Conference on Human Rights by the unprecedented consensus of 171 States, in which the world renewed its international commitment to the purposes enunciated by the Charter and UDHR once again to advance the development and implementation of international human rights standards.[43] The Vienna Declaration, in addition to reaffirming its faith in and

---

35 International Covenant on Economic, Social and Cultural Rights, G.A. res. 2200A (XXI), 21 U.N.GAOR Supp. (No. 16) at 49, U.N. Doc. A/6316 (1966), 993 U.N.T.S. 3, *entered into force* Jan. 3, 1976. Hereinafter ICESCR.

36 Ralph G. Steinhardt, Paul L. Hoffman, Christopher N. Camponovo, International Human Rights Lawyering (Cases and Materials) 6 (West Academic Publishing 2009).

37 Article 53 of the Vienna Convention on the Law of Treaties of 1969 defines Jus Congens. These norms accepted and recognized by the international community of States as a whole. Good examples are genocide, slave trading, and use of force other than in self-defense. International Law, *supra* note 14, at 107, 108.

38 Expanding The Horizons of Human Rights Law, *supra* note 30, at 117.

39 *See* Women, Law & Development International (Human Rights Watch), *supra* note 16, at 8.

40 World Conference on Human Rights was held in Vienna in 1993. It successfully presented the international community's common plan for the strengthening of human rights work around the world. *World Conference on Human Rights*, United Nations Human Rights Office of the High Commissioner, *accessed at* http://www.ohchr.org/EN/ABOUTUS/Pages/ViennaWC.aspx.

41 Women's Rights Human Rights: International Feminist Perspectives 27 (Julie Peters & Andrea Wolper eds., Routledge 1995).

42 The Vienna Declaration and Programme of Action, UN General Assembly, *Vienna Declaration and Programme of Action*, 12 July 1993, A/CONF.157/23. Hereinafter Vienna Declaration.

43 *World Conference on Human Rights*, United Nations Human Rights Office of the High Commissioner, *accessed at* http://www.ohchr.org/EN/ABOUTUS/Pages/ViennaWC.aspx.

respect for previously established general principles of equal rights of women and men and elimination of gender discrimination,[44] redefined human rights by specifically including the "human rights of women" as part of the universal human rights definition. Article 18 of Vienna Declaration reads:

> "The *human rights of women* and of the *girl-child* are an inalienable, integral and indivisible part of *universal human rights*. The full and equal participation of women in political, civil, economic, social and cultural life, at the national, regional and international levels, and the *eradication of all forms of discrimination* on grounds of *sex* are priority objectives of the international community."[45] [Emphasis Added]

In 1995 during the Fourth World Conference on Women[46] the Beijing Declaration and Platform for Action was adopted that yet again reaffirmed women's rights as human rights and that they are an inalienable, integral and indivisible part of universal human rights.[47]

44 Vienna Declaration, Preamble. *See also* JANUSZ SYMONIDES, *supra* not 29, at 249.

45 Vienna Declaration, art. 18.

46 Fourth World Conference, UN Doc. A/CONF.177/20, Sep. 15, 1995.

47 *See* Beijing Declaration, arts. 9, 14.

International law, based on a horizontal legal order,[48] exists among sovereign States, which are the primary actors, alongside non-State actors such as international organizations, non-governmental organizations[49] and individuals.[50]

Article 38 of the Statute of the International Court of Justice explicitly counts four major sources of international law: international conventions, international custom, general principles of law,[51] and judicial decisions.[52] While Article 38 does not establish a hierarchy among these sources, it gives priority of position to the international conventions including treaties where the rights and duties are determined by the agreement as expressed in treaties.[53]

Traditional international law consists of both contractual and behavioral forms of obligations such as "treaties" and "customary international law."[54] Treaties are international agreements that are a primary source of rights and

48 According to the "horizontal system" there is no supranational legislature or police force or court with universal and compulsory powers, and international law consists in the rules governing the legal relationships among States. International Human Rights Lawyering, *supra* note 36, at 23.

49 Non-governmental organizations have always played a vital role in the establishment and functioning of international human rights system. With the proliferation of Non-government organizations, the term has become increasingly difficult to define. One common definition is an organization that is not a part of a government and that has non-commercial social, cultural, legal, or environmental goals. Hereinafter NGO. International Human Rights Lawyering, *supra* note 36, at 849-850.

50 International Law, *supra* note 14, at 20.

51 General Principles are one of the potential sources of international law meaning that some principles of law seem valid across virtually all human societies or seem basic to the very idea of a civilized legal system generally. International law can arise out of the comparative exercise of finding general principles in the various domestic systems of law in the world and applying them on the international plane. International Human Rights Lawyering, *supra* note 36, at 26.

52 ICJ, art. 38. Scholarly writings also have considerable influence because the collection and evaluation of state practice plays a critical evidentiary role in determining what the law is. International Human Rights Lawyering, *supra* note 36, at 25-26.

53 *See* ICJ, art. 38(1)(a). *See also* International Law, *supra* note 14, at 112.

54 International Human Rights Lawyering, *supra* note 36, at 24.

obligations in international law and are limited to their terms.[55] In practice, the most important source of international human rights law derives from treaties because they directly create a wide range of international human rights obligations when, upon ratification, a country expressly agrees to become a State party.[56] For example, in the case of Iran, any international treaty that Iran has signed and ratified imposes international obligations for Iran as a State party upon ratification under international law.

Article 1(a) of the Vienna Convention on the Law of the Treaties 1969,[57] which is the most authoritative collection of rules concerning the interpretation of treaties,[58] defines a treaty as:

> "An international agreement concluded between States in written form and governed by international law, whether embodied in a single instrument or in two or more related instruments and whatever its particular designation."[59]

Despite the separate and freestanding nature of each treaty, the existence of certain customary principles such as "non-discrimination" and "equality" binds them all together, making them complementary to one another. The international human rights treaties upon ratification, accession or succession, create legal obligations on State parties to promote and protect human rights at the national level.[60] According to the Article 26 of the Vienna Convention 1969 "every treaty in force is binding upon the parties to it and must be performed by them in good faith."[61] The obligation to respect promises made by the State

55 INTERNATIONAL LAW, *supra* note 14, at 112.

56 GUIDE TO INTERNATIONAL HUMAN RIGHTS PRACTICE 9 (Hurst Hannum ed., 4th ed., 2004).

57 Vienna Convention on the Law of Treaties, 1155 U.N.T.S. 331, 8 I.L.M. 679, *entered into force* Jan. 27, 1980. Hereafter Vienna Convention 1969.

58 FRANK NEWMAN & DAVID WEISSBRODT, INTERNATIONAL HUMAN RIGHTS: LAW, POLICY, AND PROCESS 574 (Anderson Publishing 1990). Iran signed the Vienna Convention in 1969 but has not ratified it. Chapter XXIII Law of the Treaties: Vienna Convention on the Law of Treaties, UN TREATY COLLECTIONS (1969), *accessed at* https://treaties.un.org/doc/Publication/MTDSG/Volume%20II/Chapter%20XXIII/XXIII-1.en.pdf. Since Vienna Convention on the Law of Treaties is already generally recognized as the authoritative guide to current treaty law and practice, it is therefore binding on Iran.

59 Vienna Convention 1969, art. 1(a).

60 The United Nations Human Rights Treaty System (Fact Sheet No. 30/Rev.1), UNITED NATIONS HUMAN RIGHTS OFFICE OF THE HIGH COMMISSIONER, at 18, 19 (2012), *accessed at* http://www.ohchr.org/Documents/Publications/FactSheet30Rev1.pdf.

61 Vienna Convention 1969, art. 26.

party to comply with the provisions of a treaty is so powerful that in the case of breach, a State's domestic law cannot be used as a justification.[62] A State party may attempt to exclude or modify the legal effect of certain provisions of the treaty by making "reservations" to the treaty.[63] We will see that this tension between domestic law and treaty obligations is particularly important when analyzing issues in Iran. It becomes a battle between the universally accepted norms and jurisprudence as opposed to domestic religion and cultural norms.

Customary international law as one of the primary sources of international law is defined by the Statute of the International Court of Justice as "evidence of a general practice accepted as law."[64] The universal existence of customary international law is not because of explicit agreement to some authoritative text, but because of a general practice accepted as law.[65] A customary norm binds all governments, including those that have not recognized it.[66]

Despite protection of women's human rights by various human rights treaties, due to the inconsistency of State practice, it becomes difficult to determine the customary character of any law relating to women's human rights. The only women related rule that can be defined as a rule of customary international law with a degree of certainty is the general requirement of "non-discrimination" on the basis of "sex."[67]

---

62 *Id.* at Art. 27. *See also* International Human Rights Lawyering, *supra* note 36, at 24, 25.

63 *See* Vienna Convention 1969, art. 2(1)(d).

64 ICJ, art. 38(1)(b).

65 International Human Rights Lawyering, *supra* note 36, at 25, 26.

66 International Human Rights: Law, Policy, And Process, *supra* note 58, at 595.

67 Ekaterina Yahyaoui Krivenko, Women, Islam and International Law: Within the Context of the Convention on the Elimination of All Forms of Discrimination Against Women 20, 21 (Martinus Nijhoff Publishers 2008).

State Responsibilities under International Law

To ensure the legal enforcement of universal human rights under international law, there are many designated mechanisms at the national, regional and international levels. At the international level, most of these mechanisms provide vehicles for monitoring compliance.[68] The responsibility of States is a crucial principle in the enforcement and effectiveness of international law. In the absence of the legal responsibility of States, the obligations created by international instruments will not receive any respect by States. This crucial principle stems from the nature of the international legal system that is based on the sovereignty and equality of States, and relies on each nation to implement and be in full compliance with international human rights laws and principles.[69]

68 Women, Law & Development International (Human Rights Watch), *supra* note 16, at 13.

69 International Human Rights Law, Six Decades, *supra* note 25, at 398.

First Fundamental Sources for Women's Human Rights

Due to the essential nature of the United Nations as the birthplace of human rights, and the Universal Declaration of Human Rights as the first comprehensive statement of individual human rights, the guaranteed human rights of women will be first analyzed under these two foundational documents. Further, the human rights of women will be analyzed under human rights enforcement mechanisms and their subdivisions.

Today the explicit language used by the 1982 statute expressly prohibits women from holding judgeships in Iran. This exclusion has been made solely on the ground of sex and would not deprive a woman of becoming a judge if she were a man with same qualifications. This poses a question whether the imposed different treatment of women by the legislature counts as discrimination against women under international laws and principles. What are the guaranteed human rights for women under international law? Is the unequal treatment of women based on their gender protected by human rights mechanisms? This also raises other inquiries such as Iran's legal responsibilities under international law. Has Iran by passing the 1982 law failed to fulfill its obligations under international law?

The specific universal guaranteed human rights and principles that pertain to women serving as judges are:

- Equal rights of women and men in all their civil, political, economic, social, and cultural rights
- Non-discrimination on the prohibited ground of sex
- Right to work
- Equal Protection of the Law without discrimination

The attainment of the twin principles of "equal rights of women and men" and application of "non-discrimination" are among the earliest and most fundamental components of international human rights that are essential to the exercise and enjoyment of all human rights and freedoms, enshrined in the Charter of the United Nations and UDHR that are and reaffirmed by all other subsequent human rights instruments.[70]

The principle of "gender equality" refers to the enjoyment of equal rights, opportunities, and treatment by men and women in all spheres of life. It asserts that people's rights, responsibilities, social status, and access to resources do not depend on whether they are born male or female. This principle implies that all men and women are free to develop their personal abilities and make life choices without the limitations set by stereotypes or prejudices about gender roles or specific characteristics of men and women.[71]

According to the Committee on Economic, Social and Cultural Rights, the application of the non-discrimination clause and the guarantee of equal rights of women and men in the enjoyment of their human rights are inherently related and mutually reinforcing. Furthermore, the elimination of prohibited discrimination is fundamental to the enjoyment of the human rights on a basis of equality.[72]

The "right to work" is one of the fundamental human rights that is essential for enjoyment of other human rights and forms an inseparable and inherent part of human dignity. Not only does the right to work contribute to the survival of the individual, but also freely chosen work contributes to the recognition of the individual in her/his community.[73] Gender equality at work embraces equality of opportunity and treatment. According to the ILO, gender equality is a "matter of human rights, social justice and sustainable development."[74]

---

70 *See e.g.*, COMMITTEE ON ECONOMIC, SOCIAL AND CULTURAL RIGHTS, GENERAL COMMENT NO. 20, *infra* note 118, at 1-3.

71 ABC of Women Workers' Right and Gender Equality, INTERNATIONAL LABOUR OFFICE, at 92 (2d ed., Geneva 2007), *accessed at* http://www.ilo.org/wcmsp5/groups/public/---dgreports/---gender/documents/publication/wcms_087314.pdf.

72 Committee on Economic, Social and Cultural Rights: *General Comments No. 16: The Equal Rights of Men and Women*, ¶ 3 at 2, U.N. Doc. E/C.12/2005/4 (Aug. 11, 2005).

73 Committee on Economic, Social and Cultural Rights, *General Comments No. 18: The Right to Work*, ¶ 1 at 1, U.N. Doc. E/C.12/GC/18 (Feb. 6, 2006).

74 ILO ABC OF WOMEN WORKERS' RIGHT AND GENDER EQUALITY, *supra* note 71, at 92.

1. CHARTER OF THE UNITED NATIONS

The Charter of the United Nations is the birthstone of the international human rights obligations for the State parties.[75] The creation of the UN in 1945 was the response to the failure of States to respect and protect the dignity and human rights of their own citizens, especially during the Second World War.[76] The international journey toward ensuring and securing the human rights of people evolved with the adoption of the UDHR in 1948, which today is considered the first comprehensive human rights law that laid the foundation of modern international human rights laws.[77]

Despite some vague provisions on human rights,[78] the Charter nevertheless internationalized the concept of human rights and proved that the issue of human rights no longer stayed under the State's scope, and that there will be international obligations with regards to respecting and guaranteeing human rights for all.[79] General obligations created by the Charter are to promote universal respect for, and observance of, human rights and fundamental freedoms.[80]

Despite adoption of innovative provisions in the Charter such as faith in fundamental human rights and the equal rights of men and women,[81] particularly when women were treated as second-class citizens around the world,[82] it failed to aim specifically at women. In a more general sense, the Charter also failed to impose concrete human rights obligations on member States.[83] Also, despite creating the principle of "non-discrimination,"[84] it did not define what constitutes "discrimination," or more specifically as to women what constitutes "discrimination against women."

---

75 Women, Law & Development International (Human Rights Watch), *supra* note 16, at 8.

76 Shaheen Sardar Ali, *supra* note 20, at 198.

77 International Human Rights Law, Six Decades, *supra* note 25, at 3.

78 *See e.g.*, U.N. Charter arts. 55, 56.

79 International Law, *supra* note 14, at 958.

80 Human Rights Committee, *General Comment No. 31 [80]: The Nature of the General Legal Obligation Imposed on States Parties to the Covenant,* ¶ 2 at 1, U.N. Doc. CCPR/C/21/Rev.1/Add. 13 (May 26, 2004).

81 *See* U.N. Charter, Preamble.

82 Deller Ross, *supra* note 9, at 55.

83 International Law, *supra* note 14, at 958.

84 *See* U.N. Charter, arts. 1(3), 55(c).

The Charter also created a number of bodies that directly deal with human rights and more specifically with women's human rights to achieve the rights enumerated in the Charter. The Charter-based bodies include, for example, the Commission on Human Rights[85] that later was replaced by the Human Rights Council;[86] the Commission on the Status of Women,[87] and the process of Universal Periodic Review.[88]

According to the very first article of the Charter, the purposes of the UN are to achieve international cooperation in solving international problems of an economic, social, cultural or humanitarian character, and in promoting and encouraging respect for human rights and for fundamental freedoms for all without any kinds of distinction, and to be a center for harmonizing the action of nations in the attainment of their common ends.[89]

To codify the principles and obligations of the State party under the Charter, resolution 2625 (xxv) was passed by the General Assembly in 1970 during a commemorative session to celebrate the twenty-fifth anniversary of the United Nations. This resolution was called the Declaration on Principles of International Law concerning Friendly Relations and Co-operation among States in accordance with the Charter of the United Nations, and it emphasizes the paramount importance of the Charter and the universal application of the principles enshrined in the Charter.[90] Accordingly, States have the duty to co-operate with one another with good faith in the promotion of universal respect for, and observance of, human rights and fundamental freedoms for all.[91]

In the Preamble to the Charter the member States assert their determination "to reaffirm faith in fundamental human rights, in the dignity and worth of the human person, in the equal rights of men and women." [92]

---

85 *Infra* note 125.

86 *Infra* note 127.

87 *See* more information under Commission on the Status of Women.

88 *See* more information under Universal Periodic Review.

89 Bertrand G. Ramcharan, The Fundamentals of International Human Rights Treaty Law 20 (Martinus Nijhoff Publishers 2011).

90 *See* G.A. Res. 2625 (XXV), *Declaration on Principles of International Law concerning Friendly Relations and Co-operation among States in accordance with the Charter of the United Nations*, at 1, U.N. Doc. A/RES/25/2625 (Oct. 24, 1970).

91 *See id.* under the Duty of States to Co-Operate with one another in Accordance with the Charter, section (b).

92 U.N. Charter, Preamble. *See also* Deller Ross, *supra* note 9, at 55.

The Charter also establishes the application of the principle of "non-discrimination" to implement universal respect for human rights and fundamental freedoms for all, regardless of their race, sex, language, or religion.[93] According to Article 1(3) the purposes of the United Nations, for example, are:

> "To achieve international co-operation in solving international problems of an economic, social, cultural, or humanitarian character, and in promoting and encouraging respect for human rights and for fundamental freedoms for all without distinction as to race, sex, language, or religion."[94]

Accordingly, Article 55(c) also emphasizes the universal respect for, and observance of, human rights and fundamental freedoms for all without any kind of discrimination.[95] Member States agreed to take action for the specific obligations set forth in Article 55, which includes promotion of respect for and observance of human rights and fundamental freedoms for all without any kinds of discrimination.[96]

With regard to the right to work, Article 1(3) of the Charter uses a broad language to guarantee equal right to work for women and men as:

> "To achieve international co-operation in solving international problems of an *economic, social, cultural*, or humanitarian character, and in promoting and encouraging respect for *human rights* and for *fundamental freedoms* for all *without distinction* as to race, *sex*, language, or religion."[97] [Emphasis Added]

According to the General Comments of the Committee on Economic, Social and Cultural Rights, the "objectives of right to work reflect the fundamental purposes and principles enshrined in the United Nations as defined by Article 1(3) of the Charter."[98] The essence of the right to work is also reflected in other

93 DELLER ROSS, *supra* note 9, at 55.

94 U.N. Charter art 1(3).

95 *Id.* at Art 55(c).

96 *See id.* at Arts. 55, 56.

97 *Id.* at Art 1(3).

98 COMMITTEE ON ECONOMIC, SOCIAL AND CULTURAL RIGHTS, GENERAL COMMENTS NO. 18, *supra* note 73, ¶ 3 at 1.

paramount human rights documents such as the UDHR.[99] In addition to the broad language used by the Charter regarding the right to work, the most comprehensive human rights treaty that elaborates more on the right to work is the International Covenant on Economic, Social and Cultural Rights. Iran has ratified this Covenant. This will be discussed further under the ICESCR.[100]

The founding text of the UN, the Charter as the birthplace of human rights is binding on almost every country in the world, and Iran was one of the first countries that became a State party to the UN.[101] The Charter reaffirms its faith in fundamental human rights, equal rights of women and men, and general obligations for States to respect and promote human rights for all without discrimination.[102]

Iran as a State party to the UN is obligated to promote and encourage respect for equal human rights and for fundamental freedoms for women regardless of their gender. The passage and continuation of upholding the 1982 Law on the Qualifications for Appointment of Judges that explicitly nullifies women's equal right to enjoy their fundamental right to work—as judges—because of their gender is a clear departure from guaranteed rights enshrined in the Charter. Iran, by enforcing the de jure discriminatory statute against women, fails to respect women's equal rights in their fundamental human rights regardless of their gender. This divergence by Iran from complying with its Charter-based obligations constitutes a violation of the Charter under international law.

99 *See* UDHR, art. 23.

100 *See* discussion of "Right to Work" under ICESCR.

101 *See* Charter of the United Nations, UN Treaty Collection (June 26, 1945), *accessed at* https://treaties.un.org/doc/Publication/MTDSG/Volume%20I/Chapter%20I/I-1.en.pdf. *See also* Guide to International Human Rights Practice, *supra* note 56, at 6.

102 *See* Charter, Preamble, art. 1(3).

2. UNIVERSAL DECLARATION OF HUMAN RIGHTS

The earliest essential international human rights were collectively vested in the Charter and the Universal Declaration of Human Rights followed by establishment of the ICCPR and ICESCR.[103] The UDHR was adopted by the United Nations General Assembly in 1948,[104] and is the world's first modern comprehensive assertion of international human rights, including women's rights to equality, both in general and in marriage.[105] Despite the failure of the Charter to articulate what constitutes human rights, it was nevertheless intended that this comprehensive bill of rights would define human rights. It has been said that the UDHR can be used as an authoritative interpretation of what constitutes human rights prescribed by the Charter.[106]

While the UDHR comprises a broad range of individual rights for all, it is, however, a Declaration and does not have the nature of a binding treaty; therefore, it is not legally binding on the countries.[107] Nonetheless, despite its non-binding effects, its principles have evolved into authoritative interpretation of the rights enshrined in the Charter.[108] Given the existence of overwhelming evidence throughout the world of State practices in applying the UDHR provisions; given its being cited several times by the resolutions of General Assembly; and given its constant reference in various human rights documents, the UDHR is now clearly recognized as customary international law.[109] This makes the UDHR legally binding on all nations and since Iran is a State party to the UN, it is legally bound to be in full compliance with all its provisions and is obligated to implement the guaranteed rights enshrined in its domestic legal system.

Provisions of the UDHR have explicitly guaranteed the two key complementary principles of "equal rights of women and men" and application of "non-discrimination" regarding all the rights enshrined in the Declaration.[110] After setting

---

103 Deller Ross, *supra* note 9, at 54.

104 *See* Universal Declaration of Human Rights, G.A. Res. 217A, U.N. Doc. A/810 at 71 (1948).

105 *See* UDHR, Preamble, art. 1; Susan Deller Ross, *supra* note 9, at 56.

106 Rehman, *supra* note 6, at 57-58.

107 *See* Deller Ross, *supra* note 9, at 56.

108 *See* International Human Rights Lawyering, *supra* note 36, at 5.

109 Rehman, *supra* note 6, at 59.

110 *See* UDHR, Preamble, arts. 1, 2.

out a general prohibition against discrimination, it enumerates specific groups of rights such as economic, social and cultural rights.[111] Its Preamble starts off by recognizing the "inherent dignity" and "the equal and inalienable rights of all members of the human family" as the "foundation of freedom, justice and peace in the world."[112] Further, the Preamble reaffirms its faith in the Charter-based principles like fundamental human rights and equal rights of women and men.[113]

Article 1 of the UDHR uses a more general language to establish equality for all humans in their "dignity and rights."[114] Article 2 explicitly sets the general principal of non-discrimination by stating:

> "Everyone is entitled to *all* the *rights* and *freedoms* set forth in this Declaration, *without distinction* of any kind, such as race, colour, *sex*, language, religion, political or other opinion, national or social origin, property, birth or other status."[115] [Emphasis added]

Article 23 of the UDHR guarantees the "right to work" and "free choice of employment," by asserting:

> "Everyone has the *right to work*, to *free choice of employment*, to just and favorable conditions of work and to protection against unemployment."[116] [Emphasis Added]

With regard to the statutory prohibition of women from judgeships in Iran, it becomes essential, first, to demonstrate what constitutes "discrimination" according to international human rights laws. The Charter and the UDHR failed to define what constitutes discrimination; however, several treaties and their monitoring committees have defined discrimination explicitly. For example, the

111 U.N. HUMAN RIGHTS TREATY SYSTEM, *supra* note 60, at 5.

112 UDHR, Preamble.

113 *See id.*

114 *See id.* at Art. 1, "All human beings are born free and equal in dignity and rights."

115 *Id.* at Art. 2.

116 *Id.* at Art. 23(1).

Committee on Economic, Social and Cultural Rights[117] in its General Comment No. 20 defines discrimination as:

> "Any *distinction, exclusion, restriction* or preference or other differential treatment that is *directly* or indirectly based on the *prohibited grounds of discrimination* and which has the intention or effect of *nullifying* or *impairing* the recognition, enjoyment or exercise, on an equal footing, of Covenant rights."[118] [Emphasis added]

In a similar note, Article 1 of the Convention on the Elimination of All Forms of Discrimination against Women defines exclusively what constitutes "discrimination against women" as:

> "The term *discrimination against women* shall mean any *distinction, exclusion or restriction* made on the basis of *sex* which has the effect or purpose of *impairing or nullifying* the recognition, enjoyment or exercise by women, irrespective of their marital status, on a basis of equality of men and women, of human rights and fundamental freedoms in the political, economic, social, cultural, civil or any other field."[119] [Emphasis added]

Even though these definitions are presented by two separate international human rights bodies, and are not identical in wording, they speak with the same voice. Now in the application of the universal definition of discrimination to the 1982 Law on Qualifications for Appointment of Judges, these definitions make clear that excluding all women from judgeships because of their sex constitutes discrimination against them that was imposed directly by the legislature. The sole intention of the legislature was to nullify the right to work as judges for women only. The intention of the lawmakers to bar women from judgeship positions becomes even clearer when, a few years prior to passing the 1982 law, all existing women judges were found legally disqualified solely on the basis of

117 Committee on Economic, Social and Cultural Rights, hereinafter CESCR.

118 Committee on Economic, Social and Cultural Rights, *General Comment No. 20: Non-discrimination in economic, social and cultural rights*, at 3, U.N. Doc. E/C.12/GC/20 (July 2, 2009).

119 CEDAW, art. 1.

their sex, and were dismissed or demoted to consultant roles immediately after the 1979 Revolution.[120]

Various provisions of the UDHR[121] ban gender discrimination and guarantee women the equal enjoyment of their fundamental right to work and the freedom to choose their employment regardless of their gender. The de jure discrimination against women imposed by the 1982 law is in violation of provisions of the UDHR, and a clear failure of Iran as a State party to the UN to promote and encourage respect for human rights and fundamental freedoms for all without discrimination on the basis of sex.

120 *See* Intiqāli Bānuvān bā Rutbiyi Qażāī az Vizārati Dādgustarī bi Sāyiri Vizāratkhānihā va Tabdīli Rutbiyi Qażāīyi Ānhā bi Idārī 1358 [Transferring Women with Judicial Titles from the Ministry of Justice to other Ministries and Conversion of their Judicial Titles to Administrative 1979] (Iran) (TA). For more details *see* Chapter 2.

121 *See* e.g., UDHR, Preamble, arts. 1, 2, 23.

Human Rights Enforcement Mechanisms

The international human rights monitoring mechanisms can be divided into two main categories: Charter-based and Treaty-based mechanisms,[122] which will be discussed in the following sections.

1. CHARTER-BASED BODIES

The Charter-based bodies derive either explicitly or implicitly from the Charter of the UN setting and enforcing human rights standards.[123] All the Charter-based bodies have jurisdiction over women's international human rights, such as the Commission on Human Rights and the Commission on the Status of Women.[124]

a. Commission on Human Rights & Human Rights Council

In 1946, the Commission on Human Rights was created as a subsidiary of the UN Economic and Social Council.[125] The CHR firmly established itself as the single most important UN organ in the human rights field.[126] It was dissolved in 2006

122 Women, Law & Development International (Human Rights Watch), *supra* note 16, at 13.

123 These bodies are: the Security Council, the General Assembly, the Economic and Social Council, the Commission on Human Rights, the Sub-Commission on Prevention of Discrimination and Protection of Minorities and the UN Commission on the Status of Women. *Id.* at 13.

124 *See* Women, Law & Development International (Human Rights Watch), *supra* note 16, at 13.

125 The Commission of Human Rights was established by Economic and Social Council in 1946. Hereinafter CHR.

126 Philip Alston, The United Nations Human Rights 126 (2d ed., Oxford University Press 1992).

and replaced by the Human Rights Council[127] by General Assembly resolution 60/251.[128]

According to resolution 60/251, the UN Human Rights Council is a subsidiary organ of the General Assembly "promoting universal respect for the protection of all human rights and fundamental freedoms for all," regardless of personal characteristics.[129] As one of its obligations, it should highlight human rights violations, including "gross and systematic violations" and make recommendations thereon.[130] The primary instruments of the Human Rights Council are the Special Procedure, which can include Special Rapporteurs or Working Groups, and the Universal Periodic Review.[131]

Today, the Special Procedure of the Human Rights Council is one of the core elements of the Charter-based human rights monitoring mechanisms; including the Special Rapporteurs who originally were established by the Commission on Human Rights.[132] The Special Rapporteurs consist of independent human rights experts with orders to report and advise on human rights concerns and violations from a thematic or country-specific perspective, covering all human rights issues.[133]

The country-specific Special Rapporteur usually is appointed in response to the failure of a government to cooperate with the UN human rights bodies; or extraordinary circumstances such as when armed conflict or social unrest raise serious human right concerns within a specific country.[134] The work of Special

127 Human Rights Council, G.A. Res. 60/251, *Human Rights Council,* ¶ 1 at 2, U.N. Doc. A/RES/60/251 (April 3, 2006).

128 Human Rights Council meets in Geneva and, for example, submits an annual report to the General Assembly, and makes recommendations to the General Assembly for the further development of international law in the field of human rights. *See id.* at ¶ 1, ¶ 5(i), ¶ 5(c).

129 *See* G.A. Res. 60/251, *supra note* 127, at ¶ 2 at 2.

130 *See id.* at ¶ 3 at 2.

131 *Human Rights Monitoring Mechanisms,* Shaheedoniran.org, *accessed at* http://shaheedoniran.org/human-rights-at-the-united-nations/human-rights-monitoring-mechanisms/.

132 *See* Dag Hammarskjöld Library Research Guides, *UN Documentation: Human Rights,* United Nations Dag Hammarskjöld Library (Feb. 13, 2015), *accesses at* http://research.un.org/en/docs/humanrights/charter.

133 *Special Procedures of the Human Rights Council,* United Nations Human Rights Office of the High Commissioner, *accessed at* http://www.ohchr.org/EN/HRBodies/SP/Pages/Welcomepage.aspx.

134 UN Special Rapporteur on the Situation of Human Rights in the Islamic Republic of Iran, Video: *The UN Special Rapporteur on the situation of human rights in Iran,* Shaheedoniran.org, accessed at http://shaheedoniran.org/english/without-thumbnail-inside/video-rapporteur-iran/.

Rapporteurs is valuable for human rights scholars and lawyers for factual findings and guidance concerning human rights violations in specific countries. These reports provide a compilation of information about patterned human rights concerns drawn from various sources.[135] The working method of a Special Rapporteur includes, for example, direct communication with governments; undertaking fact-finding missions to countries and issuing reports with recommendations; preparing thematic studies to provide information on the situation; clarifying relevant norms and standards and providing guidance on their implementation; and raising public awareness.[136]

Unlike the treaty bodies, the Special Rapporteur can access human rights issues even if a country has not ratified any relevant treaties, and issue suggestions from a thematic or country-specific perspective.[137] The Special Rapporteur also complements the treaty bodies and Universal Periodic Review's work by regularly sharing information and follow-ups on their respective recommendations. Concerns raised by the Special Rapporteurs are taken into account, for example, by the General Assembly, treaty bodies and the Universal Periodic Review.[138]

Special Rapporteur on the Situation of Human Rights in the Islamic Republic of Iran

The country-specific Special Rapporteur mechanism is one of the most important Charter-based monitoring instruments and plays a key investigative and fact-finding role by communicating with and visiting a specific country.[139] The human rights situation in the IRI has been on the agenda of the UN Commission on Human Rights since early 1980s.[140] As of 2015, the IRI is among

135 International Human Rights Lawyering, *supra* note 36, at 331-332.

136 U.N. Human Rights Treaty System, *supra* note 60, at 45.

137 *Id.*

138 *See e.g., id.*

139 *Special Procedures of the Human Rights Council*, United Nations Human Rights Office of the High Commissioner, *accessed at* http://www.ohchr.org/EN/HRBodies/SP/Pages/Introduction.aspx.

140 *See e.g.,* Commission on Human Rights on its Thirty-eight session to ECOSOC, *Note verbale [sic] dated 14 September 1981 from the Permanent Mission of the Islamic Republic of Iran to the United Nations Office and the other international organizations a.t Geneva addressed to the Secretary-General,* U.N. Doc. E/CN.4/1516 (Sep. 22, 1981); Commission on Human Rights on its Thirty-eight session to ECOSOC, *Treatment of the Baha'is in Iran*, U.N. Doc. E/CN.4/1517 (Dec. 31, 1981).

14 States for which the Human Rights Council has appointed country-specific Special Rapporteurs;[141] one of the earliest country mandates belongs to Iran.[142]

The first Special Rapporteur on the situation of human rights in Iran appointed by the Human Rights Council, since the termination of the previous CHR in 2006, is Ahmed Shaheed.[143] In 2011, pursuant to the UN General Assembly resolution 65/226, resolution 16/9 was adopted by the Human Rights Council, which appointed the Special Rapporteur on the situation of human rights in the Islamic Republic of Iran.[144] The General Assembly resolution 65/226 took note of negative developments in human rights and serious ongoing human rights violations such as discrimination and gender inequality in Iran, in addition to the government's failure to permit visitation by any thematic special procedure since 2005.[145] According to Human Rights Council resolution 16/9, the Special Rapporteur should present an interim report to both the General Assembly and the Human Rights Council.[146]

For many years, starting with the appointment of the first Special Rapporteur in the 1984 concerning the human rights situation in Iran, the issue of women's human rights was neglected by the Special Rapporteur, despite enactment of a massive number of discriminatory laws against women right after the triumph of the Islamic Revolution in 1979.[147] The failure to devote a section exclusively to women among the first five allocated categories of human rights concerns

141 *See the Special Procedures*, SHAHEEDONIRAN.ORG, *accessed at* http://shaheedoniran.org/human-rights-at-the-united-nations/human-rights-monitoring-mechanisms/un-human-rights-council/the-special-procedures/.

142 *See* Ahmed Shaheed, Video: *The UN Special Rapporteur on the situation of human rights in Iran*, BERKELEY LECTURE SERIES (July 15, 2013), *accessed at* https://vimeo.com/71149943.

143 *Special Rapporteur on the situation of human rights in the Islamic Republic of Iran*, UNITED NATIONS HUMAN RIGHTS OFFICE OF THE HIGH COMMISSIONER, (2015), *accessed at* http://www.ohchr.org/EN/HRBodies/SP/CountriesMandates/IR/Pages/SRIran.aspx.

144 *See* Human Rights Council Res. 16/9, U.N. Doc. A/HRC/RES/16/9, ¶ 1 at 1 (April 8, 2011).

145 *See* G.A. Res. 65/226, *Situation of human rights in the Islamic Republic of Iran*, ¶ 1, 2, 2(f), 2(g), U.N. Doc. A/RES/65/226 (Feb. 10, 2011).

146 *See* HRC Res. 16/9, *supra* note 144.

147 Such as nullification of the Family Protection Law, dismissal of women judges, mandatory ḥijāb, and banning women in certain study fields. For more detailed discussion *see* Chapter 1.

by the Special Rapporteur[148] neglected compelling issues surrounding women's human rights in Iran. It was not until the early 1990s that for the first time the category of "situation of women" was added to the original categories of human rights concerns.[149]

Pursuant to adding the category of "situation of women," the Special Rapporteur of the Commission on Human Rights in his report to its forty-seventh session, conveyed the existence of various discriminations and unequal treatments against women in various fields such as education, family and criminal law.[150] Nonetheless, this report stayed silent regarding the dismissal and demotion of women judges that took place in the process of purification of the justice system. Likewise it did not address the passage of the 1982 Law on the Qualifications for Appointment of Judges that is an express discrimination against women obtaining or holding judgeships.

In 1992, that the interim report of the Special Rapporteur of the Commission of Human Rights briefly, yet explicitly, addressed the issue of banning women from judgeships, among other various cases of continuous discrimination against women.[151] This was the beginning of continuous reports on the issue of women being banned from becoming judges by the Special Rapporteur in the upcoming years; in addition there were, of course, reports on the existence of

148 For example, the five categories of violations submitted by Andrés Aguilar were: the right to life; the right to freedom form torture or cruel and degrading treatment; the right to liberty and security of person and to freedom from arbitrary arrest or detention; the right to a fair trial; and the right to freedom of thought, conscience, and religion. *See* REZA AFSHARI, HUMAN RIGHTS IN IRAN: THE ABUSE OF CULTURAL RELATIVISM XXI-XXII (University of Pennsylvania Press 2001).

149 *See* REZA AFSHARI, HUMAN RIGHTS IN IRAN: THE ABUSE OF CULTURAL RELATIVISM 250 (University of Pennsylvania Press 2001).

150 *See* Commission on Human Rights on its Forty-seventh session, *Report on the human rights situation in the Islamic Republic of Iran by the Special Representative (Reynaldo Galindo Pohl)*, ¶ 217-221 at 43-44, U.N. Doc. E/CN.4/1991/35 (Feb. 13, 1991).

151 *See* U.N. Secretary-General Transmits the Interim Report of the Special Representative of the Commission on Human Rights to the General Assembly, *Situation of human rights in the Islamic Republic of Iran Note by the Secretary-General,* ¶ 104 at 22, U.N. Doc. A/47/617 (Nov. 13, 1992).

systematic and systemic discrimination against women by laws and in practice in other areas.[152]

The response of the government of IRI to the allegations made by the Special Rapporteur's report and concern about the ban on women pursuing judgeships was "this allegation is unrealistic."[153]

During the 1990s, the compelling issue of pervasive discrimination against women[154] and banning women from becoming judges[155] were addressed co-

---

152 *See e.g.*, Commission on Human Rights, *Final Report on the situation of human rights in the Islamic Republic of Iran by the Special Representative*, ¶ 196, ¶ 312, at 37, 55, U.N. Doc. E/CN.4/1993/41 (Jan. 28, 1993); Commission on Human Rights, *Final report on the situation of human rights in the Islamic Republic of Iran prepared by the Special Representative*, ¶ 171 at 34, U.N. Doc. E/CN.4/1994/50 (Feb. 2, 1994); U.N. Secretary-General Transmits the Interim Report of the Special Representative of the Commission on Human Rights to the General Assembly, *Situation of human rights in the Islamic Republic of Iran Note by the Secretary-General*, ¶ 72 at 16, U.N. Doc. A/49/514 (Oct. 14, 1994); U.N. Secretary-General Transmits the Report of the Special Rapporteur of HRC to the General Assembly at its 69th Session, *Situation of human rights in the Islamic Republic of Iran Note by the Secretary-General*, ¶ 69 at 19, U.N. Doc. A/69/356 (Aug. 27, 2014).

153 *Situation of human rights in the Islamic Republic of Iran Addendum*, ¶ 59 at 10, U.N. Doc. A/48/526/Add.1 (Nov. 17, 1993).

154 *See e.g.*, Commission on Human Rights, *Final report on the situation of human rights in the Islamic Republic of Iran prepared by the Special Representative*, ¶ 171-191 at 34-37, U.N. Doc. E/CN.4/1994/50 (Feb. 2, 1994); Commission of Human Rights, *Report on the situation of human rights in the Islamic Republic of Iran prepared by the Special Representative*, ¶ 107 at 24, U.N. Doc. E/CN.4/1995/55 (Jan. 16, 1995); U.N. Secretary-General Transmits the Interim Report of the Special Representative of the Commission on Human Rights to the General Assembly, *Situation of human rights in the Islamic Republic of Iran Note by the Secretary-General*, ¶ 72 at 16, U.N. Doc. A/49/514 (Oct. 14, 1994); Commission on Human Rights, *Report on the situation of human rights in the Islamic Republic of Iran, prepared by the Special Representative*, ¶ 64 at 17, U.N. Doc. E/CN.4/1996/59 (March 21, 1996); Commission on Human Rights, *Report on the situation of human rights in the Islamic Republic of Iran, prepared by the Special Representative*, ¶ 19-26 at 7-9, U.N. Doc. E/CN.4/1997/63 (Feb. 11, 1997); U.N. Secretary-General Transmits the Interim Report of the Special Representative of the Commission on Human Rights to the General Assembly on its 52d Session, *Situation of human rights in the Islamic Republic of Iran Note by the Secretary-General*, ¶ 35, ¶ 38 at 12, 13, U.N. Doc. A/52/472 (Oct. 15, 1997); U.N. Secretary-General Transmits the Interim Report of the Special Representative of the Commission on Human Rights to the General Assembly to its 54th Session, *Situation of human rights in the Islamic Republic of Iran Note by the Secretary-General*, ¶ 21, ¶ 27 at 6, 7, U.N. Doc. A/54/365 (Sep. 21, 1999).

155 *See e.g.*, Commission on Human Rights, *Final report on the situation of human rights in the Islamic Republic of Iran prepared by the Special Representative*, ¶ 171 at 34, U.N. Doc. E/CN.4/1994/50 (Feb. 2, 1994); U.N. Secretary-General Transmits the Interim Report of the Special Representative of the Commission on Human Rights to the General Assembly, *Situation of human rights in the Islamic Republic of Iran Note by the Secretary-General*, ¶ 72 at 16, U.N. Doc. A/49/514 (Oct. 14, 1994); Commission on Human Rights, R*eport on the situation of human rights in the Islamic Republic of Iran, prepared by the Special Representative*, ¶ 40 at 12, U.N. Doc. E/CN.4/1996/59 (March 21, 1996); U.N. Secretary-General Transmits the Interim Report of the Special Representative of the Commission on Human Rights to the General Assembly to its 53th Session, *Situation of human rights in the Islamic Republic of Iran Note by the Secretary-General*, ¶ 22 at 6, U.N. Doc. A/53/423 (Sep. 23, 1998).

ntinuously in many reports prepared by the Special Rapporteurs of the Commission on Human Rights. Despite the Special Rapporteur's early reports and concerns about the general practice of banning women from judgeships, the absence of details or full investigation of this issue was apparent, and did not go further than just a few words like "women cannot become judges" in Iran. It was toward the end of the 1990s that the details and difficulties of selection and training of judges and the issue of banning women received more significant attention.[156]

For instance, in a 1996 report of the Special Rapporteur of the CHR, pursuant to a meeting of the Special Rapporteur with the Iranian Minister of Justice, one of the supposed primary problems for the Ministry was the "recruitment and training of judges," and a massive need to recruit judges within two years.[157] Notably, the Special Rapporteur asserted, "in the past persons with minimum experience and sometimes little formal education were reportedly appointed as judges."[158] Concerning female judges, his report continued, "in the last year's competitive examination for 50 female judges, there was no published list of applicants to be interviewed."[159] This report indicated that according to the Ministry the acceptance depended on obtaining the required mark in the examination.[160] It seems very unlikely that the fifty women who took the examination, all of whom had received significant legal education, could be less qualified than the male judges who were appointed previously "with minimum experience and sometimes little formal education."

By the end of the 1990s, it was well documented that the status of women, both in the laws and policies, was not recognized as equal to men in many ways.[161] As a result, the Special Rapporteur urged the government to "attach

156 *See e.g.*, Commission on Human Rights, *Report on the situation of human rights in the Islamic Republic of Iran, prepared by the Special Representative*, ¶ 36-40 at 11-12, U.N. Doc. E/CN.4/1996/59 (March 21, 1996).

157 *See id.* ¶ 37 at 11.

158 *Id.* ¶ 40 at 12.

159 *Id.*

160 *Id.*

161 *See e.g., id.* ¶ 64 at 17; U.N. Secretary-General Transmits the Interim Report of the Special Representative of the Commission on Human Rights to the General Assembly on its 52d Session, *Situation of human rights in the Islamic Republic of Iran Note by the Secretary-General*, ¶ 35 at 12, U.N. Doc. A/52/472 (Oct. 15, 1997); Commission on Human Rights, *Report on the situation of human rights in the Islamic Republic of Iran, prepared by the Special Representative*, ¶ 22 at 7, U.N. Doc. E/CN.4/1997/63 (Feb. 11, 1997).

high priority to reforming the status of women," not only to comply with its international human rights obligations but also out of respect for the dignity of its individual citizens.[162]

The discussion on the status of Iranian women also intertwined with different levels of dialogue about the status of women in other Muslim countries. These discussions led to presenting different concepts by Muslim countries, such as "equality versus equity," trying to confront the universal concept of gender equality. For example, the Special Rapporteur pointed out that some Iranian women "deny attempts to similarize [sic] women with men in all dimensions."[163] According to this principle under Islamic system, women and men are "equal in creation and in human value," and bear a "comparable weight of responsibilities and enjoy comparable benefits although in different spheres of life."[164]

The fundamental Islamic principle of equality unlike the universal definition, results in different rights, responsibilities, and punishments for women and men by all laws.[165] Article 4 of the Constitution of the IRI requires that all laws and regulations must be in accordance and conformity with Islamic jurisprudence; therefore the principle of equality as defined under Islam is used to define the rights and freedoms of the people and legislating laws pertaining to them.[166] Articles 20 and 21 of the Constitution of the IRI also confirm Islamic jurisprudence as the prevailing norm to define the rights and freedoms of the people and women in particular.[167]

In the subsequent report by the Special Rapporteur to the CHR at its fifty-third session, he made a few general points about the "nature of equality," which previously was mentioned in the report to the fifty-second session, regarding the status of women in Muslim countries and Iran. According to him, the

---

162 *See* U.N. Secretary-General Transmits the Interim Report of the Special Representative of the Commission on Human Rights to the General Assembly on its 52d Session, *Situation of human rights in the Islamic Republic of Iran Note by the Secretary-General,* ¶ 38 at 13, U.N. Doc. A/52/472 (Oct. 15, 1997).

163 Special Rapporteur of the CHR, *supra* note 156, ¶ 59 at 16.

164 *See id.*

165 For the full discussion *see* Chapter 1. *See also e.g.*, Ṣāliḥī Najaf Ābādī, Qiżāvat Zan dar Fiqhi Islāmī (Women's Judgeships in the Islamic Fiqh) 18, 20 (Umīdi Fardā Publication 2005); Murtiżā Muṭahrī, Niẓāmi Ḥuquqi Zan dar Islām [Women's Rights in Islam] 116, 121-122 (Ṣadrā Publication 2011). (TA)

166 *See* Qanuni Assassi Jumhuri'i Islamai Iran [The Constitution of The Islamic Republic of Iran] 1358 [1980], art. 4.

167 *See id.* at Arts. 20, 21.

concept of equality according to Muslim "defined a person by personal characteristics such as gender, race, or religion," judging them "unlike," and justifying differential treatment and rights. The Special Rapporteur continued that according to the majority opinion "this interpretation of equality served to perpetuate inequality in its substantive sense, that is between persons as human beings, and accordingly denied a full measure of human dignity to the members of the affected groups."[168] As a result, the Special Rapporteur rejected the argument of "non-identicality" [sic] argument and counted it as a "basis for treatment that is in substantive respects discriminatory."[169] He concluded that the rights of women are "human rights," as supposed to "women's rights," and governments should be in compliance with the universal norms, whereby the domestic culture, custom and religion cannot justify the non-existence of gender equality.[170]

As the Iranian government continued to deny and reject the existence of direct discrimination against women pursuing the judgeships, the uncertainty around the role of women in the judicial system was raised again in the interim report of the Special Rapporteur that was transmitted by the Secretary-General to the General Assembly in 1998.[171] The uncertainty was raised as the result of two contrary reports by the government of IRI. In one report the Head of the Judiciary said that there were ninety-nine women in the judicial system. By contrast, other reports indicated that of these, "four are judges in the family court and one is an assistant judge in the general court."[172]

Despite the existence of ambiguity and contrary reports about the number of women judges in the judicial system, one thing that the Special Rapporteur was certain about was that "no woman presides over trials or pronounces verdicts" in Iran.[173]

Despite all previous official reports highlighting the existence of systematic discrimination against women in Iran, and the continuous urging by the

168 Commission on Human Rights, *Report on the situation of human rights in the Islamic Republic of Iran, prepared by the Special Representative,* ¶ 20 at 7, U.N. Doc. E/CN.4/1997/63 (Feb. 11, 1997).

169 *See id.* ¶ 21 at 7.

170 *See id.* ¶ 21-22 at 7.

171 *See* U.N. Secretary-General Transmits the Interim Report of the Special Representative of the Commission on Human Rights to the General Assembly to its 53th Session, *Situation of human rights in the Islamic Republic of Iran Note by the Secretary-General,* ¶ 22 at 6, U.N. Doc. A/53/423 (Sep. 23, 1998).

172 *Id.*

173 *See id.*

international community that the government prioritize reforming the status of women and comply with its international human rights obligations and ratify CEDAW, Iran did not agree to ratify CEDAW in 1998.[174] Subsequently, when the bill to ratify CEDAW was passed by the Islamic Consultative Assembly in 2003,[175] the Guardian Council nevertheless rejected it on the ground that the provisions of the CEDAW were incompatible with Islamic jurisprudence.[176]

Article 4 of the Constitution requires that all laws be according to Islamic jurisprudence. Likewise, Article 72 of the Constitution explicitly states that the Islamic Consultative Assembly cannot enact laws contrary to Islam.[177] The Guardian Council, as one of its duties, has the duty to review and examine all laws passed by the Islamic Consultative Assembly to assure that they are in full compliance with Islam. In the case of laws rejected based on their failure to comply with Islamic laws, they will be sent back to the Islamic Consultative Assembly to be revised.[178]

In the late 1990s some early signs of change in attitude towards women and women's issues occurred in Iran. For instance, according to Āyatullāh Siyid Muḥammad Bujnurdī "many of the laws referred to in *feqh* and specific laws for men and women, which seem to be discriminatory in nature, can be revised."[179] Nonetheless, there was little substantive change with regard to the rights of women and the government failed to address the removal of discriminatory

174 *See e.g., Session 413 of the Shurāyi 'ālīyi Farhanqī [Supreme Council of the Cultural Revolution]*, Supreme Council of the Cultural Revolution (Feb 3, 1998), accessed at http://sccr.ir/pages/simpleView.aspx?provID=1036.

175 *See* Full Discussion of the Islamic Consultative Assembly 6th Term-Session 342, n. 17026, at 20-30, July 23, 2003, Library, Museum and Document Center of Iran Parliament, *accessed at* http://archive.ical.ir/files/debate/ip/06/06-342.pdf.

176 *See* Special Rapporteur on Violence against Women, its Causes and Consequences, *Mission to the Islamic Republic of Iran*, ¶ 29 at 9, U.N. Doc. E/CN.4/2006/61/Add.3 (Jan. 27, 2006). *See also* Iran MENA Gender Equality Profile: Status of Girls and Women in the Middle East and North Africa, UNICEF, at 1 (Oct. 2011), *accessed at* http://www.unicef.org/gender/files/Iran-Gender-Eqaulity-Profile-2011.pdf.

177 *See* Qanuni Assassi Jumhuri'i Islamai Iran [The Constitution of The Islamic Republic of Iran] 1358 [1980], arts. 4, 72.

178 1 Siyid Muḥammad Hāshimī, Huquqi Asāsī Jumhurīyi Islāmiyi Iran (Constitution of Islamic Republic of Iran) 167 (Dādgustar Publication 1999) (TA). *See also id.* at Art. 94.

179 Commission on Human Rights, *Report on the situation of human rights in the Islamic Republic of Iran, prepared by the Special Representative,* ¶ 13 at 6, U.N. Doc. E/CN.4/1998/59 (Jan. 28, 1998).

laws.[180] In the second half of 2000, despite certain improvements in the status of women, there was "little if any change" in the systemic discrimination against women in Iran.[181] In spite of playing an active role to pass laws to improve the status of women by the sixth Islamic Consultative Assembly,[182] the proposed reforms passed by assembly were rejected by the Guardian Council on the basis of being "un-Islamic."[183]

The Special Rapporteur on Violence against Women, its Causes and Consequences, Yakin Erturk, undertook an official mission to Iran, which took place from 29 January to 6 February 2005. In her report she asserted, "women can become judges, but they are qualified to occupy only certain judicial positions."[184] Noted were positions such as Assistant Prosecutor General, advisor to the Family Courts, and judge of the Office of Guardianship for Minors and the Interdicted Persons' Affair.[185] In her meeting with prominent judges (male and female), however, she was informed that granting women "full authority as judge" was an ongoing issue with the authorities.[186] According to her, this created a strange situation for women. Women were placed in positions that were labeled "judge" but seemed not to allow them to exercise the "full authority" of a judge, i.e. to render a final decision or verdict in any case.[187]

The status of Iranian women since the Islamic Revolution, according to the Special Rapporteur on Violence against Women, its Causes and Consequences, was viewed as "paradoxical."[188] In one way, women's participation in some aspects of public life was encouraged to legitimize the State gender policy, but

180 *See* U.N. Secretary-General Transmits the Interim Report of the Special Representative of the Commission on Human Rights to the General Assembly to its 54th Session, *Situation of human rights in the Islamic Republic of Iran Note by the Secretary-General,* ¶ 27, 64 at 7, 11, U.N. Doc. A/54/365 (Sep. 21, 1999).

181 *See* Commission on Human Rights, *Report on the situation of human rights in the Islamic Republic of Iran Prepared by the Special Representative,* ¶ 23 at 8, U.N. Doc. E/CN. 4/2001/39 (Jan. 16, 2001).

182 The Islamic Consultative Assembly (2000-2004).

183 *See* Report of Special Rapporteur, *supra* note 181, ¶ 24 at 8, U.N. Doc. E/CN. 4/2001/39.

184 Special Rapporteur on Violence against Women, its Causes and Consequences, *Mission to the Islamic Republic of Iran,* ¶ 18 at 7, U.N. Doc. E/CN.4/2006/61/Add.3 (Jan. 27, 2006).

185 *See id.*

186 *See id.*

187 For full discussion *see* Chapter 2.

188 *See* Report of the Special Rapporteur on Violence against Women, *supra* note 184, ¶ 25 at 8.

it was done under "strict surveillance and within well-defined boundaries."[189] Iranian women in comparison with other neighboring counties had access to health, education and to some extent employment and political participation but "the ground for their autonomous self-expression was precarious."[190] It was expressed that:

> "Women are praised as *mothers* but they may not exercise authority in *decisions* regarding their children; they *may become judges* but *not preside over a legal case.*"[191] [Emphasis Added]
>
> By universal standards women are confronted with economic, social and legal barriers to the full enjoyment of their human rights and are *excluded* from *equal partnership* in *determining* the parameters of social relationships in the public as well as private spheres of life. Conformity with such a gender order is ensured through the ideological and legal foundations of the Iranian State, as well as through the use of diverse forms of violence against women within the family, community and State institutions.[192] [Emphasis added]

To emphasize the general attitude in the country toward pushing for reform of discriminatory laws, this report indicated that most of the thirty-three introduced bills to modify discriminatory laws were rejected by the Guardian Council on the grounds that they were not in accordance with Islamic jurisprudence. Among the rejected bills, once again, was the proposal to ratify CEDAW.[193]

This paradox is apparent concerning women judges in Iran; they are called "women judges" but they cannot exercise the essential power of an independent judge to render the final binding decision of the court to end a dispute according to the Constitution. For many years, misleading and contrary reports by the government of IRI were provided to the Special Rapporteurs. A general term "women judges" was used to describe women in various jobs that in no way fulfill the definition of an independent judge according to Article 167 of the Constitution, which requires for judges to render verdicts and end disputes

189 *Id.* ¶ 62 at 18.

190 *Id.*

191 *Id.*

192 *Id.* ¶ 25 at 9.

193 *See id.* ¶ 29 at 9.

before them. The government conveyed the untrue idea that those women called judges exercised their primary judicial power to render a verdict in any cases. Therefore, after many years of disputed exchanges concerning the status of women as judges, and an absence of transparency from the Iranian government, the Rapporteur added a "decision-making" requirement in examining women's rights in important decision-making positions such as judgeships. This helped to determine whether those women, who Iran called judges or consultant judges, had the independent power of a judge to render the final verdict. Under Iranian law it was clear that so-called "consultant judges" did not even have "decision making" authority. According to those laws, it meant that women consultant judges worked only in the Family Courts as advisors; they could only submit an "advisory opinion" to the actual male judges who had the power to render the final decision of the court enshrined in the Constitution.

As a result, despite the government's effort to mislead, and to show the equal representation of women in high government offices like the judgeships with full power, such power was non-existent.[194] The misleading title of women judges used by the government to counteract all the allegations of discrimination against women pursuing judgeships expanded the analysis of the issue of women judges' role in the future reports. For instance, in the report submitted by the Secretary-General to the General Assembly in its sixty-seven session, the issue of the absence of women from true decision-making positions was addressed. The study went beyond accepting the mere title "judge" carried by a woman somehow connected to the judiciary. This report engaged in a true functional analysis of what so-called "women judges" actually did, and indicated that "women face restrictions in their appointment to certain decision-making positions and they may act as advisory judges, but cannot preside over a court."[195]

Once again the compelling issue of gender-based discrimination, as well as systemic and systematic violations of civil, political, economic, social and cultural rights was explicitly addressed in the 2013 report of the Human Rights Council

194 *See e.g.*, HUMAN RIGHTS COUNCIL SPECIAL RAPPORTEUR, *infra* note 207, ¶ 44 at 14; Report of the U.N. Secretary-General to General Assembly at its 67th Session, *Situation of human rights in the Islamic Republic of Iran Report of the Secretary-General,* ¶ 15 at 7, U.N. Doc. A/67/327 (Aug. 22, 2012).

195 Report of the U.N. Secretary-General to General Assembly at its 67th Session, *Situation of human rights in the Islamic Republic of Iran Report of the Secretary-General,* ¶ 15 at 7, U.N. Doc. A/67/327 (Aug. 22, 2012).

Special Rapporteur.[196] These reports explicitly elaborated on the existence of various discrimination against women and the Special Rapporteur's great concerns about the "laws and policies that continue to limit women's access to decision-making roles."[197] The report submitted by the Special Rapporteur to the twenty-second session of Human Rights Council pursuant to resolution 19/9, asserted:

> "A dearth of female representation in decision-making roles remains problematic for women's participation in public life...Women are allowed to serve as *legal counselors*, for example, but are *prohibited* from *issuing* and *signing final verdicts*."[198] [Emphasis Added]

In all the latest reports by the Special Rapporteur of the Human Rights Council and the Secretary-General in 2014, the issue of women being directly discriminated against still was an ongoing issue, despite the increase in the number of female judges reported by the government in Iran.[199] They, once again, asserted that women are "not allowed to preside over a court or to issue judgments on an equal footing with male judges,"[200] and are "permitted to serve only as female advisory judges in the Family Courts."[201]

The Islamic Republic of Iran in its response to the report of the Special Rapporteur that was transmitted by the Secretary-General to the sixty-ninth session of General Assembly, about the existence of only female advisory judges in Iran, failed to elaborate on the restrictions imposed on the female consultant judges. This response did not discuss women's inability to render the final

---

196 *See* U.N. Secretary-General Transmits the Report of the Special Rapporteur of HRC to the General Assembly at its 68th Session, *Situation of human rights in the Islamic Republic of Iran Note by the Secretary-General*, ¶ 1 at 2, U.N. Doc. A/68/503 (Oct. 4, 2013).

197 *See id.* ¶ 34 at 10.

198 Human Rights Council, *Report of the Special Rapporteur on the situation of human rights in the Islamic Republic of Iran (Ahmed Shaheed)*, ¶ 52 at 16, U.N. Doc. A/HRC/22/56 (Oct. 4, 2013).

199 *See e.g.*, Response of the Islamic Republic of Iran to Draft Report of Special Rapporteur for Submission to the 69th Session of the UN General Assembly, SHAHEEONIRAN.ORG, at 28 (2014), *accessed at* http://shaheedoniran.org/wp-content/uploads/2014/10/Response-of-the-Islamic-Republic-of-Iran-to-Draft-Report-of-Special.pdf.

200 Report of the U.N. Secretary-General to the General Assembly at its 69th Session, *Situation of human rights in the Islamic Republic of Iran Report of the Secretary-General*, ¶ 24 at 7, U.N. Doc A/69/306 (Aug. 12, 2014).

201 U.N. Secretary-General Transmits the Report of the Special Rapporteur of HRC to the General Assembly at its 69th Session, *Situation of human rights in the Islamic Republic of Iran Note by the Secretary-General*, ¶ 69 at 19, U.N. Doc. A/69/356 (Aug. 27, 2014).

decision of the court in the Family Courts. Instead the government referred only to its positive procedural steps such as an "increase in the appointment process" of women judges. This report indicated that in 2012, 743 women participants were accepted for entrance to the judicial internship and that acceptance took place equally for women and men.[202] It also emphasized:

> "Judicial internship courses take place equally for men and women judicial interns, scientifically and workshop method. Professional and skills trainings are done while the service of the judges also is without gender distinction and solely is based on the individuals' judicial and managerial positions."[203]

This report explicitly stated that according to the latest statistics, there were 670 women judges.[204] The government inserted the following chart that indicates the latest statistics for "women judges" employed in Justice Departments in 2013:

Table 1: Statistics for *Women Judges* Employed in Justice Departments Across the Nation 2013:[205]

Court Assistant	538
Judicial Consultant	96
Prosecutor's Assistant in Various Towns	8
Counselor	10
Judicial Assistant to Director General of Provinces Justice Dep.	18
Total	**670**

According to this table that indicates the latest statistics by the IRI, there were total of 670 "women judges" in 2013. None of the positions in this chart,

202 *See* 2013 Response of the Islamic Republic of Iran, *supra* note 199. *See also* Family Protection Law (2012).

203 *Id.*

204 *See id.* at 28, 29.

205 *Id.*

however, is a true judgeship. These are simply various positions held by women in the Justice Department but women assigned to true judgeship positions are completely missing, because there are none. This report once again avoids the issue raised by the Special Rapporteur that women's only opportunity to become judges is "consultant judges" in the Family Courts. The government by providing irrelevant statistics and asserting positive steps taken by them such as equally training judicial trainees is failing to fulfill in good faith its obligations under international law and procedures.[206] Calling an "assistant" or "consultant" a judge does not make them judges according to the Constitution.

Despite all official reports by the Special Rapporteurs for well over two decades, the government of IRI never once cited the Law on Qualifications for Appointment of Judges, or the law on Transferring Women with Judicial Titles from the Ministry of Justice to other Ministries and Conversion of their Judicial Titles to Administrative, or other relevant laws such as the 2012 Family Protection Law. The existing law of 1982 unquestionably expressly excludes women from serving as judges on the prohibited ground of sex. Simply, if she were a man the law in question would not deprive her from becoming a judge. This makes women victims of unequal treatment by law that discriminates against them.

Notwithstanding, the government continued to falsely insist that not only can women become judges, but also that there have been steps taken to increase the number of women judges in the judiciary. In reality, the most the government has done is add legally trained assistants and consultants to the judicial system with authority only to assist, counsel, or submit advisory opinions and only in Family Courts. Even though this may count as a positive step to increase the number of women in the judicial system, it does not count as elimination of the de jure discrimination against women who would like to pursue judgeships.

The latest recommendation by the Special Rapporteur of the UN Human Rights Council urges the IRI government to make an effort to improve female representation in decision-making positions of the judicial system.[207] It also stresses the critical need for greater transparency and closer engagement with the Human Rights Council and other UN human rights bodies in strengthening

206 *See* Vienna Convention 1969, art. 26; G.A. Res. 2625 (XXV), *Declaration on Principles of International Law concerning Friendly Relations and Co-operation among States in accordance with the Charter of the United Nations*, Under the Principle that States Shall Fulfill in Good Faith the Obligations Assumed by them in Accordance with the Charter, U.N. Doc. A/RES/25/2625 (Oct. 24, 1970).

207 *See* Human Rights Council, *Special Rapporteur on the situation of human rights in the Islamic Republic of Iran*, ¶ 44 at 14, U.N. Doc. A/HRC/19/66 (Mar. 6, 2012).

human rights for all in Iran.[208] Also the Special Rapporteur on Violence against Women, its Causes and Consequences in 2006, recommended that the Iranian regime, "if sincere about restoring women's dignity... must embark on a re-interpretation of its fundamental norms, including Islamic principles in line with the current needs and societal contributions of women as well as with universal human rights standards."[209] Continuously the Special Rapporteurs call upon the IRI government to reform its legal laws and system.[210]

b. General Assembly of the United Nations

The UN General Assembly's Social, Humanitarian and Cultural Affairs Committee commonly referred to as the "Third Committee," examines a range of social, humanitarian, and human rights issues that affect people all over the world. One of the important parts of the work of the Third Committee is focused on the examination of human rights questions, including reports of the Special Procedures of the Human Rights Council. It also discusses questions relating to the advancement of women and the protection of children among other human rights issues. The Committee passes resolutions that also include country specific resolutions related to the human rights situation in that specific country.[211]

United Nations' resolutions are formal expressions of the opinion of UN organs.[212] Resolutions adopted by the UN General Assembly, although, are only "recommendations" and do not legally bind its member States. It is noteworthy that States establish legally binding obligations for themselves in various ways, for example, by ratifying various treaties or other international agreements, or through wide acceptance of rules as binding customary international law.[213]

Among many resolutions adopted by the General Assembly concerning the human rights situation in Iran, the latest resolution adopted in 2013 expressed

---

208 *See id.* ¶ 74 at 21.

209 Report of the Special Rapporteur on Violence against Women, *supra* note 184, ¶ 65 at 18.

210 *See e.g.*, U.N. Secretary-General Transmits the Interim Report of the Special Representative of the CHR to the General Assembly to its 54th Session, *supra* note 180, ¶ 64 at 11; *id.*

211 General Assembly of the United Nations, *Social, Humanitarian & Cultural Third Committee*, United Nations, *accessed at* http://www.un.org/en/ga/third/.

212 United Nations Dag Hammarskjöld Library, *UN Resolutions*, Research UN, *accessed at* http://research.un.org/en/docs/resolutions.

213 Guide to International Human Rights Practice, *supra* note at 56, at 8.

deep concern at serious ongoing and recurring human rights violations, i.e. "pervasive gender inequality and violence against women, and increased discrimination against women and girls in law and in practice, as well as restrictions on access to government decision-making positions, and the labor market."[214] Accordingly, the UN General Assembly 2013 resolution calls upon the government "to address the substantive concerns highlighted in the reports of the Secretary-General and the Special Rapporteur, as well as calls to action found in previous resolutions of the General Assembly," to eliminate, in law and in practice, all forms of discrimination against women and promote women's participation in decision-making positions.[215]

Earlier, for instance in 2000, General Assembly resolution 55/2 reaffirmed its faith in the Charter and requested the acceptance by the governments of the essential fundamental concepts of the 21st century such as "equal rights and opportunities of women and men" all over the world.[216]

The Secretary-General, in several reports submitted to both the General Assembly and the Human Rights Council, repeatedly expressed his concerns relating to the inequality of women imposed by many laws, and the issue of "women's underrepresentation in public, political and professional life."[217] He urged the government to "adopt laws and policies that promote women's participation in decision-making positions."[218] The Secretary-General urged the IRI to address the human rights concerns raised by various reports, and called for action requested in previous resolutions of the General Assembly, as well as recommendations of various human rights mechanisms, including the Universal Periodic Review process.[219]

---

214 G.A. Third Committee, *Promotion and protection of human rights: Situation of human rights in the Islamic Republic of Iran,* ¶ 5(g) at 2, U.N. Doc. A/C.3/68/L.57 (Nov. 1, 2013). *See also* G.A. Res. 66/175, *Situation of human rights in the Islamic Republic of Iran,* ¶ 2(g) at 3, U.N. Doc. A/Res/66/175 (Feb. 17, 2012); G.A. Res. 65/226, *supra* not 145, ¶ 2(f) at 2.

215 *See* G.A. Third Committee, *Promotion and protection of human rights: Situation of human rights in the Islamic Republic of Iran,* ¶ 6, 6(d), U.N. Doc. A/C.3/68/L.57 (Nov. 1, 2013).

216 *See* G.A. Res. 55/2, *United Nations Millennium Declaration,* ¶ 6 at 2, U.N. Doc. A/RES/55/2 (Sep. 8, 2000).

217 Report of the U.N. Secretary-General to the General Assembly at its 68th Session, *Situation of human rights in the Islamic Republic of Iran,* ¶ 10 at 4, U.N. Doc. A/68/377 (Sep. 10, 2013).

218 *Id.*

219 *Id.* ¶ 49 at 15.

c. Universal Periodic Review

The Universal Periodic Review[220] is a peer-review mechanism by which a country's entire human rights record is scrutinized. It is a unique Charter-based and state-driven review mechanism for the assessment and improvement of the human rights records of all 193 UN member States.[221] The UPR was established by the General Assembly resolution 60/251 that also created the Human Rights Council in 2006.[222] Resolution 60/251 mandates the Human Rights Council to:

> Undertake a universal periodic review, based on objective and reliable information, of the fulfillment by each State of its human rights obligations and commitments in a manner which ensures universality of coverage and equal treatment with respect to all States; the review shall be a cooperative mechanism, based on an interactive dialogue, with the full involvement of the country concerned and with consideration given to its capacity-building needs; such a mechanism shall complement and not duplicate the work of treaty bodies.[223]

The UPR reviews are conducted by the UPR Working Group of the Council that includes all 47 Council Member States. The UPR Working Group reviews UPR reports in UPR Sessions three times each year in Geneva, with up to 14 countries undergoing review per session. The UPR reviews are based on an interactive dialogue between the State under review and the members and observer States of the Council. It operates on a four-and-half-year cycle and is composed of several stages in which the first cycle includes the preparation of the reports to be reviewed, reviews that lead to conclusions and recommendations. The second and subsequent cycle will focus more keenly on the implementation of the recommendations that the State has accepted in the previous cycle and further developments in their human rights matters.[224]

220 Universal Periodic Review, hereinafter UPR.

221 *Basic facts about the UPR*, United Nations Human Rights Office of the High Commissioner, (2015), *accessed at* http://www.ohchr.org/en/hrbodies/upr/pages/BasicFacts.aspx.

222 *See* G.A. Res. 60/251, *supra* note 127.

223 *Id.* ¶ 5(e), at 3.

224 U.N. Human Rights Treaty System, *supra* note 60, at 44. *See also* Basic facts about the UPR, *supra* note 221.

The function of the UPR and the treaty bodies are complementary. The UPR reviews bring to the attention of State parties the need to submit their reports to the committee regularly and to implement their recommendations. Also, the treaty bodies remind State parties to implement the recommendations made during the UPR sessions.[225]

Iran went before the Universal Periodic Review by the Working Group for the first time in 2010.[226] In its first National Report prepared by the IRI government, submitted to the Working Group, concerning economic, social and cultural rights in employment, the government explicitly stated that special attention was given to elimination of discrimination and creation of employment for women.[227] It continued:

> Relying on the progressive Islamic laws the role of women in Iran in the family institution is unparalleled and unique. All the policies relating to women's rights proceed from this principle. In respect of rights of women and elimination of discrimination against them, Iran has carried out principles, unremitting and targeted efforts to promote the status of women in education, political and cultural endeavors over the past 30 years.[228]

This report also included fundamental national jurisprudence such as Equality before the Law, Rule of Law, and Respecting Islamic Criteria.[229] Iran expressly asserted,

> "In light of the fact that the system of Government in Iran is based on principles of Islam, it is necessary that Islamic standards and criteria prevail in the society."[230]

---

225 *Id.*

226 *See* Human Rights Council Universal Periodic Review, United Nations Human Rights Office of the High Commissioner, *accessed at* http://www.ohchr.org/EN/HRBodies/UPR/Documents/uprlist.pdf.

227 *See National Report*, ¶ 89 at 17, U.N. Doc. A/HRC/WG.6/7/IRN/1 (Nov. 18, 2009).

228 *Id. at* ¶ 98 at 18.

229 *Id. at* ¶ 22, 23, 24 at 6-7.

230 *Id.* ¶ 24 at 7.

The report continued to highlight the importance of the religion jurisprudence as relates to the judgeships in Iran by stating:

> In order not to allow Islamic norms and the law to be regarded as two separate bases and for the purpose of preventing conflict of opinions by the religious jurists on a single matter, and to provide legitimacy to the judicial system, principles of religious jurisprudence (*fiqh*) need to be articulated by law and duly observed by judges. Accordingly, the qualification and the requirements needed to be a judge and the competence of courts are to be determined by law in accordance with principles of *fiqh*.[231]

This is the reaffirmation of the provisions of the Constitution of the IRI.[232] This National report under the "rights of women," explicitly highlighted the government's efforts to promote the status of women in various fields. It reads,

> Relying on the progressive Islamic laws the role of women in Iran in the family institution is unparalleled and unique. All the policies relating to women's rights proceed from this principle. In respect of rights of women and elimination of discrimination against them, Iran has carried out principles, unremitting and targeted efforts to promote the status of women in educational, political, and cultural endeavors over the past 30 years. Women rights activists, both as governmental and non-governmental entities, have been able to pass a number of reforms in the government.... These reforms have improved the status of women in comparison of international standards and the Islamic counties.... Duties in the Islamic Republic of Iran combined with the highest Islamic and human rights principles have laid the foundation for the promotion of the culture of human rights in Iran.[233]

With regard to women's participation in key positions, this report also confirmed the existence of women in high government positions without giving any details about their titles or authorities.[234]

231 *Id.*

232 *See* Qanuni Assassi Jumhuri'i Islamai Iran [The Constitution of The Islamic Republic of Iran] 1358 [1980], arts. 4, 12, 163.

233 National Report, *supra* note 227, ¶ 98 at 18-19.

234 *Id.* ¶ 101 at 19.

The compelling issue of discrimination against women in Iran was raised by many State members of the UPR Working Group in 2010.[235] In their Conclusions, for example, they asked Iran to enhance efforts to further promote the rights of vulnerable groups such as women.[236] Iran, however, in its Addendum report rejected the existence of discrimination against women and asserted that it has a "very progressive attitude toward women" and has also taken practical and effective measures in that regard.[237]

According to the Islamic Republic of Iran Mid-term Implementation Assessment, prepared to evaluate the human rights situation two years after the examination of the first UPR cycle,[238] Iran failed to implement recommendations that were offered by the member States to improve women's rights; recommendations such as adoption of measures guaranteeing women's equality under the law, and repealing or amending all domestic discriminatory provisions against women. For example, according to one NGO's report on the Mid-term assessment, the issues of systematic discrimination against women were highlighted and indicated that despite some progressive laws Iranian women are discriminated against in marriage, divorce, inheritance, and child custody matters.[239]

---

235 *See* Working Group on the Universal Periodic Review, *Islamic Republic of Iran*, ¶ 23, 27, 58, U.N. Doc. A/HRC/14/12 (March 15, 2010).

236 *Id.* at ¶ 90(7) at 13.

237 Report of the Working Group on the Universal Periodic Review, *Islamic Republic of Iran (Addendum)*, ¶ IA(2) at 2, U.N. Doc. A/HRC/14/12/Add.1 (June 3, 2010).

238 The UPR process takes place every four and half years. Some recommendations can be implemented immediately. The UPR also created an update process to evaluate the human rights situation two years after the examination at the UPR. The UPR-info seeks to ensure the respect of commitments made in the UPR; it also gives opportunity to the stakeholders to share their opinion on the commitments. About two years after the review, UPR-info invites States, NGOs, and National Institutions for Human Rights (NHRI) to share their comments on the implementation or lack of recommendations adopted at the Human Rights Council plenary session. For this purpose UPR-info publishes a Mid-term Implementation Assessment (MIA) including responses from each stakeholder. The States should implement the recommendations that they have accepted, and civil society should monitor that implementation. UPR info, Islamic Republic of Iran Mid-term Implementation Assessment, UPR-INFO.ORG (2012), *accessed at* http://www.upr-info.org/sites/default/files/document/iran_islamic_republic_of/session_07_-_february_2010/mia-iran.pdf.

239 *See e.g.*, UPR info, Islamic Republic of Iran Mid-term Implementation Assessment, UPR-INFO.ORG, at 79,81, 85, 86 (2012), *accessed at* http://www.upr-info.org/sites/default/files/document/iran_islamic_republic_of/session_07_-_february_2010/mia-iran.pdf.

"Women young and old, women with a university education, women belonging to minority groups and women of different sexual orientations, all experience discrimination."[240]

Concerning discrimination against women who pursue working as judges in Iran, many stakeholders as part of the monitoring body in the Mid-term Implementation Assessment explicitly addressed this issue as following:

"A female judge cannot issue final verdicts."[241]

"Women cannot become presiding judges."[242]

"The number has risen from 161 women in 2003 to 614 women [...]. However, Women's roles are restricted to counseling and assisting in prosecution, not directly handling down sentencing."[243]

"Women cannot be presiding judges who hand out sentencing. Women are allowed to listen to civil cases as judges, they are prohibited from becoming the verdict-speaking judge in civil courts and absolutely prevented from participating as judges in criminal courts."[244]

Recommendations offered by member States during Iran' first UPR cycle, such as to sign and ratify CEDAW, and to repeal or amend all discriminatory laws against women in national legislation were not supported by Iran because Iran considered them either to be inconsistent with the Institution-Building text, or not in conformity with its existing laws and principles.[245]

The IRI's State Report for the second cycle UPR in 2014 included the progress, or lack thereof, made by the government on the basis of some of the

240 *Id* at 79.

241 JC response. *Id.* at 80.

242 LLG response. *Id.*

243 LLG response. *Id.* at 85.

244 LLG response. *Id.* at 86.

245 *See* Universal Periodic Review, Responses to Recommendations, UPR-INFO.ORG, ¶ 92(1), 92(12) at 9, 10 (2010), *accessed at* http://www.upr-info.org/sites/default/files/document/iran_islamic_republic_of/session_7_-_february_2010/recommendationstoiran2010.pdf.

decisions, resolutions, and recommendations that were accepted previously in the first cycle.[246] Accordingly, it is Iran's legal obligation to implement previously accepted recommendations.[247]

In the 2014 Compilation Report prepared by the Office of High Commissioner for Human Rights, which contained several reports of the treaty bodies, Special Rapporteurs and other relevant official UN documents, once again the Secretary-General stressed the continuing existence of laws permitting gender discrimination in Iran. For example, regarding the status of women pursing judgeships in Iran, the UN Country Team[248] emphasized that women are banned from acting as sitting judges with the authority to issue verdicts, and the Special Rapporteur noted gender-based disparities in economic participation and political empowerment.[249]

In 2014, the Summary Report prepared by the Office of the United Nations High Commissioner for Human Rights included the summary of 49 stakeholders submissions to the UPR. This report indicated that since the 2010 UPR, "no measures were taken to amend discriminatory and restrictive laws including the Constitution."[250] According to the report of Amnesty International, for example, Iran had failed to incorporate key human rights provisions into its domestic legal system that are guaranteed by various treaties to which Iran is a State party.[251]

To improve the status of women, Iran must examine recommendations that were highlighted, once again, in 2014 by the State members of the Working Group on the UPR. For example, accede to CEDAW, reform and repeal discriminatory laws and promote equal opportunity with respect to employment. These are among recommendations proposed to the government of Iran that will be

---

246 *See* Working Group on the Universal Periodic Review, *National report,* U.N. Doc. A/HRC/WG.6/20/IRN/1 (Aug. 4, 2014).

247 *See* Islamic Republic of Iran Mid-term Implementation Assessment, *supra* note 239 at 2.

248 UN Country Team, hereinafter UNCT.

249 *See* Office of the High Commissioner for Human Rights, *Compilation prepared in accordance with paragraph 15 (b) of the annex to Human Rights Council resolution 5/1 and paragraph 5 of the annex to Council resolution 16/21 (Islamic Republic of Iran),* ¶ 11, 13, 14 at 6, U.N. Doc. A/HRC/WG.6/20/IRN/2 (Aug. 18, 2014).

250 Office of the United Nations High Commissioner for Human Rights, *Summary (Islamic Republic of Iran),* ¶ 2(2) at 2, U.N. Doc. A/HRC/WG.6/20/IRN/3 (Aug. 7, 2014).

251 *See id.* ¶ 2(3) at 2.

examined by the IRI government that is scheduled to respond not later than the twenty-eighth session of the Human Rights Council in March 2015.[252]

Iran's international obligations are not limited only to the Charter, UDHR, ratified treaties, and customary international laws. As part of its international obligations, Iran also needs to examine all the proposed recommendations concerning the improvement of women's rights made during the first and second cycle of UPR with the view to accept and implement them promptly in its domestic legal system.[253]

Out of 23 recommendations that were raised by the member States concerning the human rights of women during the first cycle of UPR, almost half of them were "accepted" by Iran. The accepted recommendations, for example, were to accept measures to guarantee women equality under the law; bring its national legislation into conformity with international obligations on women's rights; ensure the equal treatment of women in law and practice; step up efforts to enhance the participation of women in all spheres of socio-economic life, and take all steps necessary to reform the discriminatory provisions of penal and civil laws.[254] More specific to the accepted recommendations that exclusively aimed at women's equal rights under the law and reforming all de jure discriminatory laws,[255] Iran still has not implemented them promptly in its domestic legal system, which were recorded in all 2014 UPR reports. A good example of Iran's failure to reform its discriminatory laws is upholding the 1982 statute that directly discriminates against women.

Upholding de jure discriminatory laws against women such as the 1982 Law on the Qualifications for Appointment of Judges undermines Iran's international obligations arising under the UPR mechanism. Iran is required to implement all

252 *See* Report of the Working Group on the Universal Periodic Review, *Islamic Republic of Iran,* ¶ 138, 138.3-138.6, 138.8-138.9, 138.17, 138.92, 138.141, 138.191, U.N. Doc. A/HRC/28/12 (Dec. 22, 2014).

253 Ahmed Shaheed Video, *supra* note 142.

254 For example other suggested recommendations: accede to CEDAW; accept a visit to the country by the Special Rapporteurs on violence against women; repeal or amend all discriminatory provisions against women and girls in national legislation; revise legislative provisions that are discriminatory on the basis of sex, religion, political opinion or sexual orientation. *See Recommendation*, UPRInfo, accessed at http://www.upr-info.org/database/index.php?limit=0&f_SUR=79&f_SMR=All&order=&orderDir=ASC&orderP=true&f_Issue=All&searchReco=&resultMax=300&response=&action_type=&session=&SuRRgrp=&SuROrg=&SMRRgrp=&SMROrg=&pledges=RecoOnly.

255 *See* the *List of "Noted" and "Accepted" Recommendations,* UPRInfo, *accessed at* http://www.upr-info.org/database/index.php?limit=0&f_SUR=79&f_SMR=All&order=&orderDir=ASC&orderP=true&f_Issue=All&searchReco=&resultMax=300&response=&action_type=&session=&SuRRgrp=&SuROrg=&SMRRgrp=&SMROrg=&pledges=RecoOnly.

accepted recommendations such as reforming the discriminatory provisions in its civil laws and bringing its national legislation into conformity with international obligations on women's rights. Upholding the 1982 law is a clear failure of Iran to fulfill its legal obligations under the UPR mechanism. A failure of Iran to fulfill its obligation under UPR is a violation under international law.

d. Commission on the Status of Women

The Commission on the Status of Women[256] is one of the six functional commissions established by the United Nations Economic and Social Council[257] resolutions 11(II) of 21 June 1947, pursuant to Article 68 of the UN Charter.[258] In 1996, resolution 1996/6 expanded the Commission's mandate and decided that it should take a catalytic role in monitoring and reviewing progress and problems in the implementation of the Beijing Declaration and Platform for Action as key global policy documents on gender equality and its integration into the mainstream of UN wide activities.[259]

During the Commission's annual two-week session, representatives of UN member States, civil society organizations and UN entities gather at UN headquarters in New York City. They discuss progress and gaps in the implementation of the Beijing Declaration and Platform for Action. Member States agree on further actions to accelerate progress and promote women's enjoyment of their rights in political, economic, and social fields. The outcomes and recommendations of each session are forwarded to ECOSOC for follow-up.[260]

Many official statements have been presented by the IRI delegation each year before the CSW. These statements made by the government delegates, who are

256 Commission on the Status of Women, hereinafter CSW.

257 The United Nations Economic and Social Council was established in 1945 as one of the six main organs of the United Nations. Hereinafter ECOSOC.

258 *See* Economic and Social Council Res. 11(II) (June 21, 1947), *accessed at* http://www.un.org/womenwatch/daw/csw/pdf/CSW_founding_resolution_1946.pdf. *See also* ALSTON, *supra* note, 126, at 268.

259 *See* Economic and Social Council Res. 1996/6, Follow-up to the Fourth World Conference on Women (July 22, 1996). *See also* Fareda Banda, Project on a Mechanism to Address Laws that Discriminate Against Women, OFFICE OF THE HIGH COMMISSIONER FOR HUMAN RIGHTS AND GENDER UNIT, at 40 (March 6, 2008), *accessed at* http://www.ohchr.org/Documents/Publications/laws_that_discriminate_against_women.pdf.

260 *See* UN Women, *Commission on the Status of Women*, UN Women (2015), *accessed at* http://www.unwomen.org/en/csw.

women, clearly convey the IRI's view about the socio-economic, cultural, and legal status of women and what in their view constitutes gender equality in Iran.

In 2013, the IRI representative in the statement before the fifty-seventh session of the CSW reaffirmed the government's firm belief "in equality between women and men in terms of dignity and nature;"[261] stating:

> "We believe that the Almighty God has created both men and women *equally* from *essence* and for perfection and growth, *complementary* to each other whereby giving them *each a specific role* to play."[262] [Emphasis Added]

Accordingly, the only time that women and men are seen as "equal" is in their essence; their interdependence leads them to growth. Therefore, women's growth and autonomy is unbearable without men. As confirmed, women and men are equal in their dignity and human rights but "this right is not to be confused with equaling men's and women's role in family, society and in the development process."[263] The government reaffirms its belief once again in equality, complementarity, and justice as the basic concepts of the role of women and men in family and society.[264]

According to the statement of the IRI delegation to the fifty-third session of the CSW, the failure of the objectives of the Beijing Plan of Action was blamed on, for instance, the "mere domination of separation approach in women's issues."[265] The concept of Cultural Relativism[266] was used by the IRI's delegation in the statement before the fifty-fifth session of the CSW to define women's

261 U.N. Commission on the Status of Women, *Statement by Mrs. Maryam Mojtahedzadeh Advisor to the President and Head of the Center for Women and Family Affairs of the Islamic Republic of Iran before the 57th Session of CSW,* at 2 (March 5, 2013).

262 *Id.* at 1.

263 *See* U.N. Commission of the Status of Women, *Statement to the General Discussion of the 56th Session of CSW by Mr. Eshagh Al-Habib on behalf of Mrs. Maryam Mojtahedzadeh*, at 2 (Feb. 28, 2012).

264 *See id.* at 2.

265 U.N. Commission of the Status of Women, *Statement by Elham Aminzadeh to the 53d Session of CSW,* at 2 (March 4, 2009).

266 Cultural relativists argue that members of societies have different traditions, rejecting that there can be valid external critiques of culturally-based practices and claiming that no legitimate cross-cultural standards for evaluating the treatment of rights issues exist. Where Western criticisms of the treatment of women in the Middle East are concerned, the cultural relativist rejects the objects the Universalist approaches on the grounds that they reflect the values of Western culture. WOMEN'S RIGHTS HUMAN RIGHTS: INTERNATIONAL FEMINIST PERSPECTIVES, *supra* note 41, at 176.

status in Iran. Once again, the IRI delegation criticized the application of universal policies and strategies, calling them "one-dimensional," and asserted that global decisions "failed to consider the diversity of cultures and characteristics of various civilizations."[267] According to the IRI delegation in this statement, the failure to remove the obstacles and challenges faced by women in the world is because the universal policies and strategies prescribe "a single remedy for all societies."[268]

To remedy the women's problem, the IRI delegation explicitly requested the CSW to adopt a "complementary approach" towards gender issues derived from "human nature," since women and men are complementary to one another by divine rule and nature.[269]

> This divine rule ought to be carefully considered when legislating crafting laws. [sic] Neglecting the central *role of women* in the management of *family* and society while *attempting to compare men with women* in the world of work *without due attention* to their *natural rights and responsibilities* on one hand and their *similarities and differences* on the other, would lead to disregarding their rights and responsibilities and their discrepancies as well as their similarities and ultimately, derailing from the real path of the advancement of women.[270] [Emphasis Added]

The new model for the contemporary Iranian women introduced by the government is a woman with:

> "Chastity and dignity as well political insight and full responsibility shared with men towards her community and yet devoted to family and its upbringing, would be able to help raise a new civilization."[271]

Another statement on this issue:

267 U.N. Commission on the Status of Women, *Statement by Mrs. Fātimi Ajorloo in the 55th Session of CSW*, at 1 (Feb. 24, 2011).

268 *See id.*

269 *See id.*

270 *Id.* at 2.

271 STATEMENT BY ELHAM AMINZADEH, *supra* note 265, at 4.

> "We believe that by offering a *new model of contemporary women* who are *pious* and *chaste* and possess political wisdom, are accountable, self-sacrificing and promoters of spirituality in families, a new civilization will emerge."[272] [Emphasis Added]

The definition of "gender equality" for Iranian women according to the government delegations establishes an appropriate and adequate status for women in Iran. The adopted plans for the advancement of contemporary women are based on morality, equity and justice that are inspired by "religion" and "cultural ethics" of the nation.[273] The principle of considering the "family" as the fundamental unit of Islamic society;[274] the importance of recognizing women's central role in the family that leads to her role as the "main trainer" in the society, has been emphasized by several reports submitted by the Iranian delegations to the CSW and other bodies.[275]

Women's individuality to enjoy autonomous and inalienable human rights and freedoms, according to universal human rights principles, is a non-existent concept in Iran. Women are not seen as fully independent individuals who are unconditionally entitled to enjoy autonomous human rights. Rather their human rights are predefined by their chastity and dignity intertwined with their natural roles as mothers and main trainers in the society on the basis of strict religious and cultural norms imposed by the government and its Constitution. The equal rights pertaining to women, according to the government, are based on their perceived "physical and psychological" differences with men that should not to be confused with equaling men and women' roles and rights.[276]

The Iranian government's representatives considering the women's rights jurisprudence "one dimensional," and as the catalyst of failing to remove

---

272 U.N. Commission on the Status of Women, *Statement by the Delegation of the Islamic Republic of Iran in the 52d Session of CSW*, at 3 (March 3, 2008).

273 To achieve gender equity for establishing an appropriate and adequate status for women the "Charter on Women's Rights and Responsibilities" were adopted with emphasis on "morality," "justice," and "security" inspired by religious and cultural ethics in Iran. *See* STATEMENT BY ELHAM AMINZADEH, *supra* note 265, at 3.

274 *See* Qanuni Assassi Jumhuri'i Islamai Iran [The Constitution of The Islamic Republic of Iran] 1358 [1980], art. 10.

275 *See e.g.*, STATEMENT BY ELHAM AMINZADEH, *supra* note 265, at 3; STATEMENT BY MRS. MARYAM MOJTAHEDZADEH, *supra* note 262, at 2; STATEMENT BY IRI DELEGATION, *supra* note 272, at 3.

276 *See, e.g.*, SPECIAL RAPPORTEUR OF HUMAN RIGHTS COUNCIL, *supra* note 198, ¶ 42 at 13. *See also*, STATEMENT TO THE GENERAL DISCUSSION OF THE CSW 56, *supra* note 263.

women's challenges, is a clear rejection of international human rights jurisprudence as they pertain to women by the Iranian government. Good examples are many provisions of the IRI Constitution that narrow the enjoyment of political, economic, social, and cultural rights of women to Islamic criteria as the prevailing principle in the country.[277]

Gender, culture, religion and rights intersect in complicated ways. According to the Special Rapporteur in the Field of Cultural Rights, many practices and norms that discriminate against women are justified by reference to national or local culture, religion and tradition. The Special Rapporteur asserts that the justification for direct discrimination against women by reference to culture or religion should be eliminated.[278] In 2012, she asserted:

> "The time has come to question the existence of legal norms that *authorize distinguishing between women and men*, including in the internal affairs of institutions that are based on a *religious ethos or cultural identity*; in many instances, this may *lead to excluding women* from taking part in the interpretation or development of cultural or religious life."[279] [Emphasis Added]

The application of the principle of equal rights for women and men only in their dignity, and not allowing universal equality in their civil, political, economic, social and cultural rights and responsibilities, has resulted in de jure and de facto discrimination against women in Iran. Compelling examples include:

- Compulsory ḥijāb and receiving punishment in the case of failing to wear or properly comply with relevant rules
- Gender segregation
- A woman's testimony counts for half of that of a man's testimony
- Women require a male guardian's approval for marriage regardless of age
- Women are banned from becoming judges
- Polygamy and temporary-marriage allowed for men

277 *See e.g.*, Qanuni Assassi Jumhuri'i Islamai Iran [The Constitution of The Islamic Republic of Iran] 1358 [1980], art. 21.

278 General Assembly, *Secretary-General Transmit the report of the Special Rapporteur in the field of cultural rights (Farida Shaheed-Cultural rights) at its 67th Session,* ¶ 3, 62 at 2, 18, U.N. Doc. A/67/287 (Aug. 10, 2012).

279 *Id.* ¶ 62 at 18.

- Women cannot pass on their nationality to foreign-born spouses or their children
- Women remain unable to obtain a passport to travel outside the country without their husband's written permission
- Women have been excluded from many courses in universities[280]

Despite all the official reports of various international human rights bodies for almost 30 years, confirming the existence of systematic and systemic discrimination against women, it is ironic that Iran was elected by the Council as a member for a four-year term beginning at the Commission's sixtieth session's first meeting in 2015, and expiring at the close of the Commission's sixty-third session, to be held in 2019.[281]

2. TREATY-BASED BODIES

The United Nations treaty bodies monitor governments' implementation of relevant human rights treaties within their domestic legal system. Currently there are ten core international human rights treaties that set international standards for the protection and promotion of human rights in the domestic sphere of member States.[282] Each treaty creates an international committee of independent experts to monitor the implementation of its provisions,[283] such as the Human Rights Committee,[284] the Committee on Economic, Social and Cultural Rights,[285] and the Committee on the Elimination of Discrimination against Women.[286]

280 *E.g.*, ISLAMIC REPUBLIC OF IRAN MID-TERM IMPLEMENTATION ASSESSMENT, *supra* note 239, at 79-86.

281 *See* Elections, nominations, confirmations and appointments to subsidiary and related bodies of the Economic and Social Council, UN.ORG, at 2 (April 23, 2014), *accessed at* https://www.un.org/ecosoc/sites/www.un.org.ecosoc/files/documents/2014/dec.2014201.A.pdf.

282 U.N. HUMAN RIGHTS TREATY SYSTEM, *supra* note 60, at 1.

283 *See id.* at 19.

284 The Human Rights Committee was created in 1976 to review the application of the ICCPR that has 18 members. Hereinafter HR Committee.

285 The Committee on Economic, Social and Cultural Rights (CESCR) was created in 1985 to carry out the functions of the Economic, Social and Cultural Rights with 18 members.

286 The Committee on the Elimination of Discrimination against Women has reviewed the application of the CEDAW by its State parties since 1981 with 23 members.

Iran is a State party to two core international human rights treaties: ICCPR and ICESCR. Iran signed both ICCPR and ICESCR in 1968 and ratified them in 1975 without making any reservation.[287] The HR Committee and the CESCR examine and monitor the compliance of Iran with its treaty obligations to implement the guaranteed rights by the Covenants in its domestic legal system.

Treaty bodies are mandated to receive periodic reports by State parties in accordance with the treaty's provisions about the process of the application of the treaty provisions domestically. The treaty monitoring body, which is called the Committee, issues guidelines to help States with the preparation of their reports, draft "general comments"[288] interpreting the treaty provisions, and organizes discussions on themes related to the treaties.[289]

The State party is obligated to prepare and submit reports periodically to the relevant committees. The periodic reporting system by the State party not only is the fulfillment of an international obligation, but is also used as a key tool for the State to assess its achievements and failures to promote and protect human rights in the country.[290]

a. International Covenant on Civil and Political Rights

Pursuant to the adoption of the UDHR, in order to translate UN human rights principles into legally obligatory international human rights, it became essential to create legally binding documents.[291] As a result, two separate Covenants were adopted that are known as the International Covenant on Civil and Political Rights and the International Covenant on Economic, Social and Cultural Rights;[292] collectively guaranteeing civil, political, economic, social and cultural rights of individuals. The ICCPR is the most comprehensive and well-established treaty on civil and political rights.

---

287 *See* International Covenant on Civil and Political Rights, United Nations Treaties, *accessed at* https://treaties.un.org/doc/Publication/MTDSG/Volume%20I/Chapter%20IV/IV-4.en.pdf; International Covenant on Economic, Social and Cultural Rights, United Nations Treaties, *accessed at* https://treaties.un.org/doc/Publication/MTDSG/Volume%20I/Chapter%20IV/IV-3.en.pdf.

288 *See also* text *infra* note 337.

289 U.N. Human Rights Treaty System, *supra* note 60, at 21.

290 *Id.* at 24.

291 Rehman, *supra* note 6, at 62.

292 Women, Law & Development International (Human Rights Watch), *supra* note 16, at 10. *See also* International Human Rights Law, Six Decades, *supra* note 25, at 11.

The ICCPR was approved by the General Assembly resolution 2200A (XXI) in 1966 and entered into force in 1976.[293] Treaty obligations imposed by ICCPR are binding on States and do not have direct horizontal effect as a matter of international law. A failure to ensure rights enshrined in the Covenant would give rise to violations by States of those rights. This is a result of States Parties' permitting or failing to take appropriate measures, or to exercise due diligence to prevent, punish, investigate or redress the harm caused by such acts by private persons or entities.[294] Because of the contractual dimension of the treaty, the State party is obligated to comply fully with the provisions of the treaty.[295] According to Article 27 of the Vienna Convention on the Law of Treaties, concerning the domestic application of the treaty, the State party "may not invoke the provisions of its internal law as justification for its failure to perform a treaty."[296] Meaning a failure to comply with the treaty obligations cannot be justified by reference to "cultural relevance."[297]

Most treaty-based bodies establish a monitoring committee that through a periodic State reporting procedure examines the implementation of the relevant treaty-made obligations in the signatory States.[298] The HR Committee is the designated monitoring body for ICCPR according to Article 28(1) of the Covenant, which examines the State party's report and issues recommendations according to Article 40 of ICCPR.[299] Article 40(4) of the ICCPR permits the HR Committee to adopt authoritative General Comments that interpret or define specific rights enunciated in the Covenant.[300]

The Preamble and Articles 2(1), 3, and 26 of ICCPR establish equality and a comprehensive prohibition of discrimination. Similar to UDHR, the Preamble of

---

293 ICCPR *supra* note 34.

294 *See* Human Rights Committee General Comment No. 31 [80], *supra* note 80, ¶ 8 at 3. *See also* "horizontal system" *supra* note 48.

295 *Id.* ¶ 2 at 1.

296 VCLT, art. 27.

297 Human Rights Committee General Comment No. 31 [80], *supra* note 80, ¶ 14 at 6. *See also* Cultural Relativism in *supra* note 266.

298 *See* Deller Ross, *supra* note 9, at 91.

299 *See* ICCPR, arts. 28(1), 40.

300 *See id.* at Art. 40(4). *See also* Rehman, *supra* note 6, at 87.

ICCPR reaffirms the general Charter based human rights obligations to promote universal respect for, and observance of, human rights and freedoms for all.[301]

Article 2 of ICCPR sets obligations for the State parties toward individuals as the right-holders under the Covenant. Article 2(1) states:

> "Each State Party to the present Covenant undertakes to respect and to ensure to all individuals within its territory and subject to its jurisdiction the rights recognized in the present Covenant, *without distinction of any kind*, such as race, colour, *sex*, language, religion, political or other opinion, national or social origin, property, birth or other status."[302] [Emphasis Added]

Article 2(1) creates the concept of "non-discrimination" and obliges the State party to "respect" and "ensure" all the rights recognized in the Covenant to all persons within its territory with the right not to being distinguished in any way on the prohibited grounds.[303] Accordingly, this general concept of application of non-discrimination also includes elimination of gender-based discrimination.

This article imposes both negative and positive measures on the State in order to fulfill its international obligations toward its citizens. Not only must the State refrain from violating or restricting the rights enunciated in the Covenant, but it must also adopt affirmative legislative, judicial, administrative, educational and other appropriate measures to fulfill its obligations under the treaty.[304] According to the Committee, the non-discrimination clause calls for an immediate application, and upon becoming a party to the Covenant, States should eliminate all discriminatory laws to ensure the enjoyment of the rights enshrined in the Covenant.[305] Further Article 2(2) reads:

> "Where not already provided for by existing legislative or other measures, each State Party to the present Covenant *undertakes* to take the *necessary steps*, in accordance with its constitutional processes and with the provisions of the

301 *See id.* at Preamble, arts. 2(1), 3, 26. *See also* Sarah Joseph, Jenny Schultz, Melissa Castan, The International Covenant On Civil and Political Rights 518 (Oxford University Press 2000).

302 ICCPR, art 2(1).

303 *See id.* at Art. 2; Human Rights Committee, General Comment No. 18: Non-Discrimination, ¶ 1 at 1 (Nov. 10, 1989).

304 *See* Human Rights Committee General Comment No. 31 [80], *supra* note 80, ¶ 6, 7 at 3.

305 *See id.* ¶ 5 at 3.

present Covenant, *to adopt* such laws or other measures as may be *necessary to give effect* to the rights recognized in the present Covenant."[306] [Emphasis Added]

This article lays out the State responsibilities and requires State parties take "necessary steps" to give effect to the enunciated rights in the Covenant in their domestic laws. In the absence of the guaranteed rights of the Covenant in their domestic legal system, State parties are required on ratification to make such changes within their domestic system to ensure their conformity with the rights enshrined in the Covenant.[307] This emphasizes the implementation of universal human rights as a primary source of law in a domestic matter.[308] If domestic laws are contrary to the rights enunciated in the Covenant, Article 2 of the Covenant requires that the domestic laws be changed by domestic legislation to facilitate full realization of the Covenant rights.[309]

The non-discrimination principle laid down in Article 2, however, has an accessory character when it comes to imposing duties on the member States. This means that the violation of Article 2 cannot happen independently and can happen only in conjunction with the exercise of one of the fundamental numerated rights in the Covenant.[310]

Further, Article 3 of the Covenant explicitly guarantees the principle of gender equality. It reads:

"The State Parties to the present Covenant undertake to ensure the *equal right of men and women* to the enjoyment of all civil and political rights set forth in the present Covenant."[311] [Emphasis Added]

Similar to the dependent nature of the non-discrimination clause, Article 3 also has the accessory character and can be violated only when it is based on the gender-specific discrimination that affects some other rights guaranteed by the

306 ICCPR, art. 2(2).

307 *See* Human Rights Committee General Comment No. 31 [80], *supra* note 80, ¶ 13 at 5.

308 *See* Manfred Nowak, U.N. Covenant on Civil and Political Rights 27 (N.P. Engel 1993).

309 *See* Human Rights Committee General Comment No. 31 [80], *supra* note 80, ¶ 13 at 5.

310 Nowak, *supra* note 308, at 28, 33.

311 ICCPR, art. 3.

Covenant.[312] Although, it first appears that Article 3 repeats Article 2 in some ways, it is not a mere repetition. Rather, the specific additional prohibition of gender-specific discrimination is strengthened by this article and imposes additional duties on the States concerning equality between women and men.[313]

In addition to the accessory prohibition of all kinds of discrimination enshrined in Article 2(1), Article 26 provides a comprehensive and independent right to equality before the law.[314] Article 26 reads:

> "All persons are *equal before the law* and are entitled *without any discrimination to the equal protection of the law.* In this respect, the *law* shall *prohibit any discrimination* and guarantee to all persons equal and effective protection against discrimination on any ground such as race, colour, *sex*, language, religion, political or other opinion, national or social origin, property, birth or other status."[315] [Emphasis Added]

The non-discrimination principle laid down in this article is significant, because it is not only applicable to the civil and political rights guaranteed by ICCPR, but it goes beyond the scope of this Convention and will apply even if a particular subject-matter is referred to or covered in other international instruments, like economic, social and cultural rights in the ICESCR. Undisputedly, according to Maastricht Guidelines on Violations of Economic, Social and Cultural Rights, all human rights are indivisible, interdependent, interrelated and of equal importance for human dignity.[316]

The landmark decision in *S.W.M. Broeks v. Netherlands* clarified the scope of Article 26 asserting that Article 26 does not merely duplicate the guarantees already provided for in Article 2. It derives from the principle of equal protection of the law without discrimination, as contained in Article 7 of the Universal

312 NOWAK, *supra* note 308, at 69.

313 *Id.* at 69,70.

314 *Id.* at 465.

315 ICCPR, art. 26.

316 *See* S.W.M. Broeks v. Netherlands, Communication. No. 172/1984, ¶ 12(1), UN. Doc. CCPR/OP/2 at 196 (1990); International Commission of Jurists, Maastricht Guidelines on Violations of Economic, Social and Cultural Rights, ¶ 4 at 2 (Jan. 22-26, 1997).

Declaration of Human Rights, which prohibits de jure and de facto discrimination that is regulated and protected by public authorities.[317]

The prohibition of discrimination manifested in this article highlights the negative aspect of the right to equal protection the law. The State parties are obligated not to discriminate in their laws regardless of whether this has to do with the regulation of rights of the Covenant or of other human rights or with other subjective rights or duties.[318]

As part of States' obligation, Article 26 obligates the national legislature to refrain from every form of discrimination in all laws.[319] Additionally, States should take all necessary steps to enable every person to enjoy the enumerated rights. These steps, for example, include removal of obstacles to the equal enjoyment of such rights and adjustment of domestic legislation.[320]

In the case of women being barred from judgeships in Iran, the issue is whether the imposed male gender qualification for judges by the legislature constitutes discrimination against women under international law. The express provisions of ICCPR fail to define what constitutes discrimination or discrimination against women. However, the HR Committee in its General Comment No. 18 defines discrimination as:

> "Discrimination as used in the Covenant should be understand to imply any *distinction, exclusion, restriction or preference* which is based on any ground such as race, colour, *sex*, language, religion, political or other opinion, national or social origin property, birth or other status, and which has the *purpose or effect of nullifying or impairing* the recognition, enjoyment or exercise by all persons, on an equal footing, of all rights and freedoms."[321] [Emphasis Added]

According to this definition, the explicit male gender requirement for granting judgeships laid down by the 1982 Law on the Qualifications for Appointment of

317 *See* S.W.M. Broeks v. Netherlands, ¶ 12(3). *See also* Article 7 of the UDHR: "All are equal before the law and are entitled without any discrimination to equal protection of the law. All are entitled to equal protection against any discrimination in violation of this Declaration and against any incitement to such discrimination."

318 Nowak, *supra* note 308, at 469.

319 *Id.* at 473, 474.

320 *See* Human Rights Committee, *General Comment No. 28: Article 3 (The Equality of Rights between Men and Women)*, ¶ 3 at 1, U.N. Doc. HRI/GEN/1/Rev.9 (Vol. I) (May 27, 2008).

321 Human Rights Committee, General Comment No. 18: Non-Discrimination, ¶ 7 at 2 (Nov. 10, 1989).

Judges makes the distinction and exclusion purposely on the ground of sex to ban women from becoming judges. The law states judges can be selected only among men, excluding women. The intentional distinction has been made on the ground of sex to exclude women from becoming judges. If she were a man otherwise qualified, the law in question would not deprive her of a judgeship. The lawmakers purposely nullify and impair a woman's equal rights to enjoy the right to be employed as a judge and be treated equally by laws regardless of her gender. Therefore, the 1982 Law on the Qualifications for Appointment of Judges is a de jure discrimination against women in Iran.

Iran as a State party to ICCPR is legally bound to implement guaranteed rights enumerated in the Covenant in its domestic legal system upon ratification and to act with good faith at all times. A failure to comply with its treaty obligations constitutes a violation of the Covenant under international law. Articles 2, 3, and 26 require equal protection of the law without gender discrimination and prohibit discrimination in law or in practice in any field regulated by public authorities.

The de jure discrimination imposed by the 1982 law is contrary to Article 26 in conjunction with Articles 2 and 3 of the ICCPR. This law was passed in 1982 after Iran had ratified the ICCPR. The passage of the de jure discriminatory law on the basis of a prohibited ground, sex, after becoming a State party to the ICCPR, is a failure of Iran to comply with its treaty obligations. The application of Articles 2, 3, and 26 requires that upon ratification Iran must refrain from passing discriminatory laws that discriminate against women. Instead, it passed the 1982 law that explicitly discriminates against women. This is an indication of Iran's failure to comply with its treaty obligations, which is to refrain from violating or restricting the rights enunciated in the Covenant upon ratification. This counts as a violation of the Charter, UDHR, and ICCPR under international law.

Also, considering the immediate nature of the application of equal rights and non-gender discrimination in all rights enshrined in the Covenant on one hand, and Iran's passage of laws to create positions such as "consultant women judges" in Family Courts with very limited authority on the other hand, is a clear indication of Iran's deliberate retarding of, and unwillingness to, repeal its discriminatory 1982 statute, which is manifestly inconsistent with its obligation under the Covenant. This once again is a violation of the Covenant under international law.

The Human Rights Committee

In 2010, Iran submitted its Third Periodic Report according to Article 40 of ICCPR to the Human Rights Committee. In this report, Iran expressly indicated that it had taken positive measures to promote human rights of women under Article 3 of ICCPR consistent with its Islamic and cultural norms,[322] stating:

> "The strategy of the Islamic Republic of Iran is to protect human rights, justice and trust which have their roots in *Islamic and Iranian culture* and based on *non-discrimination* and respect for human rights. Accordingly, many measures and legal facilities are put in place to promote human rights of women at individual, family and social levels."[323] [Emphasis Added]

According to this report, the importance of women's rights is underlined, for example, by the Constitution, legislation based on gender balance and equity, and designation of various mechanisms for the advancement of women.[324]

Iran, however, defined what constitutes gender equality between women and men as the key principle attributed to its domestic laws. It read:

> "Gender *equity* can also include gender *equality*, but *does not entail equality in all places....* Consequently, at the *individual* level, there is full equality between men and women in respect of law and women are regarded purely as *human beings.* At social and family levels, in matters relating to *employment* and *political rights*, participation of women underlines the *importance of family and respect for all persons, be they men or women.*"[325] [Emphasis Added]

According to the report commissioned by the Office of the High Commission for Human Rights, Women's Rights and Gender Unit, "Project on a Mechanism to Address Laws that Discriminate Against Women,"

---

322 *See* Human Rights Committee, *Consideration of reports submitted by States parties under article 40 of the Covenant,* ¶ 207 at 46, U.N. Doc. CCPR/C/IRN/3 (May 31, 2010).

323 *Id.*

324 *See id.* ¶ 208-214 at 46-47.

325 *Id.* ¶ 212 at 47.

> Notwithstanding what appears to be clear normative commitments to achieving equality between the sexes, the practice of State parties, indicates that there is still *equivocation* over the principle of *non-discrimination based on sex.* States...sometimes *seek to invoke national, cultural or religious justifications for the non-implementation of equality,* claiming that the *local interpretation of the norm is at variance with the international.*[326] [Emphasis Added]

The government despite reaffirming its full compliance with the principles of "equal rights of women and men" and "non-discrimination" guaranteed by the Covenant, also cited to its cultural justification as the prevailing standard to interpret the norm in its domestic legal system as it pertains to women's rights.[327]

Concerning the ban of women from the judgeships in Iran, this State report, similar to other reports to the UPR and Human Rights Council, did not make any reference to the Law on the Qualifications for Appointment of Judges or the law Transferring Women with Judicial Titles from the Ministry of Justice to other Ministries and Conversion of their Judicial Titles to Administrative. Instead, it reaffirmed the existence of women judges in Iran by exemplifying the number of women judges in the total of 161[328] in 2003.

Despite Iran's sleight of hand in its attempt to show the existence of authoritative women judges, the Committee was not convinced. In the List of Issues report by the HR Committee after considering Iran's State Report, the Committee raised a question:

> "Why women cannot become presiding judges?"[329]

The Islamic Republic of Iran's response:

326 Fareda Banda, Project on a Mechanism to Address Laws that Discriminate Against Women, Office of the High Commissioner for Human Rights and Gender Unit, at 17 (March 6, 2008), *accessed at* http://www.ohchr.org/Documents/Publications/laws_that_discriminate_against_women.pdf.

327 *See e.g.*, Human Rights Committee States parties under article 40, *supra* note 322, ¶ 254, 251 at 59; ¶ 212 at 47.

328 *See id.* ¶ 244 at 54.

329 Human Rights Committee, *List of issues to be taken up in connection with the consideration of the third periodic report of the Islamic Republic of Iran,* ¶ 2(c) at 1, U.N. Doc. CCPR/C/IRN/Q/3 (May 17, 2011).

"The IRI has taken *promotional measures* to absorb women for incumbency of *judicial* positions.

The following is an indication of this reality:

Statistics on *Women Judges*:"[330] [Emphasis Added]

Assistant Public and Revolutionary Prosecutor	497
Judicial Counseling	82
Deputy Head	18
Counselor	10
Deputy Prosecutor	7
Total	**614**

According to this report the IRI government first asserts that measures have been taken to "absorb women for incumbency of judicial positions," providing the "chart" as evidence to this claim giving the number of 614 as its total. However, the misleading part is where the government's claim—by providing the chart as evidence for an increase in the number of women in judiciary positions—does not match the title of the chart. The title of the chart reads "Statistics on Women Judges." Clearly, the government is asserting the number of women judges as 614 by providing this chart and its title. But according to the content of the chart that indicates various positions in the judicial system and not judgeships, the title should be the "number of women working in the judicial system," and not "Statistics on Women Judges." The asserted response to the Committee is confusing, vague, and contrary to what Article 167 of the IRI's Constitution and other local laws require for judges with full authority to render a final decision of the court and end a dispute.

The nature and powers of the provided positions in this chart are very different from judgeship positions according to the supreme law of the land; none of these count as judges according to the Constitution. Over 500 of these persons

330 Human Rights Committee, *Replies from the Government of the Islamic Republic of Iran to the List of Issues*, ¶ 9 at 3, U.N. Doc. CCPR/C/IRN/Q/3/Add.1 (Sep. 12, 2011).

are prosecutors. A Prosecutor is not a judge. Likewise, while counselors may serve a useful function, a counselor is not a judge. This chart despite its title "women judges," misleadingly gives the statistics for non-judgeship positions but counts them as judges. This is an assertion to mislead the Committee and Iran fails to report and act with good faith under international law, which counts as a violation under international law.

The HR Committee in its Concluding Observation, after considering the Third Periodic Report of the IRI, explicitly stated, "women are *excluded* from certain public positions, such as the post of *judge*."[331] [Emphasis added]

The Committee recommended that Iran "should take steps to increase the number of women in decision-making and judicial bodies at all levels and in all areas."[332] The Committee also raised its concerns about Iran's system that is based on religious norms and asserted:

> "The State party *should ensure that all the obligations of the Covenant are fully respected* and that the provisions of its *internal norms* are *not invoked as justification* for its *failure* to follow its obligations under the Covenant."[333] [Emphasis Added]

b. International Covenant on Economic, Social, and Cultural Rights

The International Covenant on Economic, Social, and Cultural Rights, adopted at the same time as the ICCPR and entered into force in 1976,[334] is the fundamental treaty on economic, social and cultural rights. Unlike ICCPR that established an independent monitoring body, the provisions of ICESCR did not initially establish a similar independent monitoring body. As a result, the monitoring duty was left to the UN Economic and Social Council. It was in 1985 that the ECOSOC resolution 1985/17 established the independent expert body to supervise the

331 Human Rights Committee, *Consideration of reports submitted by States parties under article 40 of the Covenant Concluding observations of the Human Rights Committee Islamic Republic of Iran*, ¶ 8 at 2, U.N. Doc. CCPR/C/IRN/CO/3 (Nov. 29, 2011).

332 *Id.* ¶ 8 at 2.

333 *Id.* ¶ 5 at 2.

334 The International Covenant on Economic, Social, and Cultural Rights, G.A. res. 2200A (XXI), 21 U.N.GAOR Supp. (No. 16) at 49, U.N. Doc. A/6316 (1966), 993 U.N.T.S. 3, *entered into force* Jan. 3, 1976.

implementation of the ICESCR provisions that was called the Committee on Economic, Social, and Cultural Rights.[335]

The Committee on Economic, Social, and Cultural Rights[336] like the HR Committee, in numerous general comments and concluding observations on the periodic reports, adopts and elaborates on the individual economic social and cultural rights and the State's obligations under the Covenant. Despite a general comment's non-binding nature, they can still have a persuasive effect, setting out interpretive positions around which state practice may unite. No state has ever raised any formal objections to the general comments or statements of the CESCR, which suggests wide acceptance by State parties.[337]

Similar to the ICCPR, the general Charter-based State obligations to promote respect for, and observance of, human rights and freedoms are emphasized in the Preamble of the ICESCR. The Preamble of ICESCR also reaffirms the fundamental principle of equal rights for all.[338]

Identical to the HR Committee, the CESCR also explicitly defines discrimination in its General Comment No. 20 as:

> "Discrimination constitutes any *distinction, exclusion, restriction* or *preference* or other *differential treatment* that is directly or indirectly *based on* the *prohibited grounds of discrimination* and which has the intention or effect of *nullifying or impairing* the recognition, enjoyment or exercise, on an equal footing, of Covenant rights."[339] [Emphasis Added]

According to the Committee, "different treatment" based on prohibited grounds such as sex is discrimination unless it is based on a reasonable and objective justification.[340] Due to an identical definition of discrimination offered by both the Human Rights Committee and CESCR, this section will not repeat the same

335 *See* Economic and Social Council Res. 1985/17, ¶ (a), (b) at 1-2 (May 28, 1985).

336 *Supra* note 117.

337 International Human Rights Law, Six Decades, *supra* note 25, at 56.

338 *See* ICESCR, Preamble.

339 Committee on Economic, Social and Cultural Rights General Comment No. 20, *supra* note 118, ¶ 7 at 3.

340 *See id.* ¶ 13 at 5.

analysis to prove the existence of discrimination against women imposed by the 1982 statute.[341]

Article 2 of ICESCR sets key principles as well as general obligations for the State party to recognize the economic, social and cultural rights as follows:

> 1. Each State Party to the present Covenant undertakes to *take steps*, individually and through international assistance and co-operation, especially economic and technical, *to the maximum of its available resources*, with a view to *achieving progressively the full realization of the rights* recognized in the present Covenant by *all appropriate means, including particularly the adoption of legislative measures*. [Emphasis Added]
> 2. The States Parties to the present Covenant undertake to *guarantee* that the rights enunciated in the present Covenant will be exercised *without discrimination of any kind* as to race, colour, *sex*, language, religion, political or other opinion, national or social origin, property, birth or other status.[342] [Emphasis Added]

Article 2(1) of ICESCR limits the State obligations to "take steps" to the "maximum of its available resources" toward the full enjoyment of the economic, social and cultural rights[343] in the Covenant by all.[344] This requires the States to begin immediately to take steps towards full realization of these rights, and failure to comply with this obligation cannot be justified by reference to national social, cultural or economic considerations. However, what constitutes "taking steps" is left to the discretion of the State to select what it considers the most appropriate means for the full realization of ESC rights.[345]

Article 2(2) binds the State party to the principle of elimination of all kinds of discrimination, and obliges each State party to guarantee that all the rights enunciated in the Covenant be exercised without discrimination on the prohibited

341 *See* analysis of discrimination under ICCPR.

342 ICESCR, art. 2.

343 Economic, social and cultural rights, hereinafter ESC rights.

344 *See* ICESCR, art. 2(1).

345 International Human Rights Law, Six Decades, *supra* note 25, at 56. *See also* Committee on Economic, Social and Cultural Rights, General Comments No. 18, *supra* note 73, ¶ 19 at 6.

grounds such as sex.[346] According to the General Comments of the Committee, elimination of discrimination is an "immediate and cross-cutting" State obligation under the Covenant as relates to the enunciated rights. Accordingly, this makes the elimination of both formal and substantive discrimination an imminent treaty obligation of the State party to guarantee the enjoyment of the rights enshrined in the Covenant.[347] It is essential for the State party to pass a comprehensive anti-discriminatory law, guaranteeing protection against discrimination in the enjoyment of all the economic, social and cultural rights in the Covenant for all in order to be in full compliance with Article 2(2).[348]

With respect to the treaty principles being contrary to the domestic laws, as previously mentioned, Article 27 of Vienna Convention on the law of treaties states:

> "A party may not invoke the provisions of its internal law as justification for its failure to perform a treaty."[349]

Concerning the principle of gender equality, Article 3 of the Covenant states:

> "The State Parties to the present Covenant undertake to ensure the equal right of men and women to the enjoyment of all economic, social and cultural rights set forth in the present Covenant."[350]

Article 3 of the ICESCR prescribes that the State undertakes to "ensure the equal right of women and men to the enjoyment of all economic, social, and cultural rights."[351] The Committee asserts that there is a need for a comprehensive system of protection to combat gender discrimination and to ensure equal opportunities and treatment between women and men in relation to work.[352]

---

346 *See* Committee on Economic, Social and Cultural Rights General Comment No. 20, *supra* note 118, ¶ 7 at 3.

347 *Id.* ¶ 7, 8 at 3.

348 *See id.* ¶ 37 at 11.

349 VCLT, art. 27.

350 ICESCR, art. 3.

351 Committee on Economic, Social and Cultural Rights, General Comments No. 18, *supra* note 73, ¶ 13 at 5.

352 *See id.*

According to the Committee, Article 3 goes beyond a prohibition of discrimination and emphasizes "the same rights should be expressly recognized for women and men on an equal footing and suitable measures should be taken to ensure that women had the opportunity to exercise their rights."[353] Accordingly, it is necessary to reaffirm the equality rights between women and men once again and this "must be constantly emphasized, especially as there were still many prejudices preventing its full application."[354]

Unlike Article 26 of the ICCPR, Articles 2(2) and 3 of ICESCR are not independent provisions and should be applied in conjunction with other elaborated rights under the Covenant.[355]

Article 6(1) of ICESCR explicitly recognizes and guarantees the "right to work" more comprehensively than any other texts. It reads:

> "The States parties to the present Covenant recognize the *right to work*, which includes the right of everyone to the *opportunity* to gain his living by work which he *freely chooses* or accepts, and will take appropriate steps to safeguard this right."[356] [Emphasis Added]

The right to work is one of the fundamental human rights and part of economic, social, and cultural rights.[357] As part of the right to work, every individual has the right to freely decide to accept or choose her/his work, which includes the right not to be deprived of work unfairly.[358] The respect for the individual and her dignity is expressed through the freedom of the individual regarding the choice to work.[359]

---

353 Committee on Economic, Social and Cultural Rights, General Comments No. 16, *supra* note 72, ¶ 2 at 1.

354 *Id.* at 2.

355 *E.g., id.*

356 ICESCR, art. 6.

357 International Human Rights Law, Six Decades, *supra* note 25, at 51.

358 *See* ICESCR, art. 6(1); Committee on Economic, Social and Cultural Rights, General Comments No. 18, *supra* note, 73, ¶ 4 at 3.

359 *See* Committee on Economic, Social and Cultural Rights, General Comments No. 18, *supra* note, 73, ¶ 4 at 3.

Women are among the groups whose "equal opportunity" or "free choices" in employment have been repeatedly violated on the basis of their gender.[360] Stereotypical ideas about the distribution of "male" and "female" tasks and capabilities lead to direct discrimination against women in access to employment.[361] A good example would be taking women's stereotypical physical and psychological differences into account as is reflected in the 1982 Law on the Qualifications for Appointment of Judges in Iran that explicitly requires a male gender as one of the core qualifications for judges.

The guaranteed right to work enumerated in Article 6 of the Covenant is interdependent like other human rights; meaning the exercise of work in all its forms and levels requires the existence of other elements, implementation of which will depend on the conditions present in each State party. For example, "accessibility"[362] and "availability"[363] are the two interdependent essential components of the right to work.[364] Out of the two, "accessibility" is the most relevant element regarding the male gender requirement by the 1982 law in Iran. According to the Committee, the labor market must be "open to everyone" under the jurisdiction of State parties. Collectively, under Articles 2(2) and 3 in conjunction with Article 6 of the Covenant, gender-specific discrimination is prohibited in access to and maintenance of employment.[365]

The most important obligation regarding the right to work imposed on the State party with an "immediate effect" is the responsibility to guarantee that the right to work will be exercised without discrimination of any kind–Article 2(2) and the obligation to take steps toward the full realization of the rights recognized in the Covenant of to the maximum of its available resources–Article 2(1).[366]

---

360 Rehman, *supra* note 6, at 112-113.

361 ILO ABC of Women Workers' Right and Gender Equality, *supra* note 71, at 51.

362 Accessibility according to the Committee: the labor market must be open to everyone under the jurisdiction of State parties.

363 According to the Committee, availability, States must have specialized services to assist and support individuals in order to enable them to identify and find available employment.

364 Committee on Economic, Social and Cultural Rights, General Comments No. 18, *supra* note 73, ¶ 12 at 4.

365 *Id.*

366 *See id.* ¶ 19 at 6.

The Committee also distinguishes between the "inability" and "unwillingness" of the State parties to comply with their treaty obligations. In their general comments they elaborated that the State parties that are unwilling to use the maximum of their available resources for the realization of the right to work are in violation of their treaty obligations.[367]

Article 6 of the ICESCR guarantees the fundamental right to work that freely should be chosen by all regardless of their gender. As a State party to ICESCR, Iran is legally obligated to respect and protect the equal right to work for women to gain access to making a living that she freely chooses regardless of her gender including judgeship positions. The core obligation encompasses the obligation to ensure non-discrimination and equal protection of employment. This requires that Iran refrain from denying or limiting equal access to work for women in the first place, and take measures to combat discrimination and promote equal access and opportunities for them. Iran by the passing the de jure discriminatory law of 1982 after ratifying the ICESCR fails to respect the right of women to have equal access to work regardless of their gender that is guaranteed by various provisions of the ICESCR. Iran failed to refrain from violating the equal right to work for women enshrined in the Covenant. This counts as a violation of the ICESCR.

Furthermore, upholding and enforcing the 1982 law for over thirty-three years is a clear departure by Iran from its core treaty obligations to implement equal right to work for women without gender discrimination, which the Covenant requires the State to implement immediately. This also constitutes a violation of the treaty under international law. Continuous passage of additional laws to create positions with limited authority such as consultant women judges in Family Courts is an indication of the intent and unwillingness of the government to eliminate the de jure discrimination from its laws and act with good faith. This also constitutes a violation of the ICESCR under international law.

Committee on Economic, Social and Cultural Rights

In 1993, the Summary Record of the seventh meeting of the CESCR raised questions about how far the equal right to work had been expanded in Iran

367 *See id.* ¶ 32, 33 at 9.

and "whether there were any women judges" in Iran.[368] The IRI delegation in its response stated, "women could become magistrates."[369] The CESCR in its Concluding Observations (1993) states that various articles of the Constitution such as Articles 20, 24, and 28 restrict the enjoyment of universally recognized human rights, including economic, social and cultural rights, by enunciating "as long as it is not contrary to Islam," or limiting the enjoyment of rights to "in conformity with Islamic criteria."[370] The Committee concluded "such restrictive clauses negatively affect the application of the Covenant, in particular Articles 2(2) and Article 3 in conjunction with Article 6.[371] They declared that the government clearly uses "the religion as a pretext in order to abuse these rights."[372]

The Committee also asserted its particular concern with regard to the non-performance by the IRI government of its obligations under Article 3 of the Covenant to undertake to ensure the equality of women and men in their economic, social and cultural rights. With regards to the status of women pursuing judgeships, they concluded contrary to the IRI's assertion, that "women are *not* permitted to become magistrates."[373] [Emphasis Added]

Pursuant to submission of the Second Periodic Report of the IRI to the Committee in 2011, with regards to implementation of Article 3 of ICESCR, questions were raised concerning the equal rights of women and men to the enjoyment of all their ESC rights. The IRI in its response to the question "please indicate which measures are being taken to increase the number of women in decision-making positions in the public sector,"[374] indicated that the government appointed "women as judicial counselor and judges."[375]

---

368 Committee on Economic, Social and Cultural Rights, *Summary Record of the 7th Meeting,* ¶ 30 at 7, U.N. Doc. E/C.12/1993/SR.7 (June 3, 1993).

369 Committee on Economic, Social and Cultural Rights, *Summary Record of the 8th Meeting,* ¶ 36 at 7, U.N. Doc. E/C.12/1993/SR. 8 (Dec. 20, 1993).

370 Committee on Economic, Social and Cultural Rights, *Concluding observations of the Committee on Economic, Social and Cultural Rights Iran,* ¶ 4 at 2, U.N. Doc. E/C.12/1993/7 (June 9, 1993).

371 *Id.*

372 *Id.*

373 *See id.* ¶ 6 at 3.

374 *See* Committee on Economic, Social and Cultural Rights, *List of issues in connection with the consideration of the second periodic report of the Islamic Republic of Iran concerning articles 1 to 15 of the International Covenant on Economic, Social and Cultural Rights (E/C.12/IRN/2),* ¶ 6 at 2, U.N. Doc. E/C.12/IRN/Q/2 (June 8, 2012).

375 Committee on Economic, Social and Cultural Rights, *Replies of the Islamic Republic of Iran to the list of issues,* ¶ 21 at 9, U.N. Doc. E/C.12/IRN/Q/2/Add.1 (April 17, 2013).

The Committee, in its Concluding Observation pursuant to considering the Second Periodic Report of the IRI, yet again explicitly asserted its concern about the exclusion of women from becoming presiding judges over a court.[376]

Despite misleading reports submitted by the IRI government to the Committee, yet again it is proven to the Committee that women are banned from becoming judges in Iran. This is similar to other reports, for example, submitted by Iran to the Human Rights Committee and Special Rapporteurs that there are women judges in Iran. According to the Vienna Convention on the Law of Treaties, treaties should be interpreted in good faith, taking into account the object and purpose, and the ordinary meaning. The IRI government, by providing false and misleading reports to the Committee, continues to insist on the existence of women judges in Iran, which once again is a failure of government to report and act with good faith on its compliance. This constitutes a violation under international law.

376 *See* Committee on Economic, Social and Cultural Rights, *Concluding observations on the second periodic report of the Islamic Republic of Iran, adopted by the Committee at its fiftieth session (29 April-17 May 2013)*, ¶ 10 at 3, U.N. Doc. E/C.12/IRN/CO/2 (June 10, 2013).

ILO Employment and Occupation Convention (No. 111)

The International Labour Organization was found in 1919,[377] and today is a specialized agency of the United Nations that aims for the promotion of social justice and internationally recognized human and labor rights.[378] The general principles of elimination of discrimination and promotion of equality have been essential since the creation of this Convention.[379] The ILO Employment and Occupation Convention (No. 111)[380] addresses the elimination of any discrimination such as sex, race, and political opinion, and recognizes equality of opportunity and treatment in respect to employment for all, including women.[381] Like other conventions, the ILO Conventions are international treaties open to ratification by ILO member States. Upon ratification, a State party is legally bound to apply the provisions of the ratified convention in its domestic laws.[382] Iran ratified the ILO Employment and Occupation Convention (No. 111) in 1964.[383]

---

377 The Constitution of the International Labour Organization, adopted by the Peace Conference in April of 1919, established the International Labour Organization.

378 ILO has its own Constitution, membership, organs, budgets and staff. As its main activity, it sets international labor standards in the form of conventions and recommendations and supervises the application of these established norms by governments in their domestic system. Women, Law & Development International (Human Rights Watch), *supra* note 25, at 45.

379 ILO ABC of Women Workers' Right and Gender Equality, *supra* note 71, at 3.

380 ILO Convention concerning Discrimination in Respect of Employment and Occupation (C111), Discrimination (Employment and Occupation) Convention 362 U.N.T.S. 31, *entered into force* June 15, 1960. Hereinafter ILO Employment and Occupation Convention (No. 111).

381 *See* ILO Convention No. 111, arts. 1(a), 2. *See also* ILO ABC of Women Workers' Right and Gender Equality, *supra* note 71, at 6.

382 *See* ILO Convention No. 111, Preamble, art. 8(1). *See also* ILO ABC of Women Workers' Right and Gender Equality, *supra* note 71, at 5.

383 *See* International Labour Organization, *Ratifications for Islamic Republic of Iran*, International Labour Organization, *accessed at* http://www.ilo.org/dyn/normlex/en/f?p=NORMLEXPUB:11200:0::NO::P11200_COUNTRY_ID:102800.

The Preamble emphasizes the importance of combating discrimination in the field of employment and reaffirms that all humans regardless of their race or sex have the right to pursue their material well being in a condition of freedom of economic security and equal opportunity. Article 1(a) of the ILO Employment and Occupation Convention (No. 111) also defines discrimination as:

> "Any *distinction, exclusion* or preference made on the basis of race, colour, *sex*, religion, political opinion, national extraction or social origin, which has the effect of nullifying or impairing equality of opportunity or treatment in employment or occupation."[384] [Emphasis Added]

Concerning the obligation of the State party under the Convention, Article 2 obligates each State as follows:

> "Each Member for which this Convention is in force undertakes to declare and pursue a national policy designed to *promote*, by methods appropriate to national conditions and practice, *equality of opportunity* and *treatment* in respect of employment and occupation, with a view *to eliminating any discrimination* in respect thereof."[385] [Emphasis Added]

For a number of years the Committee and the Conference Committee have raised concerns regarding de jure discrimination against women in Iran, and urged the government to amend or repeal them. The Observation report published in 2013 declares that despite the IRI government's report on the increasing number of women judges, the Committee noted that the government does not address the issue of giving women access to all positions in the judiciary, including those qualified to hand down judgments. It continues that no concrete steps appear to have been taken to tackle statutory limitations on the selection of judges.[386]

The Committee emphasizes that the primary obligation of the State to ratify the ILO Employment and Occupation Convention (No. 111) is to pursue a national policy designed to promote equality of opportunity and treatment in

384 ILO Convention No. 111, art. 1(a).

385 *Id.* at Art. 2.

386 *See* International Labour Organization, *Observation (CEACR) - adopted 2012, published 102d ILC session* (2013), International Labour Organization, *accessed at* http://www.ilo.org/dyn/normlex/en/f?p=1000:13100:0::NO:13100:P13100_COMMENT_ID:3085370.

respect of employment and eliminate all discrimination according to Article 2 of the Convention. The Committee declares that repealing any statutory provisions that are discriminatory are required immediately under the Convention.[387]

The Committee, once again, strongly urges the IRI government, "to *repeal* or amend the *discriminatory laws* and regulations, and given that this is an *immediate* obligation under the Convention, the Committee strongly urges the Government to take concrete and immediate steps to ensure the repeal, effective amendment or modification of all laws, regulations, instructions or practices that *hinder women's equality of opportunity and treatment* in employment and occupation, including...the role of *female judges*."[388] [Emphasis Added]

The continuous uncertainty of the Committee about the power of women as judges and whether female judges are authorized to hand down judgments on an equal footing with male judges in Iran was addressed in 2014 and 2015.[389] In 2015, the Committee welcomed capacity building for judges according to the ILO standards and the promotion of women's participation in the labor market.[390]

387 *See id.*

388 *Id.*

389 *See* International Labour Organization, *Observation (CEACR) - adopted 2013, published 103d ILC session (2014)*, INTERNATIONAL LABOUR ORGANIZATION, *accessed at* http://www.ilo.org/dyn/normlex/en/f?p=1000:13100:0::NO:13100:P13100_COMMENT_ID:3148594; International Labour Organization, *Observation (CEACR) - adopted 2014, published 104th ILC session* (2015), INTERNATIONAL LABOUR ORGANIZATION, *accessed at* http://www.ilo.org/dyn/normlex/en/f?p=1000:13100:0::NO:13100:P13100_COMMENT_ID:3192151:NO.

390 *See id.*

Summary of the Violations of Women's Human Rights in Iran: Judgeships

The 1982 Law on the Qualifications for Appointment of Judges explicitly asserts, "Judges will be selected among qualified men."[391] The substantive issue is whether the direct statutory exclusion of women from pursuing judgeships, and giving the exclusive right to only men, constitutes discrimination against women and violates women's guaranteed human rights under international human rights mechanisms.

The de jure discrimination against women imposed by the 1982 statute requires us to examine whether the twin UN jurisprudence of prohibition of discrimination on the ground of sex, and equal rights of women and men in the exercise of right to work, were respected and ensured by Iran according to provisions of the Charter, UDHR, ICCPR, ICESCR and ILO Convention (No.111). Was the right of equality before the laws, and entitlement to equal protection of the law without gender discrimination for women, ensured by Iran according to the provisions of the UDHR, and the ICCPR?

The CEDAW, the ILO Employment and Occupation Convention, the CESCR, and the HR Committee, among others, have explicitly defined what constitutes discrimination or discrimination against women. According to the HR Committee, for example, "discrimination" is understood to imply any distinction or exclusion, which is based on any ground such as sex that has the purpose or effect of nullifying or impairing the recognition, enjoyment or exercise, on an equal footing, of all rights and freedoms by all. The 1982 law directly excludes women as a group with a purpose to nullify the exercise of the right to be employed as judges on the prohibited ground of sex. If she were a man, this law would not deprive her of becoming a judge. According to international human

391 Law on the Qualifications for Appointment of Judges in the Ministry of Justice 1982, (Iran). For detailed discussion *see* Chapter 2.

rights jurisprudence, the direct ban on women to exercise their rights to work as judges on an equal footing with men, regardless of their gender imposed by the legislature constitutes a de jure discrimination against women in Iran.

Ensuring the enjoyment to exercise the right to work for women regardless of their gender, on an equal footing, is a mandatory and immediate obligation for Iran under the Charter, UDHR, ICCPR, ICESCR, and ILO Convention (No. 111). Iran as a State party must respect and ensure women the enjoyment of all their universal human rights, on an equal footing, and regardless of their gender in its national legal system. This requires Iran, first, to refrain from violating women's guaranteed rights and discriminating against them on the basis of their sex. Guaranteeing women's human rights also requires Iran to review its legislation and practices and take the lead in implementing all measures to eliminate discrimination against women. Under international law, Iran should ensure that traditional, historical, religious, and cultural attitudes are not used to justify violations of women's right to equality before the law and to equal enjoyment of all their universal human rights. Iran's failure to refrain from violating women's guaranteed rights as its core obligation constitutes a violation under international law.

The passage of the 1982 law that directly discriminates against women after ratification of the Charter, ICCPR, ICESCR, and ILO Employment Occupation Convention by Iran is incompatible with the object and purposes laid down in the Charter, UDHR, ICCPR, ICESCR, and ILO Employment and Occupation Convention. The obligation to respect and ensure women's guaranteed rights requires that Iran take measures to combat discrimination in its laws and practice and promote equal access and opportunities for them. By passage of the de jure 1982 law, Iran has failed to fulfill this primary obligation and constitutes violations of the Charter, UDHR, ICCPR, ICESCR, and ILO Convention (No. 111).

Upholding the de jure discriminatory law for over thirty-three years is a deliberate delay and the unwillingness of Iran to repeal this discriminatory law is proof of Iran's departure from its obligations to be full compliance with the provisions of the Charter, UDHR, ICCPR, ICESCR, and ILO Employment and Occupation Convention. Instead of repealing and reforming this discriminatory law against women, the legislature has instead passed legislation that created positions like female consultant judges with limited authorities that lack decision-making power of a judge. The legislation is an assertion of Iran's unwillingness to recognize the same authority for women as judges (who serve only as consultants) in comparison with male judges who possess full decision-making power to render the final decision of a court according to the Constitution. This unwillingness to recognize equal rights for women to become judges on an equal footing as part of their guaranteed civil and ESC rights constitutes violation of provisions of the Charter, UDHR, ICCPR, ICESCR, and ILO Convention (No. 111).

States are obligated under international law to act in good faith to fulfill their obligations at all times, however, Iran has failed to do so. The IRI, for example, has continuously rejected official reports of the Special Rapporteurs and various Committees, which affirm the non-existence of women judges with decision-making authority. Instead, by submitting false and misleading reports, Iran has been insisting on the existence of women judges without making any reference to its existing law such as the 1982 or other relevant laws that either directly discriminate against them or give limited authority to women consultant judges. This compelling issue of non-existence of women judges has continuously been reported in the official reports of the HR Committee, CESCR, Special Rapporteurs of the Commission on Human Rights and Human Rights Council, Secretary-General, various NGOs and stakeholders. The international community has uniformly asserted that there is the exclusion of women from becoming judges presiding over a courtroom with the decision-making authority to render the final decision of the court in Iran. Iran by submitting false and misleading reports fail to fulfill its international obligations to act with good faith at all times. This also constitutes a violation under international law.

Iran's international obligations extend, also, to other obligations imposed by the Charter-based bodies such as UPR, Human Rights Council, and General Assembly. As part of Iran's obligation to respect and promote the equal rights of women, Iran is required to implement the accepted recommendations made during the first cycle of its Universal Periodic Review in its jurisdiction. These accepted recommendations include reforming the discriminatory provisions of its civil laws and ensuring the equal treatment of women in law and practice. This requires Iran to repeal the de jure discriminatory 1982 law against women, which is overdue since 2010. Iran has failed to repeal this law and that also constitutes a violation under international law.

Iran also is obligated to cooperate fully and comply with various resolutions adopted by the General Assembly and Human Rights Council to improve the human rights of women and eliminate de jure and de facto discrimination against women in its legal system and bring it in line with the universal human rights standards. The failure to outlaw discrimination against women in its laws and practice constitutes multiple violations under international law.

Chapter 4

Women Judges and Lawyers in the United States

Basic Comparison of the Legal Structure in the United States and Iran

Comparing legal systems is a complicated challenge. The legal standards and procedures in different systems are so dependent on their specific histories, religions, political systems and ethnic complexities that often it is difficult to really learn much from another country's legal system except that it is different. But it is fascinating that when it comes to the history of the legal status and authority of women, particularly in government decision-making positions, there is an astonishing similarity regardless of country, region, continent or religion. Until the 20th century, women had few legal rights virtually everywhere in the world.[1] This was so even in countries like England or Spain who accepted early female monarchs.[2]

In making a determination of which legal system to compare to Iran's, the United States is an obvious choice. As one of the world's most prominent legal systems, the United States is different in many critical political and cultural ways

1 For example, women did not receive universal suffrage in any country until the 20th century. Only New Zealand granted the right to vote earlier, in 1893. France did not give women the right to vote until 1944 and Switzerland until 1971. The United States granted women's universal suffrage in 1920. Suffrage was granted even later in South America, Asia, and Africa where many countries did not grant women suffrage, if at all, until after the Second World War. As we have seen, Iran granted women the right to vote in 1964. A summary of dates of women's suffrage throughout the world through 2009, and a supporting bibliography, can be found at "Women's Suffrage," Scholastic Magazine (2009). *Women's Suffrage*, Scholastic, *accessed at* http://www.scholastic.com/teachers/article/womenx2019s-suffrage. In North America and Europe in the 19th century, women and men were expected to fill separate spheres of society. Men were expected to participate in public life and women were expected to be housewives and mothers. In Great Britain, women were so bound to their husbands under the 19th century British common law traditions that they were barely considered people at all. *Feminism in the 19th Century: Women's Rights, Roles, and Limits*, Study.com, *accessed at* http://education-portal.com/academy/lesson/feminism-in-the-19th-century-womens-rights-roles-and-limits.html.

2 Paola Antolini, 1492: The Role of Women, Commission of the European Communities 32-35, *accessed at* http://aei.pitt.edu/34007/1/A484.pdf; *Elizabethan Women*, Elizabethi, *accessed at* http://www.elizabethi.org/contents/women/.

from Iran. Iran has always been an autocracy, ruled by authoritarian kings;[3] the United States has been a democracy since 1789, explicitly rejecting a monarchy in the American Revolution.[4] Iran has, for about 1300 years, been a theocracy based on Islam;[5] the United States, since its creation in 1789, has always worked to maintain a constitutional separation of religious and state power,[6] and to the degree state action in the United States is influenced by religious tradition, that tradition is not Islam, but Judeo/Christian.[7] The legal system in the United States is a common law system, meaning court decisions of individual cases not only resolve past controversies but also they set precedent that has legal effect in the future. This is contrary to the civil law system in Iran.

The political system in Iran is highly centralized;[8] the United States has carefully decentralized power in many ways, such that the central government

3 *See* Chapter 1.

4 The Declaration of Independence (1776) states: "We hold these truths to be self-evident, that all men are created equal, that they are endowed by their Creator with certain unalienable Rights, that among these are Life, Liberty and the pursuit of Happiness.--That to secure these rights, Governments are instituted among Men, deriving their just powers from the consent of the governed, --That whenever any Form of Government becomes destructive of these ends, it is the Right of the People to alter or to abolish it, and to institute new Government, laying its foundation on such principles and organizing its powers in such form, as to them shall seem most likely to effect their Safety and Happiness." *Declaration of Independence*, ARCHIVES.GOV, *accessed at* http://www.archives.gov/exhibits/charters/declaration_transcript.html.

5 *See* Chapter 1.

6 U.S. CONST. amend. I: "Congress shall make no law respecting an establishment of religion, or prohibiting the free exercise thereof; or abridging the freedom of speech, or of the press; or the right of the people peaceably to assemble, and to petition the Government for a redress of grievances." *See also* Thomas Jefferson's quote in 1802, author of the Declaration of Independence: "Believing with you that religion is a matter which lies solely between man & his god, that he owes account to none other for his faith or his worship, that the legitimate powers of government reach actions only and not opinions, I contemplate with sovereign reverence that act of the whole American people which declared that their legislature should "make no law respecting an establishment of religion, or prohibiting the free exercise thereof;" thus building a wall of eternal separation between Church & State." *Jefferson's Letter to the Danbury Baptists*, LIBRARY OF CONGRESS, *accessed at* http://www.loc.gov/loc/lcib/9806/danpost.html.

7 Russell Shorto, *How Christian Were the Founders?*, THE NEW YORK TIMES MAGAZINE (Feb. 11, 2010), *accessed at* http://www.nytimes.com/2010/02/14/magazine/14texbooks-t.html?pagewanted=all&_r=2.

8 *See e.g.*, Qanuni Assassi Jumhuri'i Islamai Iran [The Constitution of The Islamic Republic of Iran] 1358 [1980], Preamble, arts. 2(5), 109, 110.

gives way to state and local control in a wide variety of circumstances.[9] In addition, the power of the central government is also divided, so that in many circumstances no one branch of the government can dictate what the law is.[10]

Although the history and systems of the United States and Iran are dramatically different, the legal status of women in these two very different societies was remarkably similar well into the 20th century. This chapter will explore the history of women in the United States as they fought legal and customary barriers to become lawyers and judges. It will then explain the rapid developments in women's legal rights in the United States, beginning at almost the exact same time that the 1979 Islamic Revolution in Iran was also making changes in the status of women, although dramatically dissimilar to changes in the United States. Finally it will draw some key comparisons between the role and status of women in public life in the two countries since the end of the 19th century.

9 While the debate over the division of powers between the federal government and the states has been occurring since early in America's history, McCulloch v. Maryland, 17 U.S. 316 (1819), it still rages. *See also* U.S. Const. amend. X; New York v. United States, 505 U.S. 144 (1992); Printz v. United States, 521 U.S. 898 (1997); Lopez v. United States, 514 U.S. 549 (1995); United States v. Morrison, 529 U.S. 598 (2000); Abby Gluck, *Our [National] Federalism*, 123 Yale L.J. 1996, 1997-2000 (2014) (The modern allocation of state and federal power).

10 The Constitution has three separate Articles delineating the powers of the Legislature (Article I), the Executive (Article II) and the Judiciary (Article III). U.S. Const. arts. I, II, III.

Fundamental Constitutional Rules in the United States

The governmental structure of the United States was established by the Constitution of 1789; based on the "separation of powers," "federalism," and various forms of popular selection of key government officials.[11] The principle of "separation of powers" assures that the three branches of the federal government will not overstep from their constitutional roles.[12] The principle of "federalism" is based on the existence of two levels of government, national and local, which operate and govern people simultaneously.[13] The United States Constitution adopted in 1789, sets up the national government. Each of the thirteen original states, which were the component parts of this new government, was allowed to retain substantial government power, and each state has its own constitution and court system. In the United States today, there are fifty states, each with its own independent legal system.[14] The Constitution of the United

11 U.S. Const. art. I, § 2 (members of the House of Representatives are elected by the people); U.S. Const. art. I, § 3 (Senators are chosen by each state legislature). Section 3 was amended by Amendment XVII to say instead of being chosen by state legislatures, the two Senators from each state shall be "elected by the people thereof" (1913). U.S. Const. amend. XVII. *See also* William Burnham, Introduction to the Law and Legal System of the United States 1 (2d ed., West Group 1999).

12 William Burnham, Introduction to the Law and Legal System of the United States 1 (2d ed., West Group 1999).

13 *Id.*

14 *Id.*

States has a provision that dictates federal law will be supreme if any state law directly conflicts with it.[15]

The national and state governments are each sovereign in their own areas of expertise. States have independent authority in a wide range of areas, and the federal government can only intervene in limited circumstances. States elect or appoint their own officials and make their own laws. Federal courts can declare state laws unconstitutional, but only in the event of a clear conflict between the state law and either the U.S. Constitution or Congress's laws.[16]

The first ten amendments to the Constitution are known as the Bill of Rights, added in 1791, which guarantee basic rights in detail, including, for example, freedom of speech, religion, and press.[17]

15 The Supremacy Clause reads: "This Constitution, and the Laws of the United States which shall be made in Pursuance thereof; and all Treaties made, or which shall be made, under the Authority of the United States, shall be the supreme Law of the Land; and the Judges in every State shall be bound thereby, any Thing in the Constitution or Laws of any State to the Contrary notwithstanding." U.S. CONST. art. VI, § 2. *See also* Gibbons v. Ogden, where Chief Justice Marshall declared, "But the framers of our Constitution foresaw this state of things, and provided for it, by declaring the supremacy not only of itself, but of the laws made in pursuance of it. The nullity of an act, inconsistent with the Constitution, is produced by the declaration that the Constitution is the supreme law." Gibbons v. Ogden, 22 U.S. 1, 210, 211 (1824).

16 U.S. CONST. art. VI, § 2 (The Supremacy Clause). BURNHAM, *supra* not 12, at 18-19. *See also* JUDITH A. BAER, WOMEN IN AMERICAN LAW (THE STRUGGLE TOWARD EQUALITY FROM THE NEW DEAL TO THE PRESENT) 14 (2d ed., Holmes & Meier Publisher 1996). Examples of state law areas of legal control are family law, property ownership and criminal law. In Iran these areas are controlled primarily by the national government.

17 U.S CONST. amend. I through X. Rights in addition to freedom of speech, religion, press and assembly include right to a speedy trial by jury; and protection against excessive bail, cruel and unusual punishment, unreasonable search and seizure, and self-incrimination. Other rights have been added over the years such as the Thirteenth, Fourteenth and Fifteenth Amendments to the Constitution, which will be discussed later.

Article III of the U.S. Constitution speaks to the appointment of federal judges in the Constitutional Courts in the United States.[18] Supreme Court justices, judges of the intermediate Courts of Appeal, also called Circuit Courts, and District Court trial judges are all appointed to office by the President of the United States, and confirmed by a majority vote of the United States Senate. Federal judges are the only constitutional officers not popularly elected. The professional credentials and qualifications of prospective federal judges are closely evaluated by the Department of Justice and the Committee on the Federal Judiciary of the American Bar Association for positions in the federal bench.[19]

The U.S. Constitution in Article III, establishing "the judicial power of the United States," does not specify qualifications for justices or judges such as age, education, profession, or native-born citizenship.[20] The Constitution left appointment of a federal judge to the discretion of the President with the consent of the majority of the Senate. Although there are almost no formal qualifications for most federal judges written into law, there are some strong customary ones. For example, while certain judges of limited jurisdiction courts (like bankruptcy

18 U.S. CONST. art. III, § 1 states, "The judicial power of the United States shall be vested in one Supreme Court and in such inferior courts as the Congress may from time to time ordain and establish. The judges, both of the supreme and inferior courts, shall hold their offices during good behavior, and shall, at stated times, receive for their services, a compensation, which shall not be diminished during their continuance in office;" U.S. CONST. art. II, § 2 states: "He[the President] shall have power, by and with the advice and consent of the Senate, to... appoint ...judges of the Supreme Court, and all other officers of the United States, whose appointments are not herein otherwise provided for, and which shall be established by law."

19 Michael J. Yelnosky, *Who Rates Prospective Federal Judges for the American Bar Association?*, 19 Roger Williams U. L. Rev. 91, 92-96 (2014). *See also* ROBERT A. CARP & RONALD STIDHAM, JUDICIAL PROCESS IN AMERICA 244-250 (3d ed., CQ Press 1996).

20 U.S. CONST. art. III. For comparison *see* Article II, section 1, requirements for the President, reads "No Person except a natural born Citizen, or a Citizen of the United States, at the time of the Adoption of this Constitution, shall be eligible to the Office of President; neither shall any Person be eligible to that Office who shall not have attained to the Age of thirty five Years, and been fourteen Years a Resident within the United States." U.S. CONST. art. II, § 1.

courts) are required by statute to be lawyers,[21] there is no constitutional or statutory requirement that District Court judges, Courts of Appeal judges, or Supreme Court Justices be lawyers. But today it would be unheard-of for the President to nominate someone who is not an experienced lawyer. Before their appointment, most judges were private attorneys, judges in state courts or other federal courts, government attorneys or law professors.[22]

The strong tradition of legal experience as a requirement for all Supreme Court nominees is shown most clearly by the fact that all 112 members of the U.S. Supreme Court, since the formation of the Court in 1789, have had extensive legal experience or served on a lower court.[23] The ones who served on the court had engaged in at least some public service at various levels of government or had actively participated in political enterprises.[24] In the 18th and 19th centuries, the United States had few law schools, so a person who wanted to become a lawyer would "read the law" (study key treatises and writings) as a trainee under an experienced practicing attorney, or study law at the undergraduate level.

States have a wide variety of systems for selection of judges, depending on what level of court is involved. Each of the fifty states sets its own requirements for judgeships. The vast majority of the states originally had few firm qualifications and did not require judges to have a law degree. Today, judges in courts of general trial jurisdiction typically should be licensed attorneys, and most states require them to have practiced for a certain number of years.[25] For instance in California, the most populous of the fifty states,[26] under the 1879 California

---

21 Appointment and Tenure, 28 U.S.C. § 631(b)(1) (1988). *See also* Appointment of Bankruptcy Judges, 28 U.S.C. § 152 (2005).

22 Robert A. Carp & Ronald Stidham, Judicial Process in America 244 (3d ed., CQ Press 1996).

23 There are no legal or Constitutional requirements for a federal judgeship. However, an unwritten prerequisite for a place on the federal bench is having a bachelor of laws or the Juris Doctor (J.D.) degree. Henry Julian Abraham, Justices, Presidents, and Senators: A History of the U.S. Supreme Court Appointments from Washington to Bush II 39, 48 (5th ed., Rowman & Littlefield Publishers 2008).

24 *See* Henry Julian Abraham, Justices, Presidents, and Senators: A History of the U.S. Supreme Court Appointments from Washington to Bush II 48 (5th ed., Rowman & Littlefield Publishers 2008).

25 G. Larry Mays, American Courts and the Judicial Process 109 (Oxford University Press 2012); Burnham, *supra* note 12, at 178; Judicial Process in America, *supra* note 22, at 244.

26 According to the U.S. Census Bureau, the 2015 population of the United States is approaching 320,000,000. California's population exceeds 38,000,000. *National Totals: Vintage 2014,* United States Census Bureau, *accessed at* http://www.census.gov.

Constitution, any judge of a court of record has to be a member of the State Bar of California.[27] The California Constitution sets the prerequisite of being admitted to the State Bar.[28] There is a longstanding tradition in California that requires judges presiding over criminal trials of offenses punishable by a jail sentence to be attorneys.[29]

Considering the requirement for the selection of judges in the United States, though, formal qualifications for a seat on the bench are few. Tradition has established several informal criteria such as a reasonable degree of professional competence. It is clear that in order to become a judge of any constitutional court today, prospective judges must be lawyers before being selected for the bench. This has been clearly established at the federal court level by the practice since 1789; by most state courts by the legal requirements contained either in the state constitution or statutes.[30]

Therefore, in examining the history of women as judges in the United States, it is essential to examine two issues. The two are deeply intertwined. First, are the challenges women faced to even obtain admission to the bar and employment as lawyers. Second, even for those women who managed to overcome the hurdles to become attorneys, there were additional challenges before women could become judges. This chapter will provide historical analysis of the constitutional and legal evolution that took place in the fight to end discrimination against women in the legal profession and the judiciary. It also includes an examination of the modern changes that opened these positions to women, emphasizing the strong roles played by the U.S. Congress and the U.S. Supreme Court in eliminating discrimination on the ground of sex in employment.

---

27 Cal. Const. art. VI, § 15: "A person is ineligible to be a judge of a court of record unless for 10 years immediately preceding selection, the person has been a member of the State Bar or served as a judge of a court of record in this State."

28 Cal. Const. art. VI, § 9: "The State Bar of California is a public corporation. Every person admitted and licensed to practice law in this State is and shall be a member of the State Bar except while holding office as a judge of a court of record." *See also*, The State Bar of California, *accessed at* http://rules.calbar.ca.gov/Rules/Title1GlobalProvisions.aspx.

29 Gordon v. Justice Court, 12 Cal.3d 323, 334 (1974).

30 Judicial Process in America, *supra* note 22, at 285. *See also* the following gives the main qualifications and requirements needed to become a judge, obtained from the laws of the states, as provided by the U.S. Bureau of Labor Statistics. Degree level: Juris Doctor; Licensure: admitted by state to practice law; Experience: work as a lawyer for some years prior to judgeship. *Occupational Employment Statistics (Judges, Magistrate Judges, and Magistrates)*, Bureau of Labor Statistics (2014), *accessed at* http://www.bls.gov/oes/current/oes231023.htm.

Early Equality Struggles of Women in the United States

The history of the struggles of American women for legal equality in the 19th century is recorded in many exceptional works of history. This is also true regarding the history of American women in their efforts to become lawyers and judges.[31] It is necessary to briefly explore some of this history to understand the pathway of American women from the beginning of the nation until today, in order to effectively make some comparisons between the Iranian women and American women dealing with issues becoming judges.

Throughout most of the history in the U.S., women were considered legally inferior to men, viewed as the "other."[32] Women were excluded from the male definition of political equality.[33] Most of the early women legal champions faced a school of thought that believed women were by nature different from men; that they were best fitted for motherhood and housekeeping tasks. Contrary to men, women were considered compassionate, selfless, gentle, and pure, and

31 Check books such as JUDITH A. BAER, WOMEN IN AMERICAN LAW (THE STRUGGLE TOWARD EQUALITY FROM THE NEW DEAL TO THE PRESENT), (2d ed., Holmes & Meier Publisher 1996); VIRGINIA G. DRACHMAN, SISTERS IN LAW: WOMEN LAWYERS IN MODERN AMERICAN HISTORY, (Harvard University Press 1998); HEDDA GARZA, BARRED FROM THE BAR (A HISTORY OF WOMEN AND THE LEGAL PROFESSION), (Franklin Watts Publisher 1996); JOAN HOFF, LAW, GENDER, AND INJUSTICE (A LEGAL HISTORY OF U.S. WOMEN), (New York University Press 1991); SUSAN GLUCK MEZEY, IN PURSUIT OF EQUALITY: WOMEN, PUBLIC POLICY, AND THE FEDERAL COURTS (St. Martin's Press 1992); DOROTHY E MCBRIDE, WOMEN'S RIGHTS IN THE U.S.A. (POLICY DEBATES AND GENDER ROLES) (2d ed., Garland Publishing 1997); KAREN BERGER MORELLO, THE INVISIBLE BAR (THE WOMAN LAWYER IN AMERICA 1638 TO THE PRESENT), (Random House 1986); BARBARA J. HARRIS, BEYOND HER SPHERE: WOMEN AND THE PROFESSIONS IN AMERICAN HISTORY (Greenwood Press 1978).

32 HEDDA GARZA, BARRED FROM THE BAR (A HISTORY OF WOMEN AND THE LEGAL PROFESSION) 15 (Franklin Watts Publisher 1996).

33 JOAN HOFF, LAW, GENDER, AND INJUSTICE (A LEGAL HISTORY OF U.S. WOMEN) 4 (New York University Press 1991).

their minds were attuned to art and religion. The legal profession required sharp logic and shrewd negotiating skills that women lacked.[34]

The progress of women's rights has been slow because even, "We the People" did not include women or a majority of other Americans.[35] For almost 200 years, the United States functioned without having a woman on its Supreme Court.[36]

The beginnings of a women's movement did not begin until after the American Revolution.[37] The structural roots of women's political transformation in the 19th century coincided with the growth of capitalist industrialization, which sent some women into the workforce, and the growing abolitionist movement opposing slavery. Both labor issues and slavery issues motivated women to look to their own issues of inclusion and equality.[38]

The antislavery and women's movements were intertwined tightly with the goals of fighting against both slavery and the inequality of women. Women put in enormous work in antislavery societies all over the country; gathering thousands of signatures on petitions to Congress. They also fought for their own equality racing alongside the movement against slavery. The first significant historic meeting was the Women's Rights Convention held at Seneca Falls in New York, in 1848. The "Declaration of Principles" was signed at the end of the meeting, and became the first post-revolutionary female legal text that formally launched the U.S. women's rights movement. It demanded universal human rights and happiness for women. Its focus was on women's equality with men including the list of their objections to the then current legal scheme.[39] The Seneca Falls Declaration explicitly states:

---

34 Sandra Day O'Connor, The Majesty of the Law 189 (Craig Joyce, Random House 2003). *See also* Betty Friedan, The Feminine Mystique, 15-16 (Tenth Anniversary ed., Norton & Company Inc. 1974).

35 Joan Hoff, *supra* note 33, at 21.

36 Sandra Day O'Connor, The Majesty of the Law 187-188 (Craig Joyce, Random House 2003).

37 American Revolution (1775-1783) during which colonists in the Thirteen American Colonies rejected rule by the British monarchy and aristocracy, overthrew the authority of Great Britain, and founded the United States of America.

38 Steven M. Buechler, Women's Movements in the United States: Women Suffrage, Equal Rights, and Beyond 12,17-18 (Rutgers University Press 1990).

39 Howard Zinn, A People's History of the United States 123 (HarperCollins Publishers 2010). *See also id.* at 20.

> "We hold these truths to be self-evident; that all men and women are created equal."[40]

Women's representatives, then, highlighted the disappointing absence or restriction of women in various spheres of their lives such as women's economic positions, legal status, occupational possibilities, familial roles, and political disenfranchisement. They demanded a series of reforms regarding laws that prevented women from occupying public roles and treated them as inferior to men.[41] Women's advocates, for example, demanded the right to vote and educational opportunities for women; enabling women to be able to keep their own property and wages; creating equal opportunity in employment, and entering into the professions of medicine and law.[42]

Later women's suffrage movement efforts included mobilizing women voters in suffrage states toward the goal of federal enfranchisement of all women. The triumph of national women's suffrage through ratification of the Nineteenth Amendment in 1920 laid the foundation for the reemergence of a more comprehensive women's movement later in the 1960s.[43]

40 Howard Zinn, A People's History of the United States 123 (HarperCollins Publishers 2010).

41 Women did not have right to vote, right to her wages or to property, right in divorce, equal opportunities in employment and entrance to college. *Id. See also* Buechler, *supra* note 38, at 20; Karen Berger Morello, The Invisible Bar (The Woman Lawyer in America: 1638 to the Present) 10 (Random House 1986).

42 Garza, *supra* note 32, at 31.

43 Buechler, *supra* note 38, at 26.

Women Lawyers and Judges in the Early United States

a. Attorneys

One critical legal point is that in the United States all decisions about the qualifications to be a lawyer are made individually by each of the fifty states, not by the national government.[44] In comparison, in Iran all legislation controlling lawyers and judges is made by the national government.[45] So while in Iran there is only one set of rules, in the United States there are now fifty different sets of rules about the requirements to become a lawyer, as well as the requirements to become a judge.[46] This obviously makes things quite complex.

While in recent times many states have adopted similar standards as proposed by prestigious institutions, such as the American Bar Association,[47] each state still controls its rules. Just because you have been admitted to practice law in one state does not mean you can practice law in any other state.[48] There is no national legislation on admission to the bar. And even in the federal court

44 *E.g.*, Authority, Rule 4.1 (2007) states: "The California Supreme Court *exercises inherent jurisdiction over the practice of law in California*. The Committee of Bar Examiners (Committee) is authorized by law to administer the requirements for admission to practice law; to examine all applicants for admission; and to certify to the Supreme Court for admission those applicants who fulfill the requirements." [Emphasis Added]

Title 4. Admission and Educational Standards (2007), accessed at http://rules.calbar.ca.gov/LinkClick.aspx?fileticket=-2KV5j0w6Cw%3D&tabid=1227.

45 *E.g.*, Qānuni Sharāyiti Intikhābi Qużāti Dādgustarī 1361 [Law on the Qualifications for Appointment of Judges 1982] (Iran) that was passed by the Islamic Consultative assembly.

46 Garza, *supra* note 32.

47 American Bar Association (ABA) is a voluntary private organization of lawyers founded in 1878, began long campaign to establish a uniform educational requirement of attendance at a law school satisfying certain minimum standards as a prerequisite for entry into the legal professions. Burnham, *supra* note 12, at 124-125.

48 *See* Burnham, *supra* note 12, at 132.

system, which is controlled by the national government, it is required that you be an attorney admitted to practice in a state or U.S. territory before you can be admitted to the bar of the federal courts.[49] In the early days, each state has its own story concerning its acceptance of women as attorneys and judges.

The early experiences of women as lawyers are remarkable because of their extreme challenges and hardships to fight male authority in the legal field. For example, the first known woman lawyer in America was Margaret Brent. She was a master negotiator and skillful litigator, in 1638, almost 150 years before the United States ceased being a colony of Great Britain and became an independent nation. In the 17th century, she overcame all the existing restrictions against women. She was called "gentleman Margaret Brent," in person and in court records. She acted as a lawyer for the Governor of the Maryland Colony, and declared herself his executor.[50] Margaret Brent is often referred to as the first and only woman attorney in America before the American Revolution.[51]

Luce Terry in 1796 was likely the first African-American woman in the nation to argue before a court on which a member of the U.S. Supreme Court sat when she had an oral argument in a Vermont court.[52] However, she was not an attorney. She was a poet. Born in Africa and enslaved in the United States but freed via purchase by her husband and taken to Vermont, she appeared in a property dispute before the U.S. Supreme Court regarding some farmland. Though she had a lawyer, Terry presented the oral argument herself. She won the case, and Supreme Court Justice Samuel Chase, sitting on circuit, complimented her skill.[53]

---

49 According to Rule 5, Admission to the Bar: "To qualify for admission to the Bar of this Court, an applicant must have been admitted to practice in the highest court of a State, Commonwealth, Territory or Possession, or the District of Columbia for a period of at least three years immediately before the date of application; must not have been the subject of any adverse disciplinary action pronounced or in effect during that 3-year period; and must appear to the Court to be of good moral and professional character." Supreme Court of the United States, Rules of the Supreme Court of the United States, SUPREME COURT.GOV 2 (2013), *accessed at* http://www.supremecourt.gov/ctrules/2013RulesoftheCourt.pdf.

50 KAREN BERGER MORELLO, THE INVISIBLE BAR (THE WOMAN LAWYER IN AMERICA: 1638 TO THE PRESENT) 1-7 (Random House 1986).

51 *Id.* at 1. This was 150 years before the United States became a separate country.

52 REBELS IN LAW: VOICES IN HISTORY OF BLACK WOMEN LAWYERS 2 (J. Clay Smith Jr. ed., The University of Michigan Press 2000).

53 *Id.*

She is the first woman, and almost certainly the first African-American, to argue before a Supreme Court Justice.[54]

These two exceptional circumstances in America's first 225 years, however, are not the true history of women in the law during this period in the United States. Throughout the nation, states systematically denied women any legal right to be attorneys, solely because of their gender or marital status. It was not until the late 1860s that struggles began in state legislatures and courts to challenge this gender discriminatory system regarding women in the law.

The 1860s brought the worst time in American history since the American Revolution of 1776. The Civil War broke out in 1861, with northern non-slave states fighting against southern slave states in a horrific four-year war. The southern states wanted to form a new separate country in which slavery would be legal. This war shook the foundations of the country, and it was uncertain for some time whether the United States would remain one nation. The antislavery war promoted concepts of equality more broadly, and it saw the strengthening of the early women's movement.[55]

Immediately after the Civil War, which saw the slave states defeated, the United States Constitution was amended in 1866-1870 to add three new provisions. They were directed to ending slavery and promoting equality, as well as giving the federal government a larger role in enforcing these concepts on the states. The Thirteenth Amendment prohibited slavery and involuntary servitude; the Fifteenth Amendment granted the right to vote in federal elections regardless of race; and the Fourteenth Amendment guaranteed each person with "due process of law," "equal protection of the laws," and protection of the "privileges and immunities" of U.S. Citizens.[56] By 1870 these amendments were in effect. The turmoil of the War and the legal changes immediately afterward prompted a renewed effort on behalf of women's rights. This struggle manifested itself in many areas, including a push for women to enter the legal profession.[57]

---

54 *Id.*

55 History, Art & Archives-United States House of Representative, *The Women's Rights Movement*, History, Art & Archives, *accessed at* http://history.house.gov/Exhibitions-and-Publications/WIC/Historical-Essays/No-Lady/Womens-Rights/.

56 The Thirteenth Amendment was ratified in 1865; the Fourteenth Amendment was ratified in 1868; the Fifteenth Amendment was ratified in 1870. U.S. Const. amend. XIII, § 1; U.S. Const. amend. XIII, § 2; U.S. Const. amend. XV, § 1; U.S. Const. amend. XV, § 2; U.S. Const. amend. XIV, § 1; U.S. Const. amend. XIV, § 5.

57 *See* Morello, *supra* note 50, at 11.

The first known woman lawyer in the United States was Arabella Mansfield,[58] who passed the Iowa State bar in 1869.[59] Under the Iowa Code, admission to the bar had been specially limited to "any white male person," which was a common provision in many state statutes, even in non-slave states.[60] The Iowa Supreme Court ruled in the case of Mansfield that an affirmative declaration of gender is not any implied denial of the right of females.[61] As a result of this precedent, the words "white males" as a bar-admission requirement in the Iowa Code was deleted.[62]

In the same year, Myra Colby Bradwell passed the Illinois bar exam. She was found qualified to get her license to practice as an attorney and it was recommended that a license should be issued to her. Her request was denied by the Illinois courts based on the common law doctrine of *feme covert* (married). The United States adopted the French and English law, in which once a woman married she lost the right to inherit property on her own, to enter into a contract on her own and to independently obtain goods and services. The Court, by relying on the doctrine of *feme covert,* followed the old standards. In 1870, the Supreme Court of Illinois confirmed her denial of admission to the bar, simply based on her gender.[63] The court said:

> It is to be also remembered that female attorneys at law were unknown in England....That *God* designed the *sexes to occupy different spheres of action,* and that *it belonged to men to make, apply, and execute the laws,* was regarded as an almost *axiomatic truth.* We are certainly warranted in saying, that when the legislature gave to this Court the power of granting licenses to practice law, it was with not the slightest expectation that this privilege would be extended to women.[64] [Emphasis Added]

---

58 Belle Mansfield, at the age of twenty-three, was formally admitted to the bar. Even though she passed the bar, she never practiced law but made a career as an academic. In addition to her academic work, Belle Mansfield was one of the founders of the Iowa Women's Suffrage Society. MORELLO, *supra* note 50, at 11.

59 MORELLO, *supra* note 50, at 11.

60 *Id.* at 12.

61 *Id.*

62 *See* GARZA, *supra* note 32, at 12, 13.

63 Bradwell v. Illinois, 83 U.S. 130 (1873).

64 *Id at* 132, 133.

Myra Bradwell did not accept the Illinois Supreme Court decision and took her case to the U.S. Supreme Court. She insisted that she was entitled to the same "privileges and immunities" as citizens of all other states protected under the new Fourteenth Amendment, and Article IV of the United States Constitution,[65] and that the state of Illinois did not have the power to limit admission to the bar based on gender. The case was decided by the U.S. Supreme Court in the case of *Bradwell v. Illinois*, 83 U.S. 130 (1873), which was the first sex discrimination case decided by the U.S. Supreme Court.

Justice Miller, writing for the majority of the U.S. Supreme Court, ignored the rationale of the Illinois court opinion about her common law disabilities as a married woman, and held instead that the right to practice law was not a privilege or immunity of U.S. citizenship. He based his opinion on the famous *Slaughterhouse Cases*,[66] a decision that was delivered a day before Bradwell's decision. The *Slaughterhouse Cases* was the first U.S. Supreme Court interpretation of the new Fourteenth Amendment to the Constitution. Miller's decision was based on a very narrow interpretation of the privileges and immunities clause of the Fourteenth Amendment. There was no federal constitutional protection against discrimination in employment or choice of occupation, whether based on gender or any other criterion, with the possible exception of race. Seven out of eight members of the Court did not believe that the privileges and immunities clause of the Constitution guaranteed Bradwell any particular occupation, including the right to practice law. The legal result left to each state to decide, without any federal constitutional limitation, what the occupational rights of people may be.[67]

However, the most famous portion of the Bradwell decision is Justice Bradley's concurring opinion.[68] He wrote specifically to the issue of gender that had been raised by Ms. Bradwell. He said that it could not be assumed "that one

65 "The Citizens of each State shall be entitled to all Privileges and Immunities of Citizens in the several States." U.S. CONST. art. IV, § 2.

66 Slaughterhouse Cases, 83 U.S. (16 Wall.) 36 (1872).

67 In Bradwell, the Court said, "the right to control and regulate the granting of license to practice law in the courts of a state is one of those powers which are not transferred for its protection to the federal government." Bradwell, 83 U.S. 130 at 139. *See also* the opinion delivered in the Slaughterhouse Cases, 83 U.S. (16 Wall.).

68 Justice Bradley in his concurring opinion was joined by Justices Field and Swayne. Bradwell, 83 U.S. 130 at 140.

of the privileges and immunities of *women* as citizens is to engage in any and every profession occupation, or employment in civil life."[69] [Emphasis Added]

Justice Bradley continued with his restrictive view on the rights of women:

> The civil law, as *well as nature herself*, has always recognized a wide difference in the respective spheres and destinies of man and woman. *Man* is, or should be, *woman's protector* and *defender*. The *natural* and *proper timidity* and *delicacy* which belongs to the *female sex evidently unfits it for many of the occupations of civil life*. The Constitution of the family organization, which is founded in the *divine ordinance* as well as in the *nature of things*, indicates the domestic sphere as that which properly belongs to the domain and functions of womanhood. The harmony, not to say identity, of interests and views, which belong, or should belong, to the family institution is r*epugnant to the idea of a woman adopting a distinct and independent career from that of her husband*.[70] [Emphasis Added]

> It is true that many women are unmarried and not affected by any of the duties, complications, and incapacities arising out of the married state, but these are exceptions to the general rule. The *paramount destiny* and *mission* of *women* are to *fulfill* the noble and benign offices of *wife* and *mother*. This is the *law* of the *Creator*. And the rules of *civil society must be adapted* to the *general constitution of things*, and *cannot* be based upon *exceptional cases*.[71] [Emphasis Added]

While the result, barring a woman from becoming a lawyer, was not unusual for the time, it was now enshrined as federal constitutional law that women had no right to choose an occupation if the state chose to deny that right. This included being a lawyer. This opinion attributes this legal result not to constitutional or common law, but to "natural law,"[72] and expressly to the law of the Creator. And the law of the Creator is that women are "naturally timid and delicate," "unfit

69 *Id.*

70 Bradwell, 83 U.S. 130 at 141.

71 *Id.* at 141-142.

72 Definition of Natural law according to the Black's Law Dictionary "a philosophical system of legal and moral principles purportedly deriving from a universalized conception of human nature or divine justice rather than from legislative or judicial actions." BLACK'S LAW DICTIONARY, 1189 (Bryan A. Garner ed., 10th ed., Thomson Reuters 2014).

for many of the occupations of civil life," "destined to be a wife and mother," and subject to the "protection of men."

This constitutional and legal view of women, based in part on religious based arguments, remained part of American jurisprudence until the 1960s. While there were notable exceptions to barring women from becoming lawyers in the 100 years, between Bradley and the significant changes in the law in the 1960s and 1970s, women as lawyers and judges remained a rare and unusual sight in the United States. Women continued to be substantially barred from law schools, admission to the bar, and access to employment such as judgeships.[73]

With federal law providing no relief to women, much of the change, however modest, during the second half of the 19th century occurred pursuant to state law. For example, five years after the Bradwell case, in 1878, Clara Foltz began her quest to become California's first woman lawyer. A mother of five small children abandoned by her husband, Foltz fought to amend the California legislation to change the words in the state code on bar admission that exclusively gave the right to practice to "white men." Foltz paved the way for her legal career by successfully securing the passage in the California legislature, allowing admission to "any citizen or person" that included women.[74]

It was Belva A. Lockwood who then played a key role in persuading Congress to pass the special legislation called the "Lockwood Bill." This bill called for admission of a qualified woman who was a person of good moral character to practice before the U.S. Supreme Court.[75] After the passage of this bill in 1879, Lockwood became the first woman ever admitted to argue a case before the U.S. Supreme Court.[76] This, in effect, overturned the Supreme Court ruling earlier, in Lockwood, where Ms. Lockwood was denied the right to practice before the Supreme Court by Chief Justice Morrison Waite, speaking for the majority, asserting "none but men were eligible to practice as attorneys."[77]

---

73 *See* SUSAN EHRLICH MARTIN *&* NANCY C. JURIK, DOING JUSTICE, DOING GENDER 105-109, 123-126 (Sage Publications 1996); Women's Division Republican National Committee, Women in the Judicial Service, EISENHOWER PRESIDENTIAL LIBRARY, MUSEUM, AND BOYHOOD HOME (1959), *accessed at* https://www.eisenhower.archives.gov/research/online_documents/women_in_the_1950s/Women_in_Judicial_Service.pdf; *Women in Law in Canada and the U.S.*, CATALYST (2015), *accessed at* http://www.catalyst.org/knowledge/women-law-canada-and-us.

74 GARZA, *supra* note 32, at 55.

75 DIANA KLEBANOW & FRANKLIN L. JONAS, PEOPLE'S LAWYERS: CRUSADERS FOR JUSTICE IN AMERICAN HISTORY 5, 17-19 (M.E. Sharpe 2003).

76 *Id.* at 5.

77 *Id.* at 17.

Different states reached different results during this period, and even in those states allowing women to be lawyers, employment opportunities were severely limited. In Wisconsin, for example, women were allowed to practice law but were denied the right to represent their clients in the Wisconsin Supreme Court. Justice Ryan, in 1875, stated, echoing Justice Bradley in the Bradwell case as:

> The *law of nature* destined and qualifies the *female sex* for the *bearing* and *nurture of the children* of our race, and for the *custody of the homes of the world*, and *their maintenance in love and honor.* And all *life-long calling of women, inconsistent with these radical and social duties of their sex, as is the profession of law, are departures from the order of nature;* and when voluntary, treason against it. .... There are many employments in life not unfit for female character. The profession of law is surely not one of these. The *peculiar qualities of womanhood, its gentle graces, its quick sensibility, its tender susceptibility, its purity, its delicacy, its emotional impulses, its subordination of hard reason to sympathetic feeling, are surely not qualifications for forensic strife. Nature* has tempered *women as little for the judicial conflicts of the courtroom* as for the physical conflicts of the battlefield.... *Discussions are habitually necessary in courts of justice, which are unfit for female ears.*[78] [Emphasis Added]

Similarly, the Supreme Court of Oregon, in 1885, denied a woman attorney, Mary Leonard, the right to appear before it, even though she was admitted as a lawyer in Washington. This was the first application of the kind in this State that the court has recognized. Had she been a man, Mary would have been entitled to admission.[79]

And in Massachusetts, the case of Lelia Robinson was decided by the Massachusetts Supreme Judicial Court in 1876.[80] It was concluded that in Massachusetts an attorney was "almost" a public officer. To permit women to practice law implicitly granted them the right to vote. Since an attorney was "very near" to being a public officer, it was impossible for women to practice as

78 In the Matter of the Motion to Admit Miss Lavinia Goodell to the Bar of this Court, 39 Wis.232, 245, 246 (1876).

79 *Mary Leonard, 1845 - October 24, 1912,* Mary Leonard Law Society, *accessed at* http://www.maryleonardlawsociety.org/who-was-mary-leonard.html.

80 In re Lelia J. Robinson, 131 Mass. 376 (1881).

attorneys without winning the right to vote.[81] The legal argument had changed, but the result was the same. Even though Robinson lost her case, however, when Massachusetts reacted by adopting a statute specifically permitting women to practice law on the same terms as men, she gained admission to practice law the following year.[82] In those years it sometimes seemed easier to persuade state legislatures to permit women to fully practice law, as was done in Massachusetts and in California, than to persuade the male judges on the courts.

In other states, however, during the same period, some courts permitted women to practice. Connecticut was one of five states between 1882-1893 that admitted women to practice law by rejecting classical legal thoughts against women by judicial decision rather than legislative statutes.[83] Mary Hall was the first woman admitted to the bar in Connecticut. The General Statutes in Connecticut at the time stated that the Court "may admit and cause to be sworn as attorneys such persons as are qualified therefor [sic] agreeably to the rules established."[84]

The argument against Hall's admission focused on the intent of the legislation as it was originally passed. Legislators in 1750, in setting forth qualifications for attorneys, could not have contemplated that women would ever seek admission to the bar. Consequently, "persons" could only have referred to men. The Court rejected this argument, noting that public opinion on a topic may change completely although statutory language remains the same. Further, the statute had been reaffirmed by its inclusion in the 1875 statutory revision without any amendment limiting the admission of women. Since, the court reasoned, women had entered the profession of law and other professional and public occupations by 1875, and the legislature did not amend the statute, "persons" must include women.[85]

Women's struggles took different routes. Some persuaded courts to admit them as lawyers; others persuaded legislatures to change the statutes. Still others were unsuccessful in either attempt. While our ultimate goal is to compare access to judgeships for women in both the U.S. and Iran, since being a lawyer

81 *Id.* at 377, 380-383.

82 Virginia G. Drachman, Sisters in law: Women Lawyers in Modern American History 30 (Harvard University Press 1998).

83 *Id.* at 31, 32.

84 In the matter of Mary Hall, 50 Conn. 131, 134 (1882).

85 *Id.* at 134-136.

is, and has been, an essential prerequisite for a judgeship in almost all cases in the United States, understanding the long and difficult struggle of women to become lawyers helps explain why the number of women judges in the U.S. was small until the mid-20th century. There are literally dozens of individual stories of the courageous women who fought for the right to become attorneys.[86]

b. Judges

The fight of women to obtain judgeships was in its own way equal to the fight of women to become attorneys. Historically, it has only been quite recently that women began to be accorded judicial equality with men in the United States. The fact remains that the Constitution still does not explicitly protect women against discrimination. The legal status of women in the U.S. has changed more rapidly in the last four decades than in the previous two hundred years. And this includes access to judgeships. From the women lawyers' perspective in the United States, the reason for unusually low numbers of women on the bench is nothing but their gender.[87] By 1900, despite some women practicing law after the Civil War, there were only five women who served in any judicial or quasi-judicial[88] (covers an executive or administrative official's adjudicative acts) positions. By 1920, after women achieved the national right to vote, there is a record of only ten women in any judicial position at that time.[89] Even after acquiring the right to vote and sit as jurors, the percentage of women on the bench did not noticeably improve.[90]

The first woman judge in the United States was Esther Morris, appointed as a justice of the peace in the territory of Wyoming in 1870. The year before, a representative in the territorial legislature introduced a bill giving women the right to vote and hold public office. Eager to promote Wyoming territory and to attract more women settlers, the all-male territorial legislature approved the bill, making Wyoming the first state in American history to give the right to vote to women. One of the strongest supporters of the new law was the territorial governor. Morris became the governor's first and only successful female judicial

86 *Supra* note 31.

87 Joan Hoff, *supra* note 33, at 3. *See also* Morello, *supra* note 50, at 219.

88 Black's Law Dictionary 1440 (Bryan A. Garner ed., 10th ed., Thomson Reuters 2014).

89 Morello, *supra* note 50, at 219.

90 *Id.*

appointment. Although she only served for nine months, she has become an enduring symbol of women's rights. Ironically, she had no legal training at all.[91]

While there are individual stories concerning each of the very few women who became a judge before 1920, the core of the story is always the same. It was an extraordinary exception; usually the only woman judge in the state; usually in a limited or lower court judgeship, such as a master in chancery, magistrate or a justice of the peace; and never advancing beyond this first position.[92] In 1881, a woman survived challenge to her appointment as a master of chancery.[93] Ada Lee, who graduated from the University of Michigan Law School in 1884, was nominated for the Office of Circuit Court Commissioner by the Republican, Democratic and Greenback parties to which later she was elected.[94] In late 1880s, two women, Marilla Richer and Carrie Burnham Kilgore, held judicial positions. Kilgore fought a long battle in the legislature and in the courts to get the right for women to study and practice law in Pennsylvania. This was after she applied to the law department of the University of Pennsylvania and was rejected because of her gender. She became the first women graduate and later was admitted to practice before the Pennsylvania Supreme Court.[95]

During the early women's movement, as suffragettes pushed for women's equality, efforts to increase the number of women as judges also increased.[96] For example, Grace I. Rohleder, an attorney and writer who urged women's judgeships, asserted that the problem with the system was because men fail to provide the woman's viewpoint.[97] She continued that courts were almost exclusively

---

91 *Esther Hobart Morris,* Wyoming State Archives, *accessed at* http://wyoarchives.state.wy.us/Archives/Research.aspx?ID=2.

92 These are titles for the lowest level, limited jurisdiction courts in some parts of the United States. *See also* text *supra* note 21.

93 Master in Chancery: An officer appointed by a court of equity to assist the court. In English law, a senior official or clerk of a court of chancery who assists the Chancellor in various duties such as enquiring into matters referred by the court, examining cases, taking oaths and affidavits, hearing testimony, and computing damages. There were many Masters in Chancery at the same time. The office was abolished in 1897 and was replaced by the office of Master of the Supreme Court. Black's Law Dictionary, *supra* note 88, at 1123.

94 Morello, *supra* note 50, at 221.

95 Sandra Day O'Connor, *supra* note 36, at 186, 187.

96 Morello, *supra* note 50, at 224.

97 *Id.*

male: judges, clerks, marshals, policemen and even the official court stenographer were all male.[98]

98 *Id.*

Women Lawyers and Judges in the Early 20th Century: The Beginning of Change

The United States, on a national level, did not grant women the right to vote until 1920. It is interesting to note that many states, prior to 1920, limited voting to males over 21. And in almost identical language to the Iranian election laws prior to 1964, women were categorized with the insane and criminals in being barred from the franchise.[99] While women were allowed to vote in some elections in some states earlier than this,[100] the U.S. Constitution did not require or guarantee women's right to vote until the passage of the Nineteenth Amendment. This Amendment reads:

> "The right of citizens of the United States to vote shall not be denied or abridged by the United States or by any State on account of sex."[101]

However, granting to women the right to vote did not necessarily mean that women would gain access to employment, whether as attorneys and judges. While things were better than they had been immediately after the Civil War, the percentage of women lawyers in the United States in 1920 was just 3%. Indeed it was still at 3% in 1951.[102] Women judges, except in unusual local situations, were still virtually unheard of in most courts. Nevertheless, by 1923, all

99 U.S. Const. amend. XIX, (1920). *See also* Ohio Const. art. V, § 1, 6 (1851); Cal. Const. art. II, § 1 (1879). For the Iranian election laws check Chapter 1.

100 Women first were granted a right to vote in Wyoming Territory in 1869. Twenty-seven of the forty-eight states existing prior to the Nineteenth Amendment allowed women some right to vote. Constitution Center, *Centuries of Citizenship: A Constitutional Timeline*, National Constitution Center, *accessed at* http://constitutioncenter.org/experience/exhibitions/past-exhibitions/constitutional-timeline.

101 U.S. Const. amend. XIX.

102 Laura Pecenco & Mary Blair-Loy, Center for Research on Gender in the Legal Profession: The Status of Women and Men (2013), *accessed at* http://crg-stemm.ucsd.edu/_files/articles/GenderinLegalProfessionsCaseStudy.pdf.

states finally allowed women to become members of the bar.[103] This new change of opening up membership in the bar to women followed the First World War (1914-1918) and the re-examination of life and social values during that period helped the passage of the Nineteenth Amendment, and influenced the opening up of some law schools, which had begun to admit women although still in small numbers.[104]

Despite women's victory in gaining the right to vote, however, at least twenty-seven law schools continued to refuse to register women, including Columbia University, which did not admit women until 1928, and Harvard, which did not admit women until 1950. Others admitted just a tiny number.[105] For example, Yale admitted one woman in 1919 and five in 1920.[106] No law required restricting women's admission to law school. It was a deeply engrained tradition that the natural and proper timidity and delicacy which belongs to women, made them unfit for many of the occupations of civil life. Accordingly, the paramount destiny and duty of women are to fulfill the noble offices of wife and mother because this is the law of the Creator.[107]

During the 1920s and 1930s, women rarely were seen in courtrooms. There was only a small group of women attorneys with some connections to male friends or relatives who found jobs in major law firms. Women lawyers became the backbone of poverty law service, but almost never worked in the criminal division. Defending criminals was considered improper for women attorneys.[108] The reason for men's resistance to women attorneys had to do with the law's close connection to power in the society. The legal profession creates power relations between groups by shaping the rules and laws that open or limit opportunities without resort to force, making it the quintessential masculine power role.[109]

---

103 Angela Nicole Johnson, *A Timeline of Women's History in the Legal Profession*, WOMEN AS LAWYERS (2011), *accessed at* https://womenaslawyers.wordpress.com/a-timeline-of-womens-history-in-the-legal-profession/#_ftn5.

104 GARZA, *supra* note 32, at 94, 97-99.

105 SUSAN EHRLICH MARTIN & NANCY C. JURIK, DOING JUSTICE, DOING GENDER 106 (Sage Publications 1996).

106 GARZA, *supra* note 32, at 99.

107 *See* Justice Bradley concurring opinion. Bradwell, 83 U.S. 130 at 141, 142.

108 MORELLO, *supra* note 50, at 99-106.

109 DOING JUSTICE, DOING GENDER, *supra* note 105, at 103, 104.

During the 1950s, after the Second World War, women lawyers had limited choices; the government hired a few more women attorneys.[110] Still there was a firm resistance to women in fields such as criminal law. For example, the Supreme Court Justice Ruth Bader Ginsburg[111] experienced discrimination in spite of her outstanding record as a law student and no New York law firm offered her a job. She noted, "to be a woman, a Jew, and a mother to boot, that combination was a bit much."[112]

Women's entry into law, although legal and permitted in all states since 1923, nevertheless saw very modest gain through the next fifty years. In 1956 women still made up only 3% of law students.[113] Women constituted less than 5% of the enrollment at ABA approved law schools well into the 1970s.[114] Women often faced discrimination based on their gender in finding jobs. They also were rarely found on the bench as judges.[115]

It was not until after 1920 that women began to acquire judicial posts in higher courts. Florence Ellinwood[116] was a controversial woman who broke more barriers than others. It has been agreed that she would have been appointed to the United States Supreme Court in the 1940s had she not been a woman.[117] In 1922, she was the first woman elected to the Ohio Supreme Court.[118] She was re-elected to the Ohio Supreme Court in 1928.[119] Six years later, President Franklin Roosevelt appointed her to the U.S. Court of Appeals for the Sixth Circuit. She became the first woman ever appointed to an appellate federal judgeship.[120] In

110 Morello, *supra* note 50, at 99-106.

111 Justice Ruth Bader Ginsburg studied at Harvard Law School from1956. Harvard had not admitted women students until 1950. Ginsburg's class of 552 students had only nine women. The Legacy of Ruth Bader Ginsburg 13 (Scott Dodson ed., Cambridge University Press 2015).

112 People's Lawyers, *supra* note 75, at 358.

113 Paenco and Blair-Loy, *supra* note 102.

114 Doing Gender, Doing Justice, *supra* note 105, at 107.

115 *Id.* at 107-108.

116 Florence Ellinwood Allen was said to have a "masculine mind." Ten weeks after the adoption of the constitutional amendment giving women the right to vote she was elected to the court. Morello, *supra* note 50, at 231-233. *See also 13 Pioneering Women in American Law*, ABA Journal, *accessed at* http://www.abajournal.com/gallery/historical_women/764.

117 Morello, *supra* note 50, at 231.

118 *Id.* at 234.

119 *Id.*

120 *Id.*

her autobiography, she recalls that none of the judges favored her appointment to the federal bench and after the announcement one judge went to bed for almost two days.[121]

The first African-American woman judge, Jane Bolin, was appointed to the Domestic Relations Court of the city of New York in 1939, by New York's mayor.[122] Burnita Matthews was a judge of the U.S District Court for the District of Columbia. She was the first woman to serve on a federal district court, appointed by President Truman in 1949.[123]

A recently uncovered report from the Eisenhower Archives reveals that in 1959 there were only four female judges on federal courts at all levels. There were a total of 185 women judges at all levels, most of who served in specialized county or city courts such as Probate Courts. At this time there were over 5000 women lawyers in the United States, some 3% of the bar.[124] By 1977, only eight women had ever served in the federal judiciary at the District or Circuit Court level.[125] As of 1983, women held only 6% of the attorney judgeships, a percentage that was disproportionate to the 13% in practice and the 38% in law school.[126]

There are a greater number of judges in the state judicial systems than in the small federal judiciary. Improvement in the presence of women judges at the state level varies from state to state, since each of the fifty states' systems are independent. For example, the first woman judge in New York State was appointed in 1935. The first woman elected to a New York state court was in 1958.[127]

---

121 *Id.* at 234.

122 REBELS IN LAW, *supra* note 52, at 282.

123 *Id.* at 44.

124 Women's Division Republican National Committee, Women in the Judicial Service, EISENHOWER PRESIDENTIAL LIBRARY, MUSEUM, AND BOYHOOD HOME (1959), *accessed at* https://www.eisenhower.archives.gov/research/online_documents/women_in_the_1950s/Women_in_Judicial_Service.pdf.

125 DOING JUSTICE, DOING GENDER, *supra* note 105, at 108.

126 Beverly B. Cook, *Women Judges: A Preface to Their History,* 14 Golden Gate U. L. Rev. (1984), *accessed at* http://digitalcommons.law.ggu.edu/ggulrev/vol14/iss3/7. In 1981, there were 43 full-time women appellate and district court judges, 7.3 percent of the total. *Decades After O'Connor, Role of Women Judges Still Growing,* UNITED STATE COURT (2013), *accessed at* http://news.uscourts.gov/decades-after-oconnor-role-women-judges-still-growing.

127 Judge Birdie Amsterdam was elected to a state judgeship in 1958. *Birdie Amsterdam: "First lady of the Judiciary",* LAW LIBRARY OF COLUMBIA, *accessed at* http://library.law.columbia.edu/rise_of_women/judiciary/BirdieAmsterdam.html.

However, in all the years since Florence Ellinwood Allen was elected to the Ohio Supreme Court in 1923, until the 1970s, only five states had ever had a women Supreme Court judge.[128]

128 *Supra* note 116; Hawaii (1959). *Judges: Her Honor Takes the Bench,* TIME (1965), *accessed at* http://content.time.com/time/magazine/article/0,9171,839164,00.html.

The Second Civil Rights Movement: Women Lawyers and Judges in Modern Times

The first period of struggle for Civil Rights began during the period prior to the Civil War, 1861-1865, which ended with the passage of the Thirteenth, Fourteenth and Fifteenth Amendments to the U.S. Constitution, along with some strong implementing legislation.[129]

The second Civil Rights movement really started with the decision in *Brown v. Board of Education*, 347 U.S. 483, in 1954,[130] followed by the federal government's role as catalyst in altering the structure of women's rights. Not surprisingly, this movement began around issues of race, not gender, but then evolved quickly into a series of major changes in both areas. Even though slavery had been legally abolished in 1865 by the Thirteenth Amendment, implementing the earlier Emancipation Proclamation of President Abraham Lincoln in 1863, the reality of life for Blacks in America was severe, with total legally imposed segregation in the southern states, and serious discrimination in many other states.[131]

The case of *Plessy v. Ferguson*, 163 U.S. 537, in 1896[132] had recognized this legal principle of "separate but equal," and in the over fifty years since its pronouncement there had been effective and total separation, and little or no equality.[133]

---

129 *E.g.*, 42 U.S.C. § 1981 (1991), 42. U.S.C. § 1983 (1996), 42 U.S.C. § 1985 (1980) were passed immediately after the Civil War.

130 Brown v. Board of Education, 347 U.S. 483 (1954). *See also* Buechler, *supra* note 38, at 24. As women's labor force participation increased, their role in the labor force occurred in a context of sex segregation and discrimination that affected their occupational roles. In addition a hostile social climate regarding women's participation in the labor force and public roles was one of the important structural strains for many women in the post-World War II. Buechler, *supra* note 38, at 24.

131 U.S. Const. amend. XIII (1865); Richard Kluger, Simple Justice: The History of Brown v. Board of Education and Black America's Struggle for Equality, 41-42, (Vintage Books 2004); Buechler, *supra* note 38, at 26.

132 Plessy v. Ferguson, 163 U.S. 537 (1896).

133 Kluger, *supra* note 131, at 289; *See id.*

Brown overturned Plessy and ruled that legally enforced racial segregation was "inherently unequal" and violated the Fourteenth Amendment equal protection clause.[134] So began the intensive litigative and legislative change that had a profound impact not only on racial minorities in the United States, but ultimately on the status and opportunities of women.

Between 1954 and 1963, the U.S. Supreme Court issued dozens of decisions continuing to strongly demand an end to discrimination based on race.[135] A national Civil Rights Movement grew quite large, led by such iconic figures as Martin Luther King, Jr., and struggled for the elimination of racial injustice and a commitment to equality.[136] Almost simultaneously, a Women's Movement arose, not only in support of ending racial discrimination, but in support of extending the principles of Brown to gender discrimination as well.[137]

134 Brown, 347 U.S. 483, at 495.

135 *See* ERWIN CHEMERINSKY, CONSTITUTIONAL LAW PRINCIPLES AND POLICIES 704-730 (3d ed., ASPEN 2006).

136 The definitive history of the Civil Rights movement is the famous books by Taylor Branch such as: Parting the Waters: America in the King Years 1954-1963 (Simon & Schuster 1998); Pillar of Fire: America in the King Years 1963-1965 (Simon & Schuster 1999); At Canaan's Edge: America in the King Years 1965-1968 (Simon & Schuster 2007).

137 *See* FLORA DAVIS, MOVING THE MOUNTAIN: THE WOMEN'S MOVEMENT IN AMERICA SINCE 1960 (University of Illinois Press 1999).

Women's Equality & Political Branches of Government

In 1960, John F. Kennedy became President. In 1961, for the first time in history, the issue of women's equality in various spheres became part of the President's federal government agenda. President Kennedy, through an executive order, established a Commission on the Status of Women.[138] The commission's task was to explore additional affirmative steps taken through legislation, executive or administrative action to assure non-discrimination on the basis of sex and to enhance constructive employment opportunities for women.[139] Those promoting women as decision-making figures regardless of their gender, for example in the judiciary and politics, argued for women to seek elective and appointive posts at various local, state, and national levels and in all three branches of government.[140]

The Commission's Committee on Private Employment recommended legislation for equal pay for women. The Federal Equal Pay Act of 1963 bars discrimination in pay on account of sex where members of each gender are doing "equal work."[141] With the passage of this law, it became legally possible for women to win equal pay in their jobs as well as to gain unpaid wages if they had been previously cheated.[142]

---

138 American Women: The Report of the President's Commission on the Status of Women and other Publications of the Commission 3, 5, 48 (Margaret Mead & Frances Balgley Kaplan eds., Zenger Publishing Co. 1975).

139 *E.g., id* at 19, 48-53. *See also Commission on the Status of Women*, Presidential Library and Museum, *accessed at* http://www.jfklibrary.org/Asset-Viewer/Archives/JFKPOF-093-004.aspx.

140 American Women: The Report of the President's Commission on the Status of Women, *supra* note 138, at 74.

141 29 U.S.C. § 206(d) (1963); *Minimum Wage*, U.S. Equal Employment Opportunity Commission, *accessed at* http://www.eeoc.gov/laws/statutes/epa.cfm. *See also* Michael J. Zimmer, Charles A. Sullivan, Rebecca Hanner White, Cases and Material on Employment Discrimination 121 (7th ed., Aspen Publication 2008).

142 29 U.S.C. § 206(d) (1963).

While the Supreme Court spent its anti-discrimination energy on deciding more and more cases involving racial discrimination, the political branches moved ahead on both the racial and the gender front. This ended in the passage of the Civil Rights Act of 1964. It barred racial and gender discrimination in a wide range of areas.[143]

However, the passage of this law was not without sadness and irony. When the bill was introduced while John Kennedy was still President, it was given little chance to pass. At that time the bill only addressed racial discrimination. However, in November 1963, while the bill was pending, President Kennedy was assassinated in Dallas, Texas. Vice President Lyndon Johnson became President. He was also a supporter of civil rights for racial minorities, and decided that the passage of the Civil Right Act introduced by President Kennedy was not only good policy but also a fitting tribute to President Kennedy's memory.[144]

He carefully maneuvered the bill so it would pass. However, at the last minute a Representative from Virginia, a former legally segregated state, stood upon the floor of the House of Representatives, and offered an Amendment to the bill. He proposed to add the word "sex" to the list of prohibited traits for discrimination in employment in Title VII of the bill, "race, color, religion, or national origin." There is still an historical debate as to whether this amendment was meant to undermine the likelihood of passage of the bill, or was something the Representative truly believed in. Regardless of the motivation, the provision remained and so when the bill became law, it now outlawed sex discrimination on the same basis as race discrimination, a monumental achievement for women.[145] This law had a profound effect on women's employment rights.

Congress continued its work by passing another law. In 1972 Congress officially accepted the fact that sex discrimination existed in the schools and colleges

143 Civil Rights Act of 1964, 42 U.S.C. § 2000(a) et seq.; Title VII of the Civil Rights Act of 1964, 42 U.S.C. § 2000(e). *Title VII of the Civil Rights Act of 1964,* U.S. EQUAL EMPLOYMENT OPPORTUNITY COMMISSION, *accessed at* http://www.eeoc.gov/laws/statutes/titlevii.cfm.

144 Ted Gittinger & Allen Fisher, *LBJ Champions the Civil Rights Act of 1964,* NATIONAL ARCHIVES (2004), *accessed at* http://www.archives.gov/publications/prologue/2004/summer/civil-rights-act-1.html.

145 *Teaching With Documents: The Civil Rights Act of 1964 and the Equal Employment Opportunity Commission,* NATIONAL ARCHIVES, *accessed at* http://www.archives.gov/education/lessons/civil-rights-act/.

and passed a law to remedy this practice. Title IX[146] prohibits sex discrimination in any educational program or activity receiving federal financial assistance.[147] At this point women enrollment in law schools was about 9%.[148] After the passage of Title IX of the Education Amendments, law schools, along with colleges and universities in general, had to obey the law to make sure that more women were admitted. They also had to make sure that equal employment opportunities existed for those who graduated and passed the bar examination.[149] By 1980, the percentage of women in law schools was about 35%.[150] It has gradually grown until now women routinely make up nearly 50% of law school graduates.[151]

---

146 20 U.S.C. § 1681 (1972). The wording of Title IX is exactly like that of Title VI of the Civil Rights Act, except that "sex" is substituted for "race." Any educational institution receiving federal financial assistance must comply.

147 RENEE CHEROW-O' LEARY, THE STATE-BY-STATE GUIDE TO WOMEN'S LEGAL RIGHTS 45 (McGraw-Hill 1987).

148 American Bar Association, *Women in Law in Canada and the U.S. (Report on First Year and Total J.D. Enrollment by Gender 1947 – 2012)*, CATALYST (2015), *accessed at* http://www.catalyst.org/knowledge/women-law-canada-and-us.

149 MORELLO, *supra* note 50, at 162.

150 WOMEN IN LAW IN CANADA AND THE U.S., *supra* note 148.

151 CENTER FOR RESEARCH ON GENDER IN THE LEGAL PROFESSION, *supra* note 102.

Sex Discrimination & The Supreme Court of the United States

Since the Brown case was decided in 1954, reinterpreting the Equal Protection Clause and beginning the end to racial segregation, the Supreme Court had been silent on the issue of equality for women. It was in 1971 that the court decided the case of *Reed v. Reed.*[152] The court's language created a new era in constitutional law in the United States concerning gender equality. In ruling that it was unconstitutional to give males automatic preference over females in administering estates, the court said:

> To give a mandatory preference to members of either sex over members of the other, merely to accomplish the elimination of hearings on the merits, is to make the very kind of arbitrary legislative choice forbidden by the Equal Protection Clause of the Fourteenth Amendment; and whatever may be said as to the positive values of avoiding intra-family controversy, the choice in this context may not lawfully be mandated solely on the basis of sex.[153]

In the next five years, the Court handed down a series of cases all indicating that gender discrimination raised a serious equal protection of the laws issue. Such laws required the government to show a strong justification for using gender. This series of cases[154] ended in the case of *Craig v. Boren,*[155] in which the Court agreed that all gender classifications by the government were subject to

152 Reed v. Reed, 404 U.S. 71 (1971).

153 *Id.* at 76-77.

154 *E.g.*, Stanley v. Illinois, 405 U.S. 645 (1972); Frontiero v. Richardson, 411 U.S. 677 (1973); Schlesinger v. Ballard, 419 U.S. 498 (1975); Stanton v. Stanton, 421 U.S. 7 (1975); Weinberger v. Wiesenfeld, 420 U.S. 636 (1975).

155 Craig v. Boren, 429 U.S. 190 (1976).

higher scrutiny by courts, and could not be justified by custom or stereotypical assumptions about the roles of men and women in society. The Court said:

> *Reed v. Reed* has also provided the underpinning for decisions that have invalidated statutes employing gender as an inaccurate proxy for other, more germane bases of classification. Hence, 'archaic and overbroad' generalizations, *Schlesinger v. Ballard*, concerning the financial position of servicewomen, *Frontiero v. Richardson*, and working women, *Weinberger v. Wiesenfeld*, could not justify use of a gender line in determining eligibility for certain governmental entitlements. Similarly, increasingly *outdated misconceptions concerning the role of females in the home, rather than in the 'marketplace and world of ideas,'* were rejected as loose-fitting characterizations incapable of supporting state statutory schemes that were premised upon their accuracy.[156] [Emphasis Added]

Between Reed in 1971 and Craig in 1976 there were some noteworthy cases. *Stanley v. Illinois*[157] involved a law that presumed an unmarried father unfit to care for his children when the mother died. The law clearly discriminated against fathers. The Stanleys had lived together and raised their children for eighteen years. When the mother died, the state removed the children to foster care. The Supreme Court indicated that making this assumption of unfitness of the father violated the Equal Protection Clause. Note that this court said that men and women must be treated equally.[158] The case of *Frontiero v. Richardson*[159] was a case in which a female member of the Armed Forces had a much heavier burden placed on her to receive dependent benefits for a spouse than a male member. The compensation for a woman's employment was less than for a male service member. The Court said:

> Any statutory scheme which draws a sharp line between the sexes, *solely* for the purpose of achieving administrative convenience, necessarily commands 'dissimilar treatment for men and women who are . . . similarly situated,' and therefore involves the 'very kind of arbitrary legislative choice forbidden by the [Constitution]....' [Reed] We therefore conclude that, by according differential

156 *Id.* at 198-199.

157 Stanley v. Illinois, 405 U.S. 645 (1972).

158 *Id.* at 658.

159 Frontiero v. Richardson, 411 U.S. 677 (1973).

treatment to male and female members of the uniformed services for the sole purpose of achieving administrative convenience, the challenged statutes violate the Due Process Clause of the Fifth Amendment.[160]

Likewise, in the two cases of *Schlesinger v. Ballard*[161] and *Weinberger v. Wiesenfeld*,[162] the Court reasserted its concern with unjustified gender discrimination. In Schlesinger the court said that dissimilar treatment for men and women who are similarly situated violates the Equal Protection Clause.[163] Referring to the decision in Frontiero, the Court found the disparity of treatment between male and female service members with regard to benefits constitutionally invalid.[164]

In Weinberger, Social Security benefits were paid more easily to widows than to widowers in the same circumstances. The Court concluded since the gender-based classification cannot be explained as an attempt to provide for the special problems of women, the challenged section violates the Constitution.[165]

Finally, in Craig, as in some earlier cases, it was actually men who were discriminated against by laws concerning the consumption of alcoholic beverages. But the court noted that gender discrimination, whichever gender was stereotypically disadvantaged, was subject to stricter review. Craig said that statutory classifications that distinguish between males and females are subject to scrutiny under the Equal Protection Clause. To withstand constitutional challenge, "classifications by gender must serve important governmental objectives and must be substantially related to achievement of those objectives."[166]

More recently, the Supreme Court has continued to vigorously enforce its rules against most gender discriminations. In *United States v. Virginia*,[167] Justice Ruth Ginsburg wrote the opinion of the Court striking down the ban on women students at the Virginia Military Institute. Justice Ginsburg, before her appoint-

160 *Id.* at 690.

161 Schlesinger v. Ballard, 419 U.S. 498, (1975).

162 Weinberger v. Wiesenfeld, 420 U.S. 636, (1975).

163 Schlesinger, 419 U.S. at 419.

164 *Id.* at 506.

165 Weinberger, 420 U.S. at 653.

166 Craig, 429 U.S. 190 at 197.

167 United States v. Virginia, 518 U.S. 515 (1996).

ment to the Court by President Bill Clinton, had been the driving force as an attorney behind many of the earlier Supreme Court opinions striking down laws as gender discriminatory. She was, for example, the primary attorney in the Reed case and argued and won the Craig case. In gender discrimination cases, she won five arguments before the Supreme Court.[168] She stated, after a detailed analysis of why barring women from Virginia Military Institute was unjustified:

> Today's skeptical scrutiny of official action denying rights or opportunities based on sex responds to volumes of history. As a plurality of this Court acknowledged a generation ago, 'our Nation has had a long and unfortunate history of sex discrimination.' Through a century plus three decades and more of that history, women did not count among voters composing 'We the People'; not until 1920 did women gain a constitutional right to the franchise....And for a half century thereafter, it remained the prevailing doctrine that government, both federal and state, could withhold from women opportunities accorded men so long as any 'basis in reason' could be conceived for the discrimination.[169]

She continued:

> A prime part of the history of our Constitution...is the story of the extension of constitutional rights and protections to people once ignored or excluded. VMI's story continued as our comprehension of 'We the People' expanded. There is no reason to believe that the admission of women capable of all the activities required of VMI cadets would destroy the Institute rather than enhance its capacity to serve the 'more perfect Union.'[170]

By 1976 the Supreme Court, together with the Civil Rights Acts of Congress, had provided substantial constitutional and statutory protection against most—if not all—discrimination against women in education, employment, government benefits and more. Craig together with the 1963 Equal Pay Act, the 1964 Civil Rights Act and the 1972 Education Amendments provided significant gender protection.[171] The Supreme Court has continued to refine its gender discrimina-

---

168 PEOPLE'S LAWYERS, *supra* note 75, at 351, 362-372.

169 United States v. Virginia, 518 U.S. 531 (1996).

170 *Id.* at 557, 558.

171 *See* text from footnote 141-151.

tion jurisprudence, but the basic principle remains: To withstand constitutional challenge, classifications by gender must serve important governmental objectives and must be substantially related to achievement of those objectives.[172] Federal law now provides strong protection against sex discrimination in employment as well as in other areas such as education and benefits.[173] As noted earlier in Chapter 1, the years 1964-1979 were also a time of the advancement of women's rights and opportunities in Iran. Women gained the right to vote, access to more education and employment opportunities, and in particular access to judgeships.

It must be noted that given the federalism structure of the United States, each of the fifty states also has the power to pass anti-discrimination laws that can supplement the federal law. The state law may apply to more employers or types of activities than the federal law, and can also provide for different standards and remedies. As of 2014, forty-seven states provide substantial additional statutory protection against sex discrimination in employment. Only three states (Alabama, Georgia and Mississippi) do not provide separate state law protection against such sex discrimination.[174]

172 Craig, 429 U.S. at 190.

173 Title VII to the Civil Rights Act of 1964 (Discrimination), 42 U.S.C. § 2000(e); Title IX of the Education Amendments of 1972 to the Civil Rights Act of 1964, 20 U.S.C. § 1681 et seq.; Equal Credit Opportunity Act, 15 U.S.C. § 1691 et seq.

174 Listing all anti-discrimination protection by state and federal law. *Employment Discrimination in Your State*, NOLO, *accessed at* http://www.nolo.com/legal-encyclopedia/employment-discrimination-in-your-state-31017.html.

Women as Attorneys and Judges in the United States: The Picture Today

Did these changes in the law really alter the opportunities for women as lawyers and judges in the United States? What is the situation today compared with prior to these legal changes? In 1910, the number of women lawyers in the U.S. was less than 1%. Until the 1960s women continued to constitute only from 1 to 3% of the legal occupation.[175] It was not until 1923 that women were allowed to practice in all forty-eight states. Alaska did not admit women to practice until the 1950s.[176] A pattern of discrimination by law schools kept the numbers of women in most schools at about 3% in each class between 1951 and 1965,[177] and it still only averaged 5% in 1970s.[178] The passage of Title IX of the Civil Rights Act in 1972, which prohibited discrimination based on sex in the enrollment of students and hiring of faculty, began to change those numbers.[179] Graduating from law school was the first hurdle for women to become working lawyers and judges.

The next hurdle, of course, was employment. As we've seen, women's employment opportunities in the early days were severely limited. Even in those states that permitted women to practice, most law firms and government agencies openly refused jobs to women just because they were women. Even after the Second World War, when women had demonstrated their ability to handle almost any job, the discrimination remained.

Even women with training from elite schools faced employment discrimination that was openly practiced well into the 1970s. For example, a 1963 survey of 430 law firms found that "female status" was the characteristic that got the

175 Garza, *supra* note 32, at 83.

176 Johnson, *supra* note 103.

177 Doing Justice, Doing Gender, *supra* note 105, at 107.

178 *Id.*

179 *Id.*

most negative rating in selecting new recruits. Hence, it is not surprising that in 1965, fewer than 20% of the 104 law firms responding to a Harvard Law Record questionnaire employed any women lawyers. Women who were able to get legal work often were offered opportunities in low-status specialties deemed appropriate for women, such as domestic relations and probate law. They received lower pay and were denied partnerships and opportunities for leadership in bar associations.[180]

It is a famous story that when former Supreme Court Justice Sandra Day O'Connor graduated third in her class at Stanford Law School in 1953, the only job that she was offered was a secretarial job.[181] Significant changes began to occur in the 1970s and 1980s as more women graduated from law schools.[182]

Despite the increased number of women in the legal profession in the beginning of the 21st century, their numerical gains have not yielded equivalent increases in power, status, and income. Statistics showed that women and men had different employment patterns. For example, women regularly were underrepresented in private practice, and overrepresented in government, corporate/private industry, and legal aid and public defender work. Also, within each of these organizational hierarchies, women were kept at the bottom of prestige and income. They were also underrepresented in the ranks of partner, general counsel, and supervisors.[183]

Today, women are still struggling against less obvious forms of discrimination, but their integration into the bar has accelerated substantially in the last two decades. What is clear is that women's significant gains in becoming attorneys and judges are part of the much larger societal change which occurred in the United States during this period. The strength of the women's movement; and the appointment and election of women (and men supporting the rights of women) to important government positions, led to improvements in women's employment across the board. The old role models of women belong in the home began to break down, and women in the public arena gained more acceptance.[184]

180 *Id.* at 107.

181 Ann Carey McFeatters, Sandra Day O'Connor: Justice in the Balance 45 (University of New Mexico Press 2005).

182 *See e.g.*, G. Larry Mays, American Courts and the Judicial Process 353 (Oxford University Press 2012).

183 Doing Justice, Doing Gender, *supra* note 105, at 115.

184 George Guilder, *Women in the Work Force*, The Atlantic 2, 3, (1986), *accessed at* http://www.theatlantic.com/magazine/archive/1986/09/women-in-the-work-force/304924/.

It was reported in the New York Times Magazine in 1984 that from 1960 to 1983 the percentage of lawyers who were women rose from 2% to 15% and the percentage of jobs in banking and financial management held by women rose from 9% to 39%.[185]

A report from the American Bar Association in 2014 shows the following. In private practice women make up 44.8% of associates and about 20% of partners. Likewise, in corporations women occupy about 21% of counsel positions in the Fortune 500 General Council list, and only 16.8% in other Fortune Corporations. Women make up 47% of the graduates of law schools and 46% of editors on Law Reviews. Women constitute almost 21% of Law School Deans. Women now serve in 51% of Judicial Clerkships, and constitute between 24% and 33% of judges in the state and federal courts.[186]

Women judges continued to be chosen in small numbers into the 1980s. New York is a good example. Even though there were no longer any legal barriers to women serving as judges, the long history and custom of male judges continued. In 1986, five years after Sandra Day O'Connor became the first female Justice on the United States Supreme Court,[187] and three years after the first woman was appointed to the New York's highest court, New York Court of Appeals,[188] the number of women New York state judges was still quite small.[189] Then, in 1986, the Chief Justice created the New York State Judicial Committee on Women in the Courts.[190] This Committee has most recently reported that progress toward gender equity has been made but room for improvement remains.[191] By 2000, the percentage of women judges in New York had risen to 25%, with a much higher

185 The sociologist Andrew Hacker reported in the New York Times Magazine in 1984. *Id.*

186 American Bar Association, A Current Glance at Women in the Law, AMERICAN BAR ASSOCIATION (July 2014), *accessed at* http://www.americanbar.org/content/dam/aba/marketing/women/current_glance_statistics_july2014.authcheckdam.pdf.

187 SANDRA DAY O'CONNOR, *supra* note 36, at i.

188 Steven C. Krane, *Judith Smith Kaye, accessed at* https://www.nycourts.gov/history/legal-history-new-york/luminaries-court-appeals/kaye-judith.html.

189 The number of women state judges in New York in 1988 was 11%. New York State Bar Association, *Judicial Diversity: A Work in Progress*, NEW YORK STATE BAR ASSOCIATION 43, 44 (Sep. 2014), *accessed at* http://www.nysba.org/judicialdiversityreport/.

190 *Id.* at 42.

191 *Id.* at 43.

percentage of women in upper level courts. Three of the seven Court of Appeals Justices were women.[192]

The same ABA 2014 report about the number of the women judges in the United States found that on the federal courts, there are currently three women out of nine on the United States Supreme Court. The three current Justices, Ruth Ginsburg, Sonia Sotomayor, and Elena Kagan were appointed in 1993, 2009, and 2010 respectively. Out of the 169 active United States Courts of Appeal judges in 2014, 56, or 33.1% were women. Out of 1,874 active U.S. District Court judges in 2012, 451 were women, or 24%.[193]

Figures for state court judges are similar. In 2012, 27% of all state court judges were women. At the appellate court level, 32% of the judges were women.[194] This coincided with the number of women then in the legal profession, which was 34% in 2013.[195]

Nevertheless the progress made in the short span of time since the 1970s is significant. There are no laws in any state or at the federal level that restrict in any way women's right to serve as attorneys or judges. There are now powerful and influential organizations of women lawyers and women judges that have a strong voice in the legal community.[196] A study in 2010 showed there were women Chief Justices on eighteen state Supreme Courts.[197] The key historical fact is that in this period in the United States women have made continuing and consistent steps toward equality in all lawyering positions, including serving as judges. American women now serve in all levels of judgeships in all fifty states, and in the federal courts.

---

192 *Id.* at 44.

193 A CURRENT GLANCE AT WOMEN IN THE LAW, *supra* note 186, at 5.

194 *Id.* at 2, 5.

195 *Id.* at 2.

196 Such as the National Association of Women Lawyers and the National Association of Women Judges. *See The National Association of Women Lawyers,* NATIONAL ASSOCIATION OF WOMEN LAWYERS, *accessed at* http://www.nawl.org/p/cm/ld/fid=1; *Welcome to the National Association of Women Judges,* NATIONAL ASSOCIATION OF WOMEN JUDGES, *accessed at* http://www.nawj.org/.

197 *Female chief justices of state supreme courts,* BALLOTPEDIA, *accessed at* http://ballotpedia.org/Female_chief_justices_of_state_supreme_courts.

Chapter 5

Conclusion

Women as Judges in Iran

The 20th century witnessed some of the worst human rights violations in modern history, yet it was also the century in which the State's responsibility to respect and promote individual human rights and freedoms was born under international law. This led to the 1993 Vienna Declaration, which established that women's rights are human rights, and that they are an inalienable and integral part of universal human rights. These changes moved women from among marginalized groups to the center of human rights challenges.

The 20th century for Iranian women also had its dramatic ups and downs. The beginning of the century was a period in which Iranian women were treated according to hundreds of years of traditional patriarchal values that kept them illiterate and invisible to the public eye. Their social and legal rights and freedoms were restricted to domestic roles such as mothers and wives. Yet, despite all the social taboos and restrictions against women, they managed to participate in a landmark movement like the 1906 Constitution Revolution to establish a parliamentary system in Iran.

It was at the end of the first quarter of the 20th century, after the reign of Riżā Pahlavī, that the state run policies to reform and weaken the longstanding religious authority of Islamic jurisprudence and traditions began. Some of these reforms directly aimed at improving the social status of women. Bold and controversial policies, such as compulsory unveiling for women and the passage of the marriage law were among the early steps taken by the Pahlavī government to emancipate women from hundreds of years of patriarchal traditions and Islamic rules that deprived women from acquiring the most basic social, legal, and political rights. Women legally were under the "protection and guardianship" of men, incapable of making any independent decision. Despite these unprecedented policies aiming at women, the government, however, failed to reform its discriminatory legal system against women.

By the end of the reign of Riżā Pahlavī in 1941, all election laws directly discriminated against women, banning them from voting and running for elected offices. Women's non-legal existence was reflected by direct legislative language, that grouped them with murderers, criminals and mentally disabled as those ineligible to vote.

The opportunity for women to even consider high offices such as judgeships during the first quarter of the 20th century, despite the existence of gender neutral laws setting the qualifications for this position, were rare or non-existent. Women were discriminated against both by laws and in practice. Hurdles—such as the high percentage of illiteracy among women and the fact that getting a higher education for women only became available in the 1930s; de jure discriminatory election laws, and social taboos against women in public life—made it almost impossible for women to even consider key positions like judgeships, which required significant education, keen skills and freedom to work with men in public.

It was not until 1964, during the reign of Muḥammad Rizā Pahlavī that the old taboo of women being under the Islamic guardianship and protection of men, for example imposed by elections laws and Islamic jurisprudence, was broken by the passage of the law granting the equal political enfranchisement of women. This was the beginning of fast track integration of women into important government decision-making positions. Five years later, in 1969, a few women were appointed to preside as judges for the first time. Ten years later there were almost 100 women judges. However, immediately after the triumph of the 1979 Islamic Revolution, existing women judges were found summarily disqualified to work as judges and forced to step down solely because of their sex. The establishment of the government of the Islamic Republic of Iran in 1979, and the approval of the "Guardianship of the Islamic Jurisprudence" as the core principle, counts as the beginning of strict Islamization of the country. The Constitution speaks of women's rights but recognizes Shīʿa Islamic jurisprudence as its decisive and fundamental principle to scrutinize women's rights and freedoms. This justifies different treatment of women from men by the entire legal system, because Islamic jurisprudence holds different but complementary rights and responsibilities for each sex. Accordingly, women and men, due to their physical and psychological differences, deserve different rights, responsibilities, and punishments.

According to international human rights jurisprudence, such a legal interpretation introduces restrictive criteria that negatively affect the enjoyment of equal rights and freedoms of Iranian women. Different treatment of women and men solely on the basis of their sex is in direct conflict with the essence and application of universally accepted norms enforced by international human rights mechanisms. The undisputed application of the dual principles of "gender equality" and "elimination of gender-based discrimination" are among the most fundamental human rights jurisprudence enshrined by all human rights documents.

Despite continuous promises of equal rights for women and men during the turmoil of the 1979 Revolution, and despite women's immense contribution to the victory of the revolution and referendum, as the Islamic purification process took place women lost many previously acquired rights and freedoms. For the 20th century modern Iranian women, who had fought just a few decades earlier for the removal of social and religious taboos left from much of the long history of patriarchal Islamic traditions, the past returned with a vengeance. Once again women were discriminated against by laws, this time in the late 20th century. A good example was the almost instantaneous removal of existing women judges, appointed just a few years earlier, from the entire legal system.

In less than a month after the triumph of the Islamic Revolution, the service of all existing women judges was found "no longer necessary." Existing women judges were found disqualified for the sole reason of their gender, because they now failed to meet the new male only gender qualification for judgeships. This view was imposed by the application of the consensus view of Shīʿa jurists that women cannot become judges in an Islamic society and that male gender is the key qualifications for Islamic judges. The significance of a judge's role in Islamic society has been continuously emphasized by a majority of Islamic jurists and scholars as a key authority to adjudicate and end disputes. Under Islam, a judgeship counts as one of the most important positions given by God initially to the Prophet Muḥammad and infallible Imāms that over the centuries has been handing down only to qualified mujtahidīn (Islamic jurisprudents) as the ultimate protectors of Islam.

A judgeship, therefore, is considered one of the branches of Islamic leadership and prophecy that belongs exclusively to men. According to Shīʿa Islamic jurists and scholars, the challenging and demanding nature of a judgeship goes against women's physical and psychological nature and capabilities. Women are thought physically and emotionally incapable of bearing the responsibilities of judges. On the other hand men's physical and psychological nature enables them to lead and make serious decisions, which makes them suitable for this position. Therefore, women cannot become judges. This interpretation of Shīʿa Islamic jurists was implemented in the Law on the Qualifications for Appointment of Judges in the Ministry of Justice passed in 1982.

Today, the authority of qualified Islamic jurists as authoritative judges is not a foreign concept throughout the history of the Iranian legal system. This has been a long-standing principle since the Ṣafavī Dynasty when for the first time they recognized Shīʿa Islam as the official religion. In modern times, even after the adoption of the first Constitution in 1906, mujtahidīn had the exclusive constitutional jurisdiction over religious tribunals. Even during the reign of Riżā Pahlavī, and despite increasing the number and power of non-Islamic judges, the religious judges had jurisdiction over religious tribunals. Hence, after 1979, once again the exclusive right of male Islamic jurists as judges was reaffirmed by the 1982 statute—this time expanding their authority from just religious courts to all courts and jurisdictions.

Since the passage of the first statute setting the required qualifications for judges in the early 20th century, until the 1982 law, all such statutes were gender neutral. It was in 1982 that for the first time the legislature imposed the male gender requirement by passing the Law on the Qualifications for Appointment of Judges in the Ministry of Justice. The law in question expressly states, "*Judges* will be selected among qualified *men*."[1] This law is as clear as it reads. It leaves no room for any ambiguity, speculation, and interpretation. The gender specific qualification imposed by this law requires that only qualified "men" can become judges. An otherwise fully qualified woman would be denied a judgeship solely because she is a women. According to international human rights:

> "Any *distinction, exclusion, restriction* or preference or other differential treatment that is *directly* or indirectly based on the *prohibited grounds of discrimination* and which has the intention or effect of *nullifying* or *impairing* the recognition, enjoyment or exercise, on an equal footing, of Covenant Rights."[2]

The directly imposed exclusion of all women from judgeships by the legislature on the basis of the prohibited ground of sex constitutes discrimination against women according to international human rights laws.

---

1 Law on the Qualifications for Appointment of Judges in the Ministry of Justice 1982 (Iran).

2 Committee on Economic, Social and Cultural Rights, *General Comment No. 20: Non-discrimination in economic, social and cultural rights*, U.N. Doc. E/C.12/GC/20 (July 2, 2009).

Since then, positions for women labeled as "consultant judges" and "investigative judges" were created by the legislature. This, however, was a subterfuge. The lawmakers made sure that despite possessing judicial titles, these positions lacked the most essential authority of the judge, which is the decision-making power. The Constitutional decision-making power of the judge is to render the final decision of the court and end the dispute. The Constitution even asserts that judges cannot refrain from delivering such a judgment and must end the dispute among the parties.

It is critical to carefully analyze positions given titles like "female consultant judges." Why? Because to the international community, the government of the Islamic Republic of Iran has been presenting this position as true decision-making judges with the Constitutional power to end disputes in all courts, which is a false and misleading claim. These women may "advise" and "consult" but render no decisions. The government has continuously insisted on the existence of women judges in Iran, without giving much detail about the governing domestic laws. Iran, for example, in its State reports, or in responses to various human rights mechanisms reports that have raised serious concerns about the exclusion of women from becoming judges presiding over a courtroom with the decision-making authority to render the final decision of the court, has provided false and contradictory reports to mislead the international community. Iran, by submitting false and misleading reports, fails to fulfill its international obligations to act with good faith at all times, and this also constitutes a violation under international law.

The attempt to argue that consultant female judges are authoritative judges contradicts the Constitution of the IRI. Female consultant judges are statutorily banned from rendering verdicts or making any final decisions in a case. The Constitution has a clear meaning that one is not a judge just because one has the "title" of a judge, or receives the "salary" of a judge, or is being "consulted" with before rendering a verdict. The Constitution simply asserts a judge is one who "renders the final decision of the court and ends the dispute."

There is a famous story about United States President Abraham Lincoln. He asked a friend,

"How many legs does a dog have, if you call a tail a leg?" The friend replied, "Five." "No," said President Lincoln. "Calling the tail a leg would not make it a leg."[3]

This makes the point beautifully. Calling "women consultant judges", in the absence of extending the constitutional authority to them, true constitutional "judges" does not make them judges.

Contrary to the government's reports, all UN human rights monitoring bodies, NGOs, and stakeholders have rejected Iran's claim on the existence of women judges. Despite all misleading reports, the international community has uniformly asserted that women are legally excluded from becoming presiding judges over a courtroom with the full authority to render the final decision of the court in Iran, which constitutes discrimination against them in violation of international law.

The remarkable finding is that despite the government's various reports claiming that there are women judges in Iran, the key 1982 legislative statute which expressly required judges to be men was never mentioned in any State reports prepared by the IRI government.

In general the de jure discrimination against women pursuing judgeships is in violation of all international human rights jurisprudence. More specific to Iran's international obligations, Iran ratified the UN Charter, ICCPR, ICESCR and ILO Employment and Occupation Convention. Also, Iran as a State party to the UN is legally bound to be in full compliance with the provisions of the UDHR. These all impose both negative and positive measures on Iran to fulfill its international obligations toward its citizens. Iran as a State party must respect and ensure women the enjoyment of all their universal human rights, on an equal footing and regardless of their gender, in its national legal system. This requires Iran, first, to refrain from violating women's guaranteed rights and imposition of gender-based discrimination in its laws.

Iran by the passage of the discriminatory law in 1982 that directly excludes women, as a group, from judgeships on the prohibited ground of sex, fails to fulfill its negative obligation under the Charter, UDHR, ICCPR, ICESCR, and ILO Employment and Occupation Convention. Also, upholding this de jure discriminatory law for over thirty years is evidence of Iran's unwillingness to eliminate

3 *Abraham Lincoln Quote,* Wikiquote.org, *accessed at* https://en.wikiquote.org/wiki/Abraham_Lincoln. A similar story about a calf in *Reminiscences of Abraham Lincoln by distinguished men of his time* (1909) can be found in page 242.

its discriminatory law against women. This is a failure of Iran under international law to fulfill its primary legal obligation that requires it to immediately repeal its discriminatory laws. This failure, once again, counts as a violation under international law.

Iran's international obligations extend, also, to other obligations imposed by the Charter-based bodies such as the Universal Periodic Review, Human Rights Council, and General Assembly. As part of Iran's obligation to respect and promote the equal rights of women, Iran is required to implement the accepted recommendations made during the first and second cycles of its Universal Periodic Review into its domestic legal system.

Today, the de jure discrimination against women imposed by the 1982 statute is only one example of pervasive systematic and systemic discrimination against women within the Iranian legal system. The concerns regarding the systematic and systemic discrimination against women in Iran have been supported by massive official reports prepared by various international human rights mechanisms that require urgent reform. Iran, by using the concept of Cultural Relativism, attempts to maintain that gender equality does not entail equality in all places according to its national principles and rules. However, in law and practice, the application of the Islamic principle of women and men's complimentary roles, results in different treatment of women from men. In this specific case, it denies women the right to be judges. This limited interpretation of "equality" is exactly what universal human rights norms reject. Laws treating women differently perpetuates formal and substantive discrimination against women, which is a direct consequence of application of local culture and religion by the Iranian legislation.

Women as Judges: Comparison with the United States

A comparison between the status of women judges in Iran and the United States is both simple and complicated. While the history, culture and religion of the two nations are quite dissimilar, the progress of women in important social and political positions such as judges is remarkably similar until 1979. It is remarkable in some ways that countries so different should have such a similar modern history regarding woman as judges until the Islamic Revolution.

During the 19th and early 20th centuries, the role of women in the public arena lurched forward in its own ways in both countries. In the United States women continued their struggle for the right to vote, strengthened by the Fifteenth Amendment that granted the right to vote to free slaves. American women sought more access to education, including legal and medical education. There were many struggles in the courts and legislatures of the states to provide women with more opportunity, including becoming lawyers. In Iran, women took an unprecedented role during the Tobacco Revolt in 1891, joining men to fight back against the king's concessions to a foreign country. This was the beginning of women participating in public affairs despite all long-standing cultural, legal, and religious hurdles.

The first quarter of the 20th century saw significant legal changes regarding American women. In 1920, American women earned the right to vote through the enactment of the Nineteenth Amendment to the U.S. Constitution. By 1923 laws banning women from becoming lawyers were repealed or struck down in all states. However, in Iran, despite women's role in participating in the 1906 Constitutional Revolution, change in their political and legal rights did not happen. At the end of the Qājār in 1925 women explicitly were banned from voting and being elected by all elections laws. Changes began slowly with the arrival of the Pahlavī in 1925. By the mid-1930s, changes were happening to emancipate women from age-old restrictions, such as unveiling and creating more educational opportunity.

Both countries, in their own ways, seemed to be moving slowly to remove the explicit legal barriers. For American women it was also a slow process to overcome barriers in the male dominant legal field to become lawyers and judges. For Iranian women, despite the absence of direct statutory discrimination against them, as a consequence of centuries old substantive discrimination, it became impossible to even consider positions like judgeships when they were illiterate or their public appearance was restricted. Women's access to higher education was not available until the 1930s. Even though, women in the United States had better access to education than Iranian women, many U.S. law schools barred women from attending classes until well into the 1930s.

What is essential to know is that during the time when women in America were barred from practicing as lawyers, and in Iran—even today—barred from becoming judges, in both countries the exclusion of women from the role of attorneys and judges was often justified by religious principles. Even though, Iran has been an Shīʿa Islamic country for centuries, and United States constitutionally is a secular country, however, religious ideas often prevailed when it came to the rights of women. The landmark Supreme Court case of *Bradwell v. Illinois* in 1873, which allowed states to ban women from becoming lawyers, relied on the "law of the Creator." Likewise in Iran then, and even stronger today, the Constitution asserts the rights of women must be in conformity with Islamic criteria.

The great leap forward in the improvement of rights of women started in the 1960s with changes under Muḥammad Riżā Pahlavī in Iran, and Presidents Kennedy and Johnson in the United States. It was in 1964 that Iranian women were granted the right to vote and be elected to important decision-making political positions. At the same time in the United States, Congress passed the Equal Pay Act of 1963 and the Civil Rights Act of 1964, both of which provided women with powerful new protections against employment discrimination. As Iranian women's rights continued to improve, in 1969 the first women became judges. In the United States, more and more women became judges. In 1972 Congress enacted the education amendments to the Civil Rights Act, which resulted in more women attending law school and other professional schools. The U.S. Supreme Court handed down a series of decisions in the 1970s extending constitutional protection against sex discrimination.

By 1979, Iran had approximately 100 women judges. In 1981, Sandra Day O'Connor was the first woman judge appointed to the U.S. Supreme Court, and since then the percentage of women judges in the United States had risen noticeably. In both countries not only had laws barring women access to political and important government offices been eliminated; laws and attitudes now supported affirmative efforts to increase the number of women in the bar and the judiciary.

For about 75 years, despite the enormous differences between Iran and the United States, each country, in its own way, was moving toward emancipating women. This included giving women access to important decision-making roles such as judges. The definitive turning point in Iran occurred in 1979 after the fall of the Pahlavī and establishment of the government of the Islamic Republic of Iran. It was then that the road taken in Iran diverged so greatly from the road taken in the United States.

As women judges were found disqualified, first and later dismissed or demoted to lower positions in 1979 in Iran, the number and status of women judges in the United States continued to rise. Today in Iran the law mandates that only men can be judges. Today almost one-third of the judges in the United States are women. There are three women on the nine-member United States Supreme Court. While a high percent of Iranian women study law, none of them are qualified to become judges, solely because they fail to meet the male gender qualification. They are relegated to other positions such as "female consultant judges" and "investigative judges." They have the title of a judge, but are statutorily prohibited from exercising any authoritative judicial power according to the Constitution to render the final decision of the court.

A look at the United States as one model shows that progress could have continued in Iran. Iran chose to stop the progress of women with regard to judgeships after the 1979 revolution. This was not the only path available. Progress for women as judges was slow but steady in both countries and it could have continued in Iran as it did in the United States.

RECOMMENDATIONS

What should be done? Or a better question to ask would be "what are the objectives to correct these violations?" How achievable are these objectives? Is repealing or amending the 1982 Law on the Qualifications for Appointment of Judges enough to end the barrier for women to hold key government decision-making positions in Iran? Would amending this law count as a positive step toward eliminating all other de jure discrimination against women in Iran? Or is it not enough at all?

If the sole objective of this book is to tackle the issue of the statutory ban on women pursuing judgeships, the solution is straightforward. Iran must fulfill its international obligations and immediately repeal the 1982 discriminatory statute. Iran under international human rights mechanisms is obligated to guarantee women equal access to pursue judgeships, as they choose, and regardless of their gender. However, since this issue is only one compelling example of a pervasive discrimination against women in a broad range of areas, proposals should touch upon a more significant substantive problem. According to the international human rights laws, the problem is the existence of discriminatory and unequal treatment of women, and the legal supremacy of men, within the entire legal system on a wide range of matters. True equality is not simply about reversing the sexes, nor is it only about passing gender-neutral laws. Indeed gender-neutral laws may still allow discrimination against women, especially in a State like Iran where women are treated differently in all aspects of their lives starting with the Constitution, and including following old practices and customs. This is obviously a massive problem with many aspects to consider and reform that goes beyond the scope of this book. A look at the recommendations made by various United Nations mechanisms give a good indication of the wide range of issues that must be addressed by Iran.

It is essential, however, for the government of the IRI to acknowledge that basing women's rights, responsibilities, and punishments on her natural physical and psychological differences with men, in practice, results in favoring male supremacy. Assertion of the importance of "family" and task of "motherhood" as one of the most fundamental principles for women by the Constitution, is used to make women's individual rights in all other areas almost non-existent and dependent on a man and children's needs in the family as defined by laws.

The government by making reference to Cultural Relativism as a justification to treat women differently from men perpetuates discrimination against women. As it was asserted by the UN Special Rapporteur, in the report on Violence Against Women, its Causes and Consequences, the restoring of women's rights in Iran requires a complete re-interpretation of its fundamental norms and principles in line with the current needs and societal contributions of women on an equal footing with men.[4]

4 *See* Special Rapporteur on Violence against Women, its Causes and Consequences, *Mission to the Islamic Republic of Iran*, ¶ 65 at 18, U.N. Doc. E/CN.4/2006/61/Add.3 (Jan. 27, 2006).

BIBLIOGRAPHY

Constitution & Statutes & International Law

Islamic Republic of Iran (all translated by author)

Intiqāli Bānuvān bā Rutbiyi Qażāī az Vizārati Dādgustarī bi Sāyiri Vizāratkhānihā va Tabdīli Rutbiyi Qażāīyi Ānhā bi Idārī 1358 [Transferring Women with Judicial Titles from the Ministry of Justice to other Ministries and Conversion of their Judicial Titles to Administrative 1979] (Iran).

lāyiḥiyi Qānunīyi Iṣlāḥi Sāzmāni Dādgustarī va Qānuni Istikhdāmi Qużāt 1357 [Law Amending the Ministry of Justice and the Law of Employment of the Judges 1979] (Iran).

Mutamami Qānuni Āsāsī [Amendment to the Constitution] 1286 [1907].

Niẓāmnāmi Intikhābāti Majlisi Shurāyi Millī 1285 [Election Law of the National Consultative Assembly 1906] (Iran).

Qanun'i Assass'i Iran (Iranian Constitution) 1906.

Qānuni Āīni Dādrisī Dādgāhhāyi Umumī va Inqilāb dar Muridi Umuri Madanī 1379 [Codes of Civil Procedure in the Public and Revolutionary Courts 2000] (Iran).

Qānuni Alḥāqi Panj Tabṣari bi Qānuni Sharāyiti Intikhābi Qużāti Dādgustarī 1363 [Five Notes Affixed to the Law on the Qualifications for Appointment of Judges in the Ministry of Justice 1985] (Iran).

Qānuni Anjumanhāyi Iyālatī va Vilāyatī 1286 [Law of the State and Provincial Associations 1907] (Iran).

Qanuni Assassi Jumhuri'i Islamai Iran [The Constitution of The Islamic Republic of Iran] 1358 [1980].

Qānuni Ḥimāyati Khānivādi 1346 [Family Protection Law 1967] (Iran).

Qānuni Ḥimāyati Khānivādi 1353 [Family Protection Law 1975] (Iran).

Qānuni Ḥimāyati Khānivādi 1391 [Family Law Protection 2012] (Iran).

Qānuni Ijāziyi Ijrāyi Niẓāmnāmiyi Intikhābāti Majlisi Sinā 1328 [Law Allowing the Enforcement of the Senate Election 1949] (Iran).

Qānuni Ikhtiṣāṣi Tiʿdādī az Dādgāhāyi Mujud bi Dādgāhāyi Mużuʿi Aṣli (21) Qānuni Asāsī (Dādgāhi Khānivādi) 1376 [Allocating the Number of Existing Courts to the Family Courts 1997] (Iran).

Qānuni Intikhābāti Majlisi Shurāyi Millī 1290 [Election Law of the National Consultative Assembly 1911] (Iran).

Qānuni Intikhābāti Majlisi Shurāyi Millī 1304 [Election Law of the National Consultative Assembly 1925] (Iran).

Qānuni Iṣlāḥi Muqararāti Marbut bi Ṭalāq 1371 [Law Amending the Law of Divorce 1992] (Iran).

Qānuni Iṣlāhi Qānuni Istikhdāmi Qużāt va Sharāyiti Karāmuzī 1347 [Amendment to the Law of the

Employment of Judges and Internship 1969] (Iran).
Qānuni Iṣlāḥi Qānuni Tashkīli Dādgāhhāyi ʿumumī va Inqilāb 1381 [Amendment to the Law of Public and Revolutionary Courts 2002] (Iran).
Qānuni Iṣlāḥi Qismatī az Qāuni Uṣuli Tashkīlāti ʿdlīyi va Istikhdāmi Qużāt 1315 [Amending Parts of the Principals Governing the Justice Department and the Employment of Judges 1936] (Iran).
Qānuni Iṣlāḥi Tabṣiriyi Panji Qānuni Alḥāqi Panj Tabṣiri bi Qānuni Sharāyiti Intikhābi Qużāti Dādgustarī Muṣavabi 1363 [Amendment to the Note Five of the Five Notes Affixed to the Law on the Qualifications for Appointment of Judges of 1985 (1995)] (Iran).
Qānuni Iṣlāḥi Tashkīli Dādgāhhāyi Umumī va Inqilāb 1381 [Amendment to the Law of Public and Revolutionary Courts 1994] (Iran).
Qānuni Istikhdāmi Ḥukāmi Maḥākimi ʿdlīyi va Ṣāḥibmanṣabāni Pārki 1302 [Employment Law of the Justice Tribunals' Judges and the Officers of the Public Prosecutor Office 1923] (Iran).
Qānuni Maḥākimi Sharʿ 1310 [Law of the Religious Tribunals 1931] (Iran).
Qānuni Mujāzāti Islamī 1362 [Islamic Penal Code 1982] (Iran).
Qānuni Mujāzāti Islam*ī* 1375 [Islamic Penal Code 1996] (Iran).
Qānuni Rāji bi Istikhdāmi Qużāt va Sharāyiti Kārāmuzī 1343 [Employment Law of the Judges and the Internship 1964] (Iran).
Qānuni Rājiʿ Bi Shirkati Bānuvān Dar Intikhābāt 1343 [Law on Women's Participation in Election 1964] (Iran).
Qānuni Sharāyiti Intikhābi Qużāti Dādgustarī 1361 [Law on the Qualifications for Appointment of Judges in the Ministry of Justice 1982] (Iran).
Qānuni Tashkīli Dādgāhhāyi Umumī va Inqilāb 1373 [Public and Revolutionary Courts 1994] (Iran).
Qānuni Umuri Ḥisbī 1319 [Law of Non-Litigious Matters 1940] (Iran).
Qānuni Uşuli Tashkīlāi ʿdlīyi va Maḥāżiri Sharʿīyi va Āḥkāmi Şulḥīyi 1290 [Law of Principles Governing Justice Department, Religious Offices and Peace Courts 1911] (Iran).
Qanuni-i- Madani [Civil Code] Tehran 1313 [1934], art. 1041.
Qununi Istikhdāmi Qużāt va Ṣāḥibmanṣabāni Pārki va Mubāshirini S̱abti Asnād 1306 [Employment Law of the Judges and Officials of the Public Prosecutor's Office and Registration office 1928] (Iran).
Ruznamehi Rasmi Jumhuri Islami Iran [The Official Gazette of the Islamic Republic of Iran], *Fihristi Qavānini Mansukh Ṣarīḥ 1285-1335* [*The List of Nullified Laws from 1906-1956*] (Iran, 2012), *accessed at* http://www.rooznamehrasmi.ir/Laws/ShowLaw.aspx?Code=666.
Uṣuli Muḥākimāti Ḥuquqī 1290 [Rules of Legal Procedure 1911] (Iran).

UNITED STATES

Appointment and Tenure, 28 U.S.C. § 631(b)(1) (1988).

CALIFORNIA CONSTITUTION, art. II, § 1 (1879).

CALIFORNIA CONSTITUTION, art. VI, § 15.

CALIFORNIA CONSTITUTION, art. VI, § 9.

Civil Rights Act of 1964, 42 U.S.C. § 2000(a) et seq.

Equal Credit Opportunity Act, 15 U.S.C. § 1691 et seq.

Minimum Wage, 29 U.S.C. § 206(d) (1963).

OHIO CONSTITUTION, art. V, § 1, 6 (1851).

Prohibition of sex discrimination in payment of wages, 29 U.S.C. § 206(d)

Title IX of the Civil Rights Act of 1964, 20 U.S.C. § 1681 (1972).

Title VI of the Civil Rights Act of 1964, 42 U.S.C. § 2000(d).

Title VII of the Civil Rights Act of 1964, 42 U.S.C. § 2000(e).

UNITED STATES CONSTITUTION, amend. I.

UNITED STATES CONSTITUTION, amend. XIII, § 1.

UNITED STATES CONSTITUTION, amend. XIII, § 2.

UNITED STATES CONSTITUTION, amend. XIII.

UNITED STATES CONSTITUTION, amend. XIV, § 1.

UNITED STATES CONSTITUTION, amend. XIV, § 5.

UNITED STATES CONSTITUTION, amend. XIX.

UNITED STATES CONSTITUTION, amend. XV, § 1.

UNITED STATES CONSTITUTION, art. I, § 2.

UNITED STATES CONSTITUTION, art. II, § 2.

UNITED STATES CONSTITUTION, art. III, § 1.

UNITED STATES CONSTITUTION, art. VI, § 2.

UNITED STATES CONSTITUTION, arts. I, II, III, V, VI,

INTERNATIONAL LAW

Beijing Declaration and Platform for Action, Fourth World Conference on Women, 15 September 1995, A/CONF.177/20 (1995) and A/CONF.177/20/Add.1 (1995).

Convention Concerning Discrimination in Respect of Employment and Occupation (Entry into force: 15 Jun 1960) Adoption: Geneva, 42nd ILC session (25 Jun 1958).

Convention on the Elimination of All Forms of Discrimination against Women, G.A. res. 34/180, 34 U.N. GAOR Supp. (No. 46) at 193, U.N. Doc. A/34/46, *entered into force* Sept. 3, 1981.

G.A. Res. 2625 (XXV), *Declaration on Principles of International Law concerning Friendly Relations and Co-operation among States in accordance with the Charter of the United Nations*, U.N. Doc. A/RES/25/2625 (Oct. 24, 1970).

International Covenant on Civil and Political Rights, G.A. res. 2200A (XXI), 21 U.N. GAOR Supp. (No. 16) at 52, U.N. Doc. A/6316 (1966), 999 U.N.T.S. 171, *entered into force* Mar. 23, 1976.

International Covenant on Economic, Social and Cultural Rights, G.A. res. 2200A (XXI), 21 U.N.GAOR Supp. (No. 16) at 49, U.N. Doc. A/6316 (1966), 993 U.N.T.S. 3, *entered into force* Jan. 3, 1976.

Proclamation of Tehran, Final Act of the International Conference on Human Rights, Teheran, 22 April to 13 May 1968, U.N. Doc. A/CONF. 32/41 at 3 (1968).

The Charter of the United Nations, June 26, 1945, 59 Stat. 1031, T.S. 993, 3 Bevans 1153, *entered into force* Oct. 24, 1945.

The Vienna Declaration and Programme of Action, UN General Assembly, *Vienna Declaration and Programme of Action*, 12 July 1993, A/CONF.157/23.

Universal Declaration of Human Rights, G.A. Res. 217A, U.N. Doc. A/810 at 71 (1948).

Vienna Convention on the Law of Treaties, 1155 U.N.T.S. 331, 8 I.L.M. 679, *entered into force* Jan. 27, 1980.

BOOKS

1 & 2 SIYID MUḤAMMAD HĀSHIMĪ, HUQUQI ASĀSĪ JUMHURĪYI ISLĀMIYI IRAN (CONSTITUTION OF ISLAMIC REPUBLIC OF IRAN), (Dādgustar Publication 1999). (Translated by Author).

1 HAMMED SHAHIDIAN, WOMEN IN IRAN: GENDER POLITICS IN THE ISLAMIC REPUBLIC (Greenwood Press 2002).

1 SHAHĪD AVVAL, LUMʿI DAMSHAQĪYI (Asad Allāh Lutfī trans., 2d ed., Khursandī Publication 2011). (Translated by Author)

1, 3, 4, 5, 13, 14 IMAM KHOMEINI, SAHIFEH-YE IMAM (Majid Karimi & Mansoor Limba eds., the Institute for Compilation and Publication of Imam Khomeini's Work 2008).

2 MUḤAMMAD MUʿĪN, FARHANGI FĀRSĪ [PERSIAN ENCYCLOPEDIC DICTIONARY], (Amīrkabīr Publication 1963). (Translated by Author)

3 MURTIżā RĀVANDĪ, TĀRĪKHI IJTIMĀʿĪYI IRĀN [THE SOCIAL HISTORY OF IRAN], (Amīr Kabīr Publication 1978). (Translated by Author)

4 IMĀM KHUMIYNĪ, TARJUMIYI TAḤRĪR AL VASĪLI [TRANSLATION OF TAḤRĪR AL VASĪLI], (trans. Siyid Muḥamad Bāqir Musavī Hamidānī, Dār Ul ʿilm Publication 2007). (Translated by Author)

AḤMAD KASRAVĪ, TĀRĪKHI MASHRUTIYI IRĀN [THE IRANIAN CONSTITUTIONAL REVOLUTION], (Amīr Kabīr Publication 1999). (Translated by Author)

ALI VAFĀDĀR, ḤUQUQI ASĀSĪ VA TAḤAVULĀTI SĪYĀSĪ [CONSTITUTIONAL LAW AD POLITICAL EVOLUTIONS], (Shirvīn Publication 1995). (Translated by Author)

AMERICAN WOMEN: THE REPORT OF THE PRESIDENT'S COMMISSION ON THE STATUS OF WOMEN AND OTHER PUBLICATIONS OF THE COMMISSION (Margaret Mead & Frances Balgley Kaplan eds., Zenger Publishing Co. 1975).

AMĪR SAʿĪD VAKĪLĪ & PURĪYĀ ASKARĪ, QĀNUNI ASĀSĪ DAR ZAMĀNI ḤUQUQI KUNUNĪ [THE CONSTITUTIONAL LAW DURING CURRENT TIMES], (Mujd Publication). (Translated by Author)

ANN CAREY MCFEATTERS, SANDRA DAY O'CONNOR: JUSTICE IN THE BALANCE (University of New Mexico Press 2005).

ANN LAMBTON, CONTINUITY AND CHANGE IN MEDIEVAL PERSIA, (Yaʿqub Ajand trans., Niy Publication 1993).

AREZOO OSANLOO, POLITICS OF WOMEN'S RIGHTS IN IRAN, (Princeton University Press 2009).

BANAFSHIH ḤIJĀZĪ, ŻAʿĪFI: BARASĪYI JĀYGĀHI ZANI IRĀNĪ DAR ʿṢRI ṢAFAVĪ

[The Weak Sex: The Examination of Women's Status During the Ṣafavī Dynasty], (Qaṣīdi Sarā Publication 1992). (Translated by Author)

Barbara J. Harris, Beyond Her Sphere: Women And The Professions In American History, (Greenwood Press 1978).

Bertrand G. Ramcharan, The Fundamentals of International Human Rights Treaty Law, (Martinus Nijhoff Publishers 2011).

Betty Friedan, The Feminine Mystique, (Tenth Anniversary ed., Norton & Company Inc. 1974).

Black's Law Dictionary (Bryan A. Garner ed., 10th ed., Thomson Reuters 2014).

Camron Michael Amin, The Making of the Modern Iranian Women (University Press of Florida 2002).

Diana Klebanow & Franklin L. Jonas, People's Lawyers: Crusaders for Justice in American History (M.E. Sharpe 2003).

Dorothy E McBride, Women's Rights in the U.S.A. (Policy Debates and Gender Roles), (2d ed., Garland Publishing 1997).

Ekaterina Yahyaoui Krivenko, Women, Islam and International Law: Within the Context of the Convention on the Elimination of All Forms of Discrimination Against Women, (Martinus Nijhoff Publishers 2008).

Erwin Chemerinsky, Constitutional Law Principles and Policies (3d ed., ASPEN 2006).

Expanding The Horizons of Human Rights Law (Ineta Ziemele ed., Martinus Nijhoff Publishers 2005).

Fatima Mernissi, Beyond the Veil: Male-Female Dynamics in Modern Iran, (2d ed., Indiana University Press 1987).

Flora Davis, Moving the Mountain: The Women's Movement in America since 1960, (University of Illinois Press 1999).

Frank Newman & David Weissbrodt, International Human Rights: Law, Policy, And Process (Anderson Publishing 1990).

G. Larry Mays, American Courts and the Judicial Process (Oxford University Press 2012).

Gender in Contemporary Iran: Pushing the Boundaries, (Roksana Bahramitash & Eric J. Hooglund eds., Routledge 2011).

Hamideh Sedghi, Women and Politics in Iran: Veiling, Unveiling, and Reveiling, (Cambridge University Press 2007).

Hammed Shahidian, Women in Iran: Gender Politics in the Islamic Republic, (Greenwood Press 2002).

Ḥasan Pīrnīyā, Tārīkhi Irān: Qabl az Islām [Iranian History before Islam], (8th ed., Niqāh Publication 2012). (Translated by Author)

Hassan Toqranegar, Ḥuquqi Sīyāsī va Ijtimāʿyi Zanān Qabl va Baʿd az Pīruzīyi Inqilābi Islāmīyi Irān [Political and Social Rights of Women, before and after the Islamic Revolution of Iran], (The Center for Islamic Revolution Documents, 2010). (Translated by Author)

Hedda Garza, Barred from the Bar (A History of Women and the Legal Profession), (Franklin Watts Publisher 1996).

Henry Julian Abraham, Justices, Presidents, and Senators: A History of the U.S. Supreme Court Appointments from Washington to Bush II (5th ed., Rowman & Littlefield Publishers 2008).

Hidāyatullāh ʿalavī, Zan Dar Irāni Bāstān [Women During Ancient Iran], (Hīrmand Publication 2001). (Translated by Author)

Hossein Mehrpour, Mabāḥiṣī az Ḥuquqi Zan [Certain Issues on Women's Rights], (Ettela'at Publications 2000). (Translated by Author)

Howard Zinn, A People's History of the United States (HarperCollins Publishers 2010).

Human Rights: Concept and Standards, (Janusz Symonides ed., Ashgate Publishing 2000).

Hurst Hannum, Guide to International Human Rights Practice (4th ed., 2004).

Imā Alī, Nahjul Balāghi, (Muhammad Dashtī trans., Tehran Badr Publication 2011). (Translated by Author)

International Human Rights Law, Six Decades after the UDHR and Beyond, (Mashood A. Baderin & Manisuli Ssenyonjo eds., Ashgate Publishing 2010).

Jack Donnelly, Universal Human Rights in Theory and Practice, (2d ed., Cornell University Press 2003).

Janet Afary, Sexual Politics in Modern Iran, (Cambridge University Press 2009).

Javaid Rehman, International Human Rights Law: A Practical Approach (Pearson 2003).

Joan Hoff, Law, Gender, and Injustice (A Legal History of U.S. Women), (New York University Press 1991).

Judith A. Baer, Women in American law (The Struggle Toward Equality from the New Deal to the Present), (2d ed., Holmes & Meier Publisher 1996).

Karen Berger Morello, The Invisible Bar (The Woman Lawyer in America 1638 to the Present), (Random House 1986).

Larry Mays, American Courts and the Judicial Process (1st ed., Oxford University Press 2011).

Leila Ahmed, Women, and Gender in Islam: Historical Roots of a Modern Debate, (Yale University Press 1992).

Lori F. Damrosch, Louis Henkin, Sean D. Murphy, Hans Smit, International Law: Cases and Materials, (5th ed., West Publishing 2009).

Manfred Nowak, U.N. Covenant on Civil and Political Rights, (N.P. Engel 1993).

Manṣuri Tadvīnpur, Asnādi Ruḥānīyat va Majlis [Documentation of Clergy and Assembly], (The Library of the Islamic Consultant Assembly 2000).

Maria Brosius, Women in Ancient Persia (559-331 BC), (Oxford University Press 1996).

Marvin Zonis, Majestic Failure: The Fall of the Shah (Esmail Zan, Batol Saidi trans., Noor Publication 1992).

Mihrangīz Kār, Mushārikati Sīyāsī Zanān [Women's Participation in Politics], (Rushangarān va Muṭāliʿti Zanān Publication 2001). (Translated by Author)

Mohammad Reza Pahlavi, Answer to History (Stein & Day publisher 1981).

Muḥamad Hāshim Kamālī, Principles of Islamic Jurisprudence (3d ed., The Islamic Texts Society 2003). (Translated by Author)

Muḥammad Ḥusiyni Khusru Panāh, Hadafhā va Mubārizāti Zan dar Irān az Inqilābi Mashruṭi tā Salṭanati Pahlavī [Iranian Woman's Goals and Battles From the Constitutional Revolution until the Pahlavi Dynasty], (Payāmi Imruz Publication 2002). (Translated by Author)

Muḥaqiq Ḥillī, Sharāyiʿ Alislām, (Abul Qāsim Ibni Aḥmad Yazdī trans., 6th ed., Tehran University Publication 1996). (Translated by Author)

Murtiżā Muṭaharī, Niẓāmi Ḥuqūqi Zan dar Islām [Women's Rights in Islam], (Ṣadrā Publication 2011). (Translated by Author)

Philip Alston, The United Nations Human Rights (2d ed,, Oxford University Press 1992).

Ralph G. Steinhardt, Paul L. Hoffman, Christopher N. Camponovo, International Human Rights Lawyering (Cases and Materials) (West Academic Publishing 2009).

Renee Cherow-O' Leary, The State-by-State Guide to Women's Legal Rights, (McGraw-Hill 1987).

Reza Afshari, Human Rights in Iran: The Abuse of Cultural Relativism, (University of Pennsylvania Press 2001).

Richard Kluger, Simple Justice: The History of Brown v. Board of Education and Black America's Struggle for Equality, (Vintage Books 2004).

Riżā Āyirmilu, Zan dar Girdābi Sharīʿt [The Women and the Islamic Fundamentalists], (Invand Publication 2002). (Translated by Author)

Robert A. Carp & Ronald Stidham, Judicial Process in America, (3d ed., CQ Press 1996).

Rushanʿalī Shikārī, Uṣuli Fiqh [The Foundation of Islamic Jurisprudence], (Ṭarḥi Nuvīn Andīshi Publication 2008). (Translated by Author)

Ṣāliḥī Najaf Ābādī, Qiżāvati Zan dar Fiqhi Islāmī [Women's Judgeships in the Islamic Fiqh], (Umīdi Fardā Publication 2005). (Translated by Author)

Sandra Day O'Connor, The Majesty of the Law, (Craig Joyce, Random House 2003).

Sarah Joseph, Jenny Schultz, Melissa Castan, The International Covenant On Civil and Political Rights (Oxford University Press 2000).

Sean Wilentz, The Rise of American Democracy, Slavery and the Crisis of American Democracy (1st ed., W. W. Norton & Company 2007).

Shaheen Sardar Ali, Gender and Human Rights in Islam and International Law: Equal Before Allah, Unequal Before Man?, (Kluwer Law International 2000).

Shahīd S̱ānī, Sharḥi Lumʿi, (Assad Allah Lotfi trans., 7th ed., Mujd Publication 2010). (Translated by author)

Siyid Ḥasan Amīn, Tārīkhi Ḥuqūqi Irān [The History of Law in Iran] 42 (3d ed., Dāʾratulmaʿārifi Irān Shināsī Publication 2012). (Translated by Author)

Siyid Ja'far Hāshimī Bājgānī, Barasīyi Taṭbīqīi Uṣuli Muḥākimāti Madanī [The Comparative review of the principles of civil trials], (1st ed., The Islamic Documentation Center Publication 1999). (Translated by Author)

Steven M. Buechler, Women's Movements in the United States: Women Suffrage, Equal Rights, and Beyond, (Rutgers University Press 1990).

Susan Deller Ross, Women's Human Rights: The International and Comparative Law Casebook (University of Pennsylvania Press 2008).

Susan Ehrlich Martin & Nancy C. Jurik, Doing Justice, Doing Gender (Sage Publications 1996).

Susan Gluck Mezey, In Pursuit of Equality: Women, Public Policy, and the Federal Courts, (St. Martin's Press 1992).

Taylor Branch, At Canaan's Edge: America in the King Years, 1965-1968, (Simon & Schuster 2007).

Taylor Branch, Parting the Waters: America in the King Years 1954-1963, (Simon & Schuster 1989).

Taylor Branch, Pillar of Fire: America in the King Years 1963-1965, (Simon & Schuster 1999).

The Legacy of Ruth Bader Ginsburg (Scott Dodson ed., Cambridge University Press 2015).

Tony Weir, An Introduction to Comparative Law (K. Zweigert & H. Kotz trans., 3d eds., Oxford University Press 1998).

Virginia G. Drachman, Sisters in law: Women Lawyers in Modern American History, (Harvard University Press 1998).

Voices in History of Black Women Lawyers (J. Clay Smith Jr. ed., The University of Michigan Press 1998).

William Burnham, Introduction to the Law and Legal System of the United States (2d ed., West Group 1999).

Women, Law & Development International; Human Rights Watch Women's Rights Project, Women's Human Rights Step by Step: A Practical Guide to Using International Human Rights Law and Mechanisms to Defend Women's Human Rights, (Margaret A. Schuler & Dorothy Q. Thomas, eds., Women, Law & Development International and Human Rights Watch 1997).

Women's Rights Human Rights: International Feminist Perspectives, (Julie Peters & Andrea Wolper ed., Routledge 1995).

'llāmi Ḥillī, Tabṣaral Muti'alimīn, ('llāmi Shi'rānī trans., 6th ed., Islāmīyi Publication 2006). (Translated by Author)

TABLE OF CASES

Bradwell v. Illinois, 83 U.S. 130 (1873).
Brown v. Board of Education, 347 U.S. 483 (1954).
Craig v. Boren, 429 U.S. 190 (1976).
Frontiero v. Richardson, 411 U. S. 677 (1973).
Gibbons v. Ogden, 22 U.S. 1 (1824).
Gordon v. Justice Court, 12 Cal.3d 323 (1974).
In re Lelia J. Robinson, 131 Mass. 376 (1881).
In the Matter of the Motion to Admit Miss Lavinia Goodell to the Bar of this Court, 39 Wis.232 (1876).
McCulloch v. Maryland, 17 U.S. 316 (1819).
New York v. United States, 505 U.S. 144 (1992).
Plessy v. Ferguson, 163 U.S. 537 (1896).
Printz v. United States, 521 U.S. 898 (1997).
Reed v. Reed, 404 U.S. 71 (1971).
S.W.M. Broeks v. Netherlands, Communication. No. 172/1984, UN. Doc. CCPR/OP/2 at 196 (1990).
Schlesinger v. Ballard, 419 U.S. 498 (1975).
Slaughterhouse Cases, 83 U.S. (16 Wall.) 36 (1872).
Stanley v. Illinois, 405 U. S. 645 (1972).
Stanton v. Stanton, 421 U. S. 7 (1975).
United States v. Virginia, 518 U.S. 515 (1996).
Weinberger v. Wiesenfeld, 420 U.S. 636 (1975).

FULL DISCUSSION OF THE NATIONAL CONSULTATIVE ASSEMBLY & ISLAMIC CONSULTATIVE ASSEMBLY (ALL TRANSLATED BY AUTHOR)

Full Discussion of the Islamic Consultative Assembly 1st Term-Session 227, n.10689, Oct. 22, 1981, Library, Museum and Document Center of Iran Parliament, *accessed at* http://archive.ical.ir/files/debate/ip/01/01-227.pdf.
Full Discussion of the Islamic Consultative Assembly 1st Term-Session 252, n. 10735, Dec. 22, 1981, Library, Museum and Document Center of Iran Parliament, *accessed at* http://archive.ical.ir/files/debate/ip/01/01-252.pdf.
Full Discussion of the Islamic Consultative Assembly 1st-Term Session 253, n. 10736, Dec. 23, 1981, Library, Museum and Document Center of Iran Parliament, *accessed at* http://archive.ical.ir/files/debate/ip/01/01-253.pdf.
Full Discussion of the Islamic Consultative Assembly 2d Term-Session 69, n. 11635, Dec. 25, 1984, Library, Museum and Document Center of Iran Parliament, *accessed at* http://archive.ical.ir/files/debate/ip/02/02-069.pdf.
Full Discussion of the Islamic Consultative Assembly 3d Term-Session 471, n.13774, March 11, 1992, Library, Museum and Document

Center of Iran Parliament, *accessed at* http://archive.ical.ir/files/debate/ip/03/03-471.pdf.

Full Discussion of the Islamic Consultative Assembly 4th Term-Session 322, n.14624, April 18, 1995, Library, Museum and Document Center of Iran Parliament, *accessed at* http://archive.ical.ir/files/debate/ip/04/04-322.pdf.

Full Discussion of the Islamic Consultative Assembly 5th Term-Session 111, n.15428, July 30, 1997, Library, Museum and Document Center of Iran Parliament, *accessed at* http://archive.ical.ir/files/debate/ip/05/05-111.pdf.

Full Discussion of the Islamic Consultative Assembly 6th Term-Session 342, n. 17026, July 23, 2003, Library, Museum and Document Center of Iran Parliament, *accessed at* http://archive.ical.ir/files/debate/ip/06/06-342.pdf.

Full Discussion of the National Consultative Assembly 21st Term-1st Session, Library, Museum and Document Center of Iran Parliament, *accessed at* http://www.ical.ir/index.php?option=com_mashrooh&view=session&id=23732&Itemid=38.

Full Discussion of the National Consultative Assembly 2d Term-280 Session, Library, Museum and Document Center of Iran Parliament, *accessed at* http://ical.ir/index.php?option=com_mashrooh&view=session&id=20566&Itemid=38.

Full Discussion of the National Consultative Assembly 4th Term-71 Session, Library, Museum and Document Center of Iran Parliament, *accessed at* http://www.ical.ir/index.php?option=com_mashrooh&view=session&id=20768&Itemid=38.

ARTICLES (STATUTES, BOOKS, ARTICLES, OFFICIAL DOCUMENTS, LAW REVIEW ARTICLES)

13 Pioneering Women in American Law, ABA Journal, *accessed at* http://www.abajournal.com/gallery/historical_women/764.

2 Āyatullāh Ḥusiin Alī Muntaẓirī, Page 101, Official Website of Montazeri, *accessed at* https://amontazeri.com/book/mabani/volume-2/101#cref-3. (Translated by Author)

Abby Gluck, *Our [National] Federalism*, 123 Yale L.J. 1996, (2014) (The modern allocation of state and federal power).

ABC of Women Workers' Right and Gender Equality, International Labour Office (2d ed., Geneva 2007), *accessed at* http://www.ilo.org/wcmsp5/groups/public/---dgreports/---gender/documents/publication/wcms_087314.pdf.

Afsāni Rushan, Masāʿili Kashfi Ḥijāb bi Rivāyati Asnādi Kitābkhāniyi Majlisi Shurāyi Millī Irān [Issues Surrounding Unveiling According to the Documents of the Library of the National Consultative Assembly], Institute for Humanities and Cultural Studies (Winter 2009), *accessed at* http://www.ensani.ir/storage/Files/20101205135852-

Pages%20from%20payam6-54.pdf. (Translated by Author)

Alī Muḥammad Jahāngīrī, *Niẓāmi Jumhurīyi Islāmī va Ḥaqi Qiżāvati Zanān [The Islamic Republic of Iran and the Rights of Women Judges]*, ASRE-NOU.NET (Dec. 11, 2012), *accessed at* http://asre-nou.net/php/view.php?objnr=24459. (Translated by Author)

American Bar Association, A Current Glance at Women in the Law, AMERICAN BAR ASSOCIATION (July 2014), *accessed at* http://www.americanbar.org/content/dam/aba/marketing/women/current_glance_statistics_july2014.authcheckdam.pdf.

Angela Nicole Johnson, *A Timeline of Women's History in the Legal Profession*, WOMEN AS LAWYERS (2011), *accessed at* https://womenaslawyers.wordpress.com/a-timeline-of-womens-history-in-the-legal-profession/#_ftn5.

Are there qualifications to be a Justice? SUPREME COURT OF THE UNITED STATES, *accessed at* http://www.supremecourt.gov/faq.aspx#faqgi2.

Bā Ishāri bi Ilzāmi Qānun Barāyi Jazbi Zanān dar Dādgāhāyi Khānivādi [According to The Legal Necessity of Attracting Women in Family Law Courts], ICANA (Nov. 2, 2013), *accessed at* http://icana.ir/Fa/News/240234. (Translated by Author)

Bāshgāhi Khabarnigārān, *Ḥujatul Islām Rahbar Hushdār Dād [Ayatullāh Rahbar Warned]*, KHABARNIGĀRĀN (June 22, 2012), *accessed at* http://www.yjc.ir/fa/news/3996965/YJC.IR, (Translated by Author)

Basic facts about the UPR, UNITED NATIONS HUMAN RIGHTS OFFICE OF THE HIGH COMMISSIONER, (2015), *accessed at* http://www.ohchr.org/en/hrbodies/upr/pages/BasicFacts.aspx.

Bāzbīnī Dar Aṣli 115 Barāyi Salāmatīyi Intikhābāt [Review of Article 115 for a Fair Election], GUARDIAN COUNCIL, *accessed at* http://www.shora-gc.ir, http://www.shora-gc.ir/Portal/Home/ShowPage.aspx?Object=News&CategoryID=1649831b-f60a-44a8-ac21-51d63e34cdb9&WebPartID=bffcf800-40b2-46a5-931c-4a56db364e44&ID=b9895649-6051-40fb-b09e-7c18b60d44cc. (Translated by Author)

Beverly B. Cook, *Women Judges: A Preface to Their History*, 14 Golden Gate U. L. Rev. (1984), *accessed at* http://digitalcommons.law.ggu.edu/ggulrev/vol14/iss3/7.

Birdie Amsterdam: "First lady of the Judiciary", LAW LIBRARY OF COLUMBIA, *accessed at* http://library.law.columbia.edu/rise_of_women/judiciary/BirdieAmsterdam.html.

Commission on the Status of Women, PRESIDENTIAL LIBRARY AND MUSEUM, *accessed at* http://www.jfklibrary.org/Asset-Viewer/Archives/JFKPOF-093-004.aspx.

Comprehensive Guide to Bar Admission Requirements, ABA & NABE (2015), *accessed at* http://www.ncbex.org/assets/media_files/Comp-Guide/CompGuide.pdf.

Constitution Center, *Centuries of Citizenship: A Constitutional Timeline*, NATIONAL CONSTITUTION CENTER, *accessed at* http://constitutioncenter.org/experience/exhibitions/past-exhibitions/constitutional-timeline.

Dag Hammarskjöld Library Research Guides, *UN Documentation: Human*

Rights, United Nations Dag Hammarskjöld Library (Feb. 13, 2015), *accesses at* http://research.un.org/en/docs/humanrights/charter.

Dar Āzmuni *Qāżī 93 [In the Judiciary Exam 93]*, Ekhtebar, (Sep. 29, 2014), *accessed at* http://www.ekhtebar.com/ -و-درم-رایداد-348-،-93-تواضق-نومزآ-رد 64-رایداد-ز/. (Translated by Author)

Decades After O'Connor, Role of Women Judges Still Growing, United State Court (2013), *accessed at* http://news.uscourts.gov/decades-after-oconnor-role-women-judges-still-growing.

Declaration of Independence, Archives.gov, *accessed at* http://www.archives.gov/exhibits/charters/declaration_transcript.html.

Definition of key terms used in the UN Treaty Collection: Treaties, United Nations Treaty Collection, *accessed at* https://treaties.un.org/Pages/overview.aspx?path=overview/definition/page1_en.xml#treaties.

Dukhti Iran, *Farāz va Furudi Zanān Qāżī dar Iran* [*Ups and Downs of the Women's Judgeships*], Dukhti Iran (July 8, 2013), *accessed at* http://www.dokhtiran.com/interview/1392_04/001375.php. (Translated by Author)

Elections, nominations, confirmations and appointments to subsidiary and related bodies of the Economic and Social Council, UN.org (April 23, 2014), *accessed at* https://www.un.org/ecosoc/sites/www.un.org.ecosoc/files/documents/2014/dec.2014201.A.pdf.

Elizabethan Women, Elizabethi, *accessed at* http://www.elizabethi.org/contents/women/.

Employment Discrimination in Your State, NOLO, *accessed at* http://www.nolo.com/legal-encyclopedia/employment-discrimination-in-your-state-31017.html.

Esther Hobart Morris, Wyoming State Archives, *accessed at* http://wyoarchives.state.wy.us/Archives/Research.aspx?ID=2.

Faraj Allāh Hidāyat Nīyā Ganjī, *Rīyāsati Jumhurīyi Zanān* [*Women's Presidency*], The Guardian Council Information Website, (2004), *accessed at* http://www.shora-gc.ir/Portal/Home/ShowPage.aspx?Object=News&CategoryID=8fac823a-5745-41b6-a9e2-b879c74deb7b&WebPartID=9e3f5a95-7363-42d7-8e58-e450d9975ad4&ID=28259be1-dd05-40a7-8234-33487258e6c1. (Translated by Author)

Fareda Banda, Project on a Mechanism to Address Laws that Discriminate against Women, Office of the High Commissioner for Human Rights and Gender Unit (March 6, 2008), *accessed at* http://www.ohchr.org/Documents/Publications/laws_that_discriminate_against_women.pdf.

Fatḥullāh Yāvarī, *Dādgāhi Madanīyi Khāṣ dar Niẓāmi Jumhurīyi Islāmīyi Iran* [*The Special Civil Courts in the Islamic Republic of Iran*], Ghavanin (1991), *accessed at* http://www.ghavanin.ir/PaperDetail.asp?id=664. (Translated by Author)

Female chief justices of state supreme courts, Ballot Pedia, *accessed at* http://ballotpedia.org/Female_chief_justices_of_state_supreme_courts.

Feminism in the 19th Century: Women's Rights, Roles, and Limits, Study.com, *accessed at* http://education-portal.com/academy/lesson/feminism-in-the-19th-century-womens-rights-roles-and-limits.html.

General Assembly of the United Nations, *Social, Humanitarian & Cultural Third Committee*, UNITED NATIONS, *accessed at* http://www.un.org/en/ga/third/.

George Guilder, *Women in the Work Force*, THE ATLANTIC (1986), *accessed at* http://www.theatlantic.com/magazine/archive/1986/09/women-in-the-work-force/304924/.

History, Art & Archives-United States House of Representative, *The Women's Rights Movement*, HISTORY, ART & ARCHIVES, *accessed at* http://history.house.gov/Exhibitions-and-Publications/WIC/Historical-Essays/No-Lady/Womens-Rights/.

Human Rights Monitoring Mechanisms, SHAHEEDONIRAN.ORG, *accessed at* http://shaheedoniran.org/human-rights-at-the-united-nations/human-rights-monitoring-mechanisms/.

Ilhām: Tafsīri Shurāyi Nigahbān az Vāzhiyi Rijāli Sīyāsī Tagyīrī Nakardi Ast [Elham: the Guardian Council's Interpretation of the Term "Rijāl" has not Changed], JAMEJAM ONLINE (Jan. 22, 2005), *accessed at* http://www1.jamejamonline.ir/newstext.aspx?newsnum=100004167229. (Translated by Author)

International Labour Organization, *Observation (CEACR) - adopted 2012, published 102nd ILC session* (2013), INTERNATIONAL LABOUR ORGANIZATION, *accessed at* http://www.ilo.org/dyn/normlex/en/f?p=1000:13100:0::NO:13100:P13100_COMMENT_ID:3085370.

International Labour Organization, *Observation (CEACR) - adopted 2014, published 104th ILC session* (2015), INTERNATIONAL LABOUR ORGANIZATION, *accessed at* http://www.ilo.org/dyn/normlex/en/f?p=1000:13100:0::NO:13100:P13100_COMMENT_ID:3192151:NO.

International Labour Organization, *Ratifications for Islamic Republic of Iran*, INTERNATIONAL LABOUR ORGANIZATION, *accessed at* http://www.ilo.org/dyn/normlex/en/f?p=NORMLEXPUB:11200:0::NO::P11200_COUNTRY_ID:102800.

Iran MENA Gender Equality Profile: Status of Girls and Women in the Middle East and North Africa, UNICEF (Oct 2011), *accessed at* http://www.unicef.org/gender/files/Iran-Gender-Eqaulity-Profile-2011.pdf.

Jefferson's Letter to the Danbury Baptists, LIBRARY OF CONGRESS, *accessed at* http://www.loc.gov/loc/lcib/9806/danpost.html.

Judges: Her Honor Takes the Bench, TIME (1965), *accessed at* http://content.time.com/time/magazine/article/0,9171,839164,00.html.

Khāniyi Millat, *Qiżāvat bā Ruḥīyiyi Zanān Sāzigār Nīst [A Judgeship is not Compatible with Women's Nature]*, ISLAMIC CONSULTATIVE ASSEMBLY NEWS AGENCY (July 9, 2012), *accessed at* http://www.icana.ir/Fa/News/200733. (Translated by Author)

Laura Pecenco & Mary Blair-Loy, Center for Research on Gender in the Professions Legal Professions: The Status of Women and men (2013), *accessed at* http://crgp.ucsd.edu/documents/GenderinLegalProfessionsCaseStudy.pdf.

Mary Leonard, 1845 - October 24, 1912, MARY LEONARD LAW

SOCIETY, *accessed at* http://www.maryleonardlawsociety.org/who-was-mary-leonard.html.

Michael J. Yelnosky, *Who Rates Prospective Federal Judges for the American Bar Association?*, 19 Roger Williams U. L. Rev. 91, (2014).

Mobin Edalat, *Ilzāmī Budani Ḥużuri Qāżīyi Mushāviri Zan dar Daʿāvīyi Khānivādi* [*The Necessety of the Presence of a Female Consultant Judge*],HEDAYATMOBIN (AUG. 16, 2014), *available at* http://hedayatmobin.com/%D8%A7%D9%84%D8%B2%D8%A7%D9%85%DB%8C-%D8%A8%D9%88%D8%AF%D9%86-%D8%AD%D8%B6%D9%88%D8%B1-%D9%82%D8%A7%D8%B6%DB%8C-%D9%85%D8%B4%D8%A7%D9%88%D8%B1-%D8%B2%D9%86-%D8%AF%D8%B1-%D8%AF%D8%B9%D8%A7%D9%88%DB%8C/. (Translated by Author)

Mukhālifat bā Lāyiḥiyi Anjumanhāyi Iyālatī va Vilāyatī [*Opposition to the Bill of State And Provincial Associations*], IMAM-KHOMEINI, *accessed at* http://www.imam-khomeini.ir/fa/c2688/زندگی_نامه/دوران_مبارزات/مخالفت_با_لایحه_انجمنهای_ایالتی_و_ولایتی. (Translated by Author)

National Totals: Vintage 2014, UNITED STATES CENSUS BUREAU, *accessed at* http://www.census.gov/popest/data/national/totals/2014/index.html.

New York State Bar Association, *Judicial Diversity: A Work in Progress*, NEW YORK STATE BAR ASSOCIATION (Sep. 2014), *accessed at* http://www.nysba.org/judicialdiversityreport/.

Noushin Ahmadi Khorasani, Iranian Women's Equality Calendar With Chronology of One Million Signatures Campaign Demanding Changes to Discriminatory Laws, (Sahar Mofakham & Mahsa Shekarloo & Leila Tavakoli trans., 2008), *accessed at* http://www.feministschool.com/english/IMG/pdf/Iranian_Women_s_equality_calendar-2.pdf.

Occupational Employment Statistics (Judges, Magistrate Judges, and Magistrates), BUREAU OF LABOR STATISTICS (2014), *accessed at* http://www.bls.gov/oes/current/oes231023.htm.

OFFICIAL WEBSITES

Abraham Lincoln Quote, WIKIQUOTE.ORG, *accessed at* https://en.wikiquote.org/wiki/Abraham_Lincoln

Paola Antolini, 1492: The Role of Women, Commission of the European Communities, *accessed at* http://aei.pitt.edu/34007/1/A484.pdf.

Rasmīyat Yāftani Qānuni Asāsīyi Jumhurīyi Islāmīyi Irān [*Finalized Constitution of the Islamic Republic of Iran*], THE CENTER FOR ISLAMIC DOCUMENTATIONS 1979, *accessed at* http://www.irdc.ir/fa/calendar/65/default.aspx. (Translated by Author)

Recommendation, UPRINFO, *accessed at* http://www.upr-info.org/database/index.php?limit=0&f_SUR=79&f_SMR=All&order=&orderDir=ASC&orderP=true&f_Issue=All&searchReco=&resultMax=300&response=&action_type=&session=&SuRRgrp =&SuROrg=&SMRRgrp=&SMROrg=&pledges=RecoOnly.

Rules of the Supreme Court of the United States, SUPREME COURT.GOV (2013), *accessed at* http://www.supremecourt.gov/ctrules/2013RulesoftheCourt.pdf.

Russell Shorto, *How Christian Were the Founders?*, THE NEW YORK TIMES MAGAZINE (Feb. 11, 2010), *accessed at* http://www.nytimes.com/2010/02/14/magazine/14texbooks-t.html?pagewanted=all&_r=2.

Session 413 of the Shurāyi ʿālīyi Farhanqī [Supreme Council of the Cultural Revolution], SUPREME COUNCIL OF THE CULTURAL REVOLUTION (Feb 3, 1998), *accessed at* http://sccr.ir/pages/simpleView.aspx?provID=1036.

Special Procedures of the Human Rights Council, UNITED NATIONS HUMAN RIGHTS OFFICE OF THE HIGH COMMISSIONER, *accessed at* http://www.ohchr.org/EN/HRBodies/SP/Pages/Welcomepage.aspx.

Special Procedures of the Human Rights Council, UNITED NATIONS HUMAN RIGHTS OFFICE OF THE HIGH COMMISSIONER, *accessed at* http://www.ohchr.org/EN/HRBodies/SP/Pages/Introduction.aspx.

Special Rapporteur on the situation of human rights in the Islamic Republic of Iran, UNITED NATIONS HUMAN RIGHTS OFFICE OF THE HIGH COMMISSIONER, (2015), *accessed at* http://www.ohchr.org/EN/HRBodies/SP/CountriesMandates/IR/Pages/SRIran.aspx.

Steven C. Krane, *Judith Smith Kaye*, *accessed at* https://www.nycourts.gov/history/legal-history-new-york/luminaries-court-appeals/kaye-judith.html.

Tamilla F. Ghodsi, *Tying a Slipknot: Temporary Marriages in Iran*, 15 MICH. J. INT'L L. 645, (1994).

Taṣvībi Lāyihiyi Anjumanhāyi Iyālatī va Vilāyatī Dar Dulati Asadullāhi Aʿlam [Passage of the Bill of State And Provincial Associations by the Government of Asadullāhi Aʿlam], ISLAMIC REVOLUTION DOCUMENT CENTER (1962), *accessed at* http://www.irdc.ir/fa/calendar/154/default.aspx. (Translated by Author)

Teaching With Documents: The Civil Rights Act of 1964 and the Equal Employment Opportunity Commission, NATIONAL ARCHIVES, *accessed at* http://www.archives.gov/education/lessons/civil-rights-act/.

Ted Gittinger & Allen Fisher, *LBJ Champions the Civil Rights Act of 1964*, NATIONAL ARCHIVES (2004), *accessed at* http://www.archives.gov/publications/prologue/2004/summer/civil-rights-act-1.html.

The Declaration of Sentiments and Resolutions Seneca Falls Conference (1848), *accessed at* https://www.mccarter.org/Education/mrs-packard/html/MRS.%20PACKARD%20The%20Declaration%20of%20Sentiments,%20Seneca%20Falls%20Hyperlink.pdf.

The Iran Heritage Foundation (America), *What is the Cyrus Cylinder?*, IHF AMERICA (Oct. 12, 2012), *accessed at* http://cyruscylinder2013.com/2012/10/what-is-the-cyrus-cylinder/.

The National Association of Women Lawyers, NATIONAL ASSOCIATION OF WOMEN LAWYERS, *accessed at* http://www.nawl.org/p/cm/ld/fid=1.

The Special Procedures, SHAHEEDONIRAN.ORG, *accessed at* http://shaheedoniran.org/human-rights-at-the-united-nations/human-rights-monitoring-mechanisms/un-human-rights-council/the-special-procedures/.

The State Bar of California, *accessed at* http://rules.calbar.ca.gov/Rules/Title1GlobalProvisions.aspx.

The United Nations Human Rights Treaty System (Fact Sheet No. 30/Rev.1), United Nations Human Rights Office of the High Commissioner, (2012), *accessed at* http://www.ohchr.org/Documents/Publications/FactSheet30Rev1.pdf.

Thirty-Five Years of Forced Hijab, Justice4Iran (2014), *accessed at* http://justice4iran.org/wp-content/uploads/2014/03/Hejab-Report-JFI-English.pdf.

UN Women, *Commission on the Status of Women*, UN Women (2015), *accessed at* http://www.unwomen.org/en/csw.

United Nations Dag Hammarskjöld Library, *UN Resolutions*, Research UN, *accessed at* http://research.un.org/en/docs/resolutions.

Valentine M. Moghadam, Women in the Islamic Republic of Iran: Legal Status, Social Positions, and Collective Action, Wilsoncernter.org (2004), *accessed at* https://www.wilsoncenter.org/sites/default/files/ValentineMoghadamFinal.pdf.

Welcome to the National Association of Women Judges, National Association of Women Judges, *accessed at* http://www.nawj.org/.

Women in Law in Canada and the U.S., Catalyst (2015), *accessed at* http://www.catalyst.org/knowledge/women-law-canada-and-us.

Women, Power and Politics in 21st Century Iran (Tara Povery & Elaheh Rostami Povery eds., Ashgate Publishing 2012).

Women's Division Republican National Committee, Women in the Judicial Service, Eisenhower Presidential Library, Museum, and Boyhood Home (1959), *accessed at* https://www.eisenhower.archives.gov/research/online_documents/women_in_the_1950s/Women_in_Judicial_Service.pdf.

Women's Suffrage, Scholastic, *accessed at* http://www.scholastic.com/teachers/article/womenx2019s-suffrage.

World Conference on Human Rights, United Nations Human Rights Office of the High Commissioner, *accessed at* http://www.ohchr.org/EN/ABOUTUS/Pages/ViennaWC.aspx.

ʿbāsi Muḥamadī Aṣl, Mavāniʿi Mushārikati Sīyasīyi Zanān Dar Irān [Restriction against Women's Political Participation in Iran], Scientific Information Database (2004), *accessed at* http://www.sid.ir/fa/VEWSSID/J_pdf/62113831204.pdf. (Translated by Author)

OFFICIAL IRANIAN NEWSPAPERS (ALL TRANSLATED BY AUTHOR)

Iṭṭilāʿāt Newspaper (Iran), Feb. 1, 1979, N. 15774.

Itṭilāʿāt Newspaper (Iran), Feb. 26, 1979, N. 15794.

Itṭilāʿāt Newspaper (Iran), March 7, 1979, N. 15802.

Itṭilāʿāt Newspaper (Iran), March 8, 1979, N. 15803.

Iṭṭilāʿāt Newspaper (Iran), March 10, 1979, N. 15804.
Iṭṭilāʿāt Newspaper (Iran), March 11, 1979, N. 15805.
Iṭṭilāʿāt Newspaper (Iran), March 14, 1979, N. 15808.
Iṭṭilāʿāt Newspaper (Iran), March 31, 1979, N. 15818.
Iṭṭilāʿāt Newspaper (Iran), May 19, 1979, N. 15857.
Iṭṭilāʿāt Newspaper (Iran), June 11, 1979, N. 15876.
Āyandigān Newspaper (Iran), June 13, 1979, N. 3374.
Iṭṭilāʿāt Newspaper (Iran), June 19, 1979, N. 15883.
Iṭṭilāʿāt Newspaper (Iran), July 28, 1979, N. 15915.
Iṭṭilāʿāt Newspaper (Iran), July 31, 1979, N. 15918.
Iṭṭilāʿāt Newspaper (Iran), Aug. 4, 1979, N. 15921.
Iṭṭilāʿāt Newspaper (Iran), Aug. 6, 1979, N.15922.
Iṭṭilāʿāt Newspaper (Iran), Oct. 12, 1979, N. 15928.
Inqilābi Islāmī Newspaper (Iran), Oct. 25, 1980, N. 384.

OFFICIAL VIDEOS

Ahmed Shaheed, Video: *The UN Special Rapporteur on the situation of human rights in Iran*, Berkeley Lecture Series (July 15, 2013), *accessed at* https://vimeo.com/71149943.
Television Interview by Barbara Walters with Shāh of Iran, YouTube (1977), *accessed at* https://www.youtube.com/watch?v=UDE4ZUcFR-I&list=FLHlAZQ_N2c1DM6_sOq0KZ3Q.
UN Special Rapporteur on the Situation of Human Rights in the Islamic Republic of Iran, Video: *Dr. Shaheed Addresses United Nations Press Corps-a press conference to preview his 2014 report*, Shaheedoniran.org (Oct. 28, 2014), *accessed at* http://shaheedoniran.org/english/english/dr-shaheeds-addresses-united-nations-press-corps/.
UN Special Rapporteur on the Situation of Human Rights in the Islamic Republic of Iran, Video: *The UN Special Rapporteur on the situation of human rights in Iran*, Shaheedoniran.org, *accessed at* http://shaheedoniran.org/english/without-thumbnail-inside/video-rapporteur-iran/.

OFFICIAL INTERNATIONAL DOCUMENTS

Chapter XXIII Law of the Treaties: Vienna Convention on the Law of Treaties, UN Treaty Collections (1969), *accessed at* https://treaties.un.org/doc/Publication/MTDSG/Volume%20II/Chapter%20XXIII/XXIII-1.en.pdf.
Charter of the United Nations, UN Treaty Collection (June 26, 1945), *accessed at* https://treaties.un.org/doc/Publication/MTDSG/Volume%20I/Chapter%20I/I-1.en.pdf.
Commission Human Rights on its Thirty-eight session to ECOSOC, *Note verbale [sic] dated 14 September 1981 from the Permanent Mission of the Islamic Republic of Iran to the*

United Nations Office and the other international organizations a.t Geneva addressed to the Secretary-General, U.N. Doc. E/CN.4/1516 (Sep. 22, 1981).

Commission of Human Rights, *Final Report on the situation of human rights in the Islamic Republic of Iran by the Special Representative*, U.N. Doc. E/CN.4/1993/41 (Jan. 28, 1993).

Commission on Human Rights on its Forty-seventh session, *Report on the human rights situation in the Islamic Republic of Iran by the Special Representative (Reynaldo Galindo Pohl)*, U.N. Doc. E/CN.4/1991/35 (Feb. 13, 1991).

Commission on Human Rights on its Thirty-eight session to ECOSOC, *Treatment of the Baha'is in Iran*, U.N. Doc. E/CN.4/1517 (Dec. 31, 1981).

Commission on Human Rights, *Final report on the situation of human rights in the Islamic Republic of Iran prepared by the Special Representative*, U.N. Doc. E/CN.4/1994/50 (Feb. 2, 1994).

Commission on Human Rights, *Report on the situation of human rights in the Islamic Republic of Iran prepared by the Special Representative*, U.N. Doc. E/CN.4/1995/55 (Jan. 16, 1995).

Commission on Human Rights, *Report on the situation of human rights in the Islamic Republic of Iran, prepared by the Special Representative*, U.N. Doc. E/CN.4/1996/59 (March 21, 1996).

Commission on Human Rights, *Report on the situation of human rights in the Islamic Republic of Iran, prepared by the Special Representative*, U.N. Doc. E/CN.4/1997/63 (Feb. 11, 1997).

Commission on Human Rights, *Report on the situation of human rights in the Islamic Republic of Iran, prepared by the Special Representative*, U.N. Doc. E/CN.4/1998/59 (Jan. 28, 1998).

Commission on Human Rights, *Report on the situation of human rights in the Islamic Republic of Iran Prepared by the Special Representative*, U.N. Doc. E/CN. 4/2001/39 (Jan. 16, 2001).

Committee on Economic, Social and Cultural Rights, *Concluding observations of the Committee on Economic, Social and Cultural Rights Iran*, U.N. Doc. E/C.12/1993/7 (June 9, 1993).

Committee on Economic, Social and Cultural Rights, *Concluding observations on the second periodic report of the Islamic Republic of Iran, adopted by the Committee at its fiftieth session (29 April-17 May 2013)*, U.N. Doc. E/C.12/IRN/CO/2 (June 10, 2013).

Committee on Economic, Social and Cultural Rights, *General Comment No. 20: Non-discrimination in economic, social and cultural rights*, U.N. Doc. E/C.12/GC/20 (July 2, 2009).

Committee on Economic, Social and Cultural Rights, *General Comments No. 18: The Right to Work*, U.N. Doc. E/C.12/GC/18 (Feb. 6, 2006).

Committee on Economic, Social and Cultural Rights, *General Comments No. 16: The Equal Rights of Men and Women*, U.N. Doc. E/C.12/2005/4 (Aug. 11, 2005).

Committee on Economic, Social and Cultural Rights, *General Comment No. 9: The Domestic Application of the Covenant*, U.N. Doc. E/C.12/1998/24 (Dec. 3, 1998).

Committee on Economic, Social and Cultural Rights, *List of issues in connection with the consideration of the second periodic report of the Islamic Republic of Iran concerning articles 1 to 15 of the International Covenant on Economic, Social and Cultural Rights (E/C.12/IRN/2)*, U.N. Doc. E/C. 12/IRN/Q/2 (June 8, 2012).

Committee on Economic, Social and Cultural Rights, *Replies of the Islamic Republic of Iran to the list of issues*, U.N. Doc. E/C.12/IRN/Q/2/Add. 1 (April 17, 2013).

Committee on Economic, Social and Cultural Rights, *Summary Record of the 7th Meeting*, U.N. Doc. E/C.12/1993/SR.7 (June 3, 1993).

Committee on Economic, Social and Cultural Rights, *Summary Record of the 8th Meeting*, U.N. Doc. E/C.12/1993/SR. 8 (Dec. 20, 1993).

Economic and Social Council Res. 11(II) (June 21, 1947), *accessed at* http://www.un.org/womenwatch/daw/csw/pdf/CSW_founding_resolution_1946.pdf.

Economic and Social Council Res. 1985/17 (May 28, 1985).

Economic and Social Council Res. 1996/6, *Follow-up to the Fourth World Conference on Women* (July 22, 1996).

Economic, Social and Cultural Rights, UNITED NATIONS TREATIES, *accessed at* https://treaties.un.org/doc/Publication/MTDSG/Volume%20I/Chapter%20IV/IV-3.en.pdf.

G.A. Res. 55/2, *United Nations Millennium Declaration*, U.N. Doc. A/RES/55/2 (Sep. 8, 2000).

G.A. Res. 60/251, *Human Rights Council*, U.N. Doc. A/RES/60/251 (April 3, 2006).

G.A. Res. 65/226, *Situation of human rights in the Islamic Republic of Iran*, U.N. Doc. A/RES/65/226 (Feb. 10, 2011).

G.A. Res. 66/175, *Situation of human rights in the Islamic Republic of Iran*, U.N. Doc. A/Res/66/175 (Feb. 17, 2012).

G.A. Res. S-23/3, *Further actions and initiatives to implement the Beijing Declaration and Platform for Action*, U.N. Doc. A/RES/S-23/3 (Nov. 16, 2000).

G.A. Third Committee, *Promotion and protection of human rights: Situation of human rights in the Islamic Republic of Iran*, U.N. Doc. A/C.3/68/L.57 (Nov. 1, 2013).

G.A., *Situation of human rights in the Islamic Republic of Iran Note by the Secretary-General*, U.N. Doc. A/48/526 (Nov. 8, 1993).

General Assembly at its 63d Session, *Report of the Secretary-General on the situation of human rights in the Islamic Republic of Iran*, U.N. Doc. A/63/459 (Oct. 1, 2008).

General Assembly, *Secretary-General Transmit the report of the Special Rapporteur in the field of cultural rights (Farida Shaheed-Cultural rights) at its 67th Session*, U.N. Doc. A/67/287 (Aug. 10, 2012).

Human Rights Committee, *Consideration of reports submitted by States parties under article 40 of the Covenant: Islamic Republic of Iran*, U.N. Doc. CCPR/C/IRN/Q/3/Add.1 (Sept. 12, 2011).

Human Rights Committee, *Consideration of reports submitted by States parties under article 40 of the Covenant*, U.N. Doc. CCPR/C/IRN/3 (May 31, 2010).

Human Rights Committee, *Consideration of reports submitted by States parties under article 40 of the Covenant Concluding observations of the Human Rights Committee Islamic Republic of Iran*, U.N. Doc. CCPR/C/IRN/CO/3 (Nov. 29, 2011).

Human Rights Committee, *Consideration of Reports Submitted by States Parties Under Article 40 of the Covenant*, U.N. Doc. CCPR/C/79/Add.25 (Aug. 3, 1993).

Human Rights Committee, *General Comment No. 18: Non-discrimination* (Nov. 10, 1989).

Human Rights Committee, *General Comment No. 28: Article 3 (The Equality of Rights between Men and Women)*, U.N. Doc. HRI/GEN/1/Rev.9 (Vol. I) (May 27, 2008).

Human Rights Committee, *General Comment No. 31 [80]: The Nature of the General Legal Obligation Imposed on States Parties to the Covenant*, U.N. Doc. CCPR/C/21/Rev.1/Add.13 (May 26, 2004).

Human Rights Committee, *List of issues to be taken up in connection with the consideration of the third periodic report of the Islamic Republic of Iran*, U.N. Doc. CCPR/C/IRN/Q/3 (May 17, 2011).

Human Rights Council Res. 16/9, U.N. Doc. A/HRC/RES/16/9 (April 8, 2011).

Human Rights Council Universal Periodic Review, United Nations Human Rights Office of the High Commissioner, *accessed at* http://www.ohchr.org/EN/HRBodies/UPR/Documents/uprlist.pdf.

Human Rights Council, *Report of the Special Rapporteur on the situation of human rights in the Islamic Republic of Iran (Ahmed Shaheed)*, U.N. Doc. A/HRC/22/56 (Oct. 4, 2013).

Human Rights Council, *Special Rapporteur on the Situation of Human Rights in the Islamic Republic of Iran (Ahmed Shaheed)*, U.N. Doc. A/HRC/28/70 (March 12, 2015).

Human Rights Council, *Special Rapporteur on the situation of human rights in the Islamic Republic of Iran*, U.N. Doc. A/HRC/19/66 (Mar. 6, 2012).

Interim Report of the U.N. Secretary-General to the HRC at its 22d Session, *Secretary-General on the situation of human rights in the Islamic Republic of Iran*, U.N. Doc. A/HRC/22/48 (May 7, 2003).

Interim Report of the U.N. Secretary-General to the HRC at its 31st Session, *Secretary-General on the Situation of Human Rights in Iran Note by the Secretary-General*, U.N. Doc. A/HRC/31/26 (March 3, 2016).

International Commission of Jurists, Maastricht Guidelines on Violations of Economic, Social and Cultural Rights, 26 January 1997.

International Covenant on Civil and Political Rights, United Nations Treaties, *accessed at* https://treaties.un.org/doc/Publication/MTDSG/Volume%20I/Chapter%20IV/IV-4.en.pdf.

International Labour Organization, *Observation (CEACR) - adopted 2012, published 102d ILC session* (2013), International Labour Organization, *accessed at* http://www.ilo.org/dyn/normlex/en/f?p=1000:13100:0::NO:13100:P13100_COMMENT_ID:3085370.

National Report, U.N. Doc. A/HRC/WG.6/7/IRN/1 (Nov. 18, 2009).

Office of the High Commissioner for Human Rights, *Compilation Prepared in Accordance with Paragraph 15(B) of the Annex to Human Rights Council Resolution 5/1(Islamic Republic of Iran)*, U.N. Doc. A/HRC/WG.6/7/IRN/2 (Nov. 25, 2009).

Office of the High Commissioner for Human Rights, *Compilation prepared in accordance with paragraph 15 (b) of the annex to Human Rights Council resolution 5/1 and paragraph 5 of the annex to Council resolution 16/21 (Islamic Republic of Iran)*, U.N. Doc. A/HRC/WG.6/20/IRN/2 (Aug. 18, 2014).

Office of the United Nations High Commissioner for Human Rights, *Summary (Islamic Republic of Iran)*, U.N. Doc. A/HRC/WG.6/20/IRN/3 (Aug. 7, 2014).

Report of the U.N. Secretary-General to General Assembly at its 67th Session, *Situation of human rights in the Islamic Republic of Iran Report of the Secretary-General*, U.N. Doc. A/67/327 (Aug. 22, 2012).

Report of the U.N. Secretary-General to the General Assembly at its 69th Session, *Situation of human rights in the Islamic Republic of Iran Report of the Secretary-General*, U.N. Doc A/69/306 (Aug. 12, 2014).

Report of the U.N. Secretary-General to the General Assembly at its 68th Session, *Situation of human rights in the Islamic Republic of Iran*, U.N. Doc. A/68/377 (Sep. 10, 2013).

Report of the Working Group on the Universal Periodic Review, *Islamic Republic of Iran (Addendum)*, U.N. Doc. A/HRC/14/12/Add.1 (June 3, 2010).

Report of the Working Group on the Universal Periodic Review, *Islamic Republic of Iran*, U.N. Doc. A/HRC/14/12 (March 15, 2010).

Report of the Working Group on the Universal Periodic Review, *Islamic Republic of Iran*, U.N. Doc. A/HRC/28/12 (Dec. 22, 2014).

Report of the Working Group on the Universal Periodic Review, *National report*, U.N. Doc. A/HRC/WG.6/20/IRN/1 (Aug. 4, 2014).

Response of the Islamic Republic of Iran to Draft Report of Special Rapporteur for Submission to the 69th Session of the UN General Assembly, SHAHEEONIRAN.ORG (2014), *accessed at* http://shaheedoniran.org/wp-content/uploads/2014/10/Response-of-the-Islamic-Republic-of-Iran-to-Draft-Report-of-Special.pdf.

Situation of human rights in the Islamic Republic of Iran Addendum, U.N. Doc. A/48/526/Add.1 (Nov. 17, 1993).

Special Rapporteur on Violence against Women, its Causes and Consequences, *Mission to the Islamic Republic of Iran*, U.N. Doc. E/CN.4/2006/61/Add.3 (Jan. 27, 2006).

Summary Prepared by the Office of the High Commissioner for Human Rights in Accordance with Paragraph 15(c) of the Annex to Human Rights Council Resolution 5/1 Islamic Republic of Iran, U.N. Doc. A/HRC/WG.6/7/IRN/3 (Nov. 30, 2009).

U.N. Commission of the Status of Women, *Statement by Elham Aminzadeh to the 53d Session of CSW* (March 4, 2009).

U.N. Commission of the Status of Women, *Statement to the General Discussion of the CSW 56th by Mr. Eshagh Al-Habib on behalf of Mrs. Maryam Mojtahedzadeh* (Feb. 28, 2012).

U.N. Commission on the Status of Women, *Statement by Mrs. Fātimi Ajorloo in the 55th Session of CSW* (Feb. 24, 2011).
U.N. Commission on the Status of Women, *Statement by Mrs. Maryam Mojtahedzadeh Advisor to the President and Head of the Center for Women and Family Affairs of the Islamic Republic of Iran before the 57th Session of CSW* (March 5, 2013).
U.N. Commission on the Status of Women, *Statement by the Delegation of the Islamic Republic of Iran in the 52d Session of CSW* (March 3, 2008).
U.N. General Assembly, *Situation of Human Rights in the Islamic Republic of Iran*, U.N. Doc. A/70/352 (Aug. 31, 2015).
U.N. Secretary-General Transmits the Interim Report of the Special Representative of the Commission on Human Rights to the General Assembly, *Situation of human rights in the Islamic Republic of Iran Note by the Secretary-General*, U.N. Doc. A/47/617 (Nov. 13, 1992).
U.N. Secretary-General Transmits the Interim Report of the Special Representative of the Commission on Human Rights to the General Assembly, *Situation of human rights in the Islamic Republic of Iran Note by the Secretary-General*, U.N. Doc. A/49/514 (Oct. 14, 1994).
U.N. Secretary-General Transmits the Interim Report of the Special Representative of the Commission on Human Rights to the General Assembly on its 52d Session, *Situation of human rights in the Islamic Republic of Iran Note by the Secretary-General*, U.N. Doc. A/52/472 (Oct. 15, 1997).
U.N. Secretary-General Transmits the Interim Report of the Special Representative of the Commission on Human Rights to the General Assembly to its 54th Session, *Situation of human rights in the Islamic Republic of Iran Note by the Secretary-General*, U.N. Doc. A/54/365 (Sep. 21, 1999).
U.N. Secretary-General Transmits the Interim Report of the Special Representative of the Commission on Human Rights to the General Assembly to its 53th Session, *Situation of human rights in the Islamic Republic of Iran Note by the Secretary-General*, U.N. Doc. A/53/423 (Sep. 23, 1998).
U.N. Secretary-General Transmits the Report of the Special Rapporteur of HRC to the General Assembly at its 69th Session, *Situation of human rights in the Islamic Republic of Iran Note by the Secretary-General*, U.N. Doc. A/69/356 (Aug. 27, 2014).
U.N. Secretary-General Transmits the Report of the Special Rapporteur of HRC to the General Assembly at its 68th Session, *Situation of human rights in the Islamic Republic of Iran Note by the Secretary-General*, U.N. Doc. A/68/503 (Oct. 4, 2013).
Universal Periodic Review, Responses to Recommendations, UPR-INFO.ORG (2010), *accessed at* http://www.upr-info.org/sites/default/files/document/iran_islamic_republic_of/session_7_-_february_2010/recommendationstoiran2010.pdf.
UPR info, Islamic Republic of Iran Mid-term Implementation Assessment,

UPR-INFO.ORG (2010), *accessed at* http://www.upr-info.org/sites/default/files/document/iran_islamic_republic_of/session_07_-_february_2010/mia-iran.pdf.

www.ingramcontent.com/pod-product-compliance
Lightning Source LLC
LaVergne TN
LVHW052302200926
848481LV00002B/441